Law and Society
Recent Scholarship

Edited by Melvin I. Urofsky

A Series from LFB Scholarly

Congress, the Constitution, and Divided Government

Matthew O. Field

LFB Scholarly Publishing LLC
El Paso 2013

Library of Congress Cataloging-in-Publication Data

Field, Matthew O., 1978-
Congress, the constitution, and divided government / Matthew O. Field.
pages cm
Includes bibliographical references and index.
ISBN 978-1-59332-628-9 (hardcover : alk. paper)
1. Legislative power--United States. 2. Separation of powers--United States. 3. Constitutional law--United States. I. Title.
KF4930.F54 2013
342.73'042--dc23
2013014121

ISBN 978-1-59332-628-9

Printed on acid-free 250-year-life paper.

Manufactured in the United States of America.

Table of contents

Acknowledgements

I would like to thank Western Illinois University and the University of Oklahoma, more specifically the History Department in particular at the former and the Department of Political Science and Carl Albert Congressional Research and Studies Center at the latter, for affording me opportunities I had only dreamed about prior. I hope to, in some small but measurable ways, repay both in due time.

CHAPTER 1

Introduction: Congress and the Constitution

No doubt the political branches have a role in interpreting and applying the Constitution.[1]

Regardless of the fact that the second portion of former Chief Justice Rehnquist's statement leaves proper delineation of the first part ambiguous, if the first half is accurate, it begs the obvious question: what role has the branch of government mentioned in Article I of the Constitution (Congress) played in "interpreting" and "applying" the Constitution? At the most elementary level, Congress is quite literally connected with the Constitution. Not only are members of Congress constitutionally required to take an oath "to support and defend the Constitution of the United States,"[2] but many observers agree that, at

[1] Supreme Court Justice William Rehnquist, *United States v. Morrison*, 529 U.S. 598, 616 (2000). Rehnquist continues, "but ever since *Marbury* [*v. Madison*] this Court has remained the *ultimate* expositor of the constitutional text." Emphasis added.

[2] U.S. Constitution, art. 6, cl. 3; 5 U.S.Code. § 3331 (1982). As Louis Fisher states, "[m]embers of Congress take an oath of office to defend the Constitution, not the President." Congress, Senate, Committee on the Judiciary, Statement by Louis Fisher, Specialist in Constitutional Law: Exercising Congress's Constitutional Power to End a War, hearing, 110th Cong., 1st sess., 30 Jan. 2007. Currie reminds us that "judges are not alone in this regard. Others swear to uphold the Constitution as well: presidents, cabinet officers, members of Congress – indeed every federal, state, and local officer in the land." David P. Currie, "Prolegomena for a Sampler:

least to some degree, "Congress as a political institution exerts influence on constitutional development,"[3] and that "Congress is a particularly important site for extrajudicial constitutional interpretation, and it is often crucial for both raising new constitutional controversies and settling old ones."[4] As the branch of our government tasked with legislating, an ever-changing and never-ending endeavor involving contested first principles and ubiquitous policy prescriptions, how could it not?

More specifically, in terms of exegetical appreciation for the Constitution, "[m]any scholars have recently expressed interest in examining – and defending – the role of Congress in interpreting the Constitution,"[5] a desire more fully validated if it is true that "Congress can be, and frequently has been, a responsible interpreter of the Constitution."[6] Critics of "Congress's ability to do so will invoke historical experience and recent episodes in which members of Congress disclaimed interest in assessing the constitutionality of a proposal before them. To that extent, the question is empirical: Do

---

Extrajudicial Interpretation of the Constitution, 1789-1861," in Congress and the Constitution, eds. Neal Devins and Keith E. Whittington (Durham: Duke University Press, 2005), 19.

[3] Gerald L. Neuman, "Review: Variations for Mixed Voices," Review of Constitutional Dialogues: Interpretation as Political Process by Louis Fisher, University of Pennsylvania Law Review 137, no. 5 (May 1989): 1871.

[4] Neal Devins and Keith E. Whittington, "Introduction," in Congress and the Constitution, 7.

[5] Mark Tushnet, "Evaluating Congressional Constitutional Interpretation: Some Criteria and Two Informal Case Studies," in Congress and the Constitution, 269.

[6] Mark Tushnet, "Evaluating Congressional Constitutional Interpretation: Some Criteria and Two Informal Case Studies," in Congress and the Constitution, 288. Tushnet's chapter is devoted to only two case studies, and within those two at a very broad level. As he notes in his first footnote, "[o]f course in the end one needs to evaluate congressional performance – and judicial performance – across the entire range of action. My informal case studies are designed to give some credibility to the claim that Congress does *generally* act in a constitutionally responsible manner, but they cannot establish that claim." 290.

members of Congress engage in constitutional interpretation, and when they do, how well do they perform? "[7] Furthermore, even when it may desire otherwise, sometimes "Congress must interpret the Constitution in areas that the Supreme Court has never reached and may never reach in the course of deciding cases or controversies."[8]

HISTORICAL ANTECEDENTS

Each chapter will detail more fully their respective issue's deliberative history. Nevertheless, a brief précis will not impede an effort at contextualizing Congress' previous constitutionally deliberative efforts. Historically, Congress has frequently demonstrated its prerogative to engage in serious and often intense constitutional debate. David Currie has documented in great detail how "[i]n the early Congress virtually everything became a constitutional question – from great controversies like those over the national bank and the president's removal power to ephemera of exquisite obscurity."[9] Virtually "the whole business of legislation [was] practical construction of the Constitution"[10] and

[7] Mark Tushnet, "Evaluating Congressional Constitutional Interpretation: Some Criteria and Two Informal Case Studies," 269.

[8] John C. Yoo, "Lawyers in Congress," in Congress and the Constitution, eds. Neal Devins and Keith E. Whittington (Durham: Duke University Press, 2005), 134. Yoo cites Gerhard Casper, Separating Power: Essays on the Founding Period (Cambridge: Harvard University Press, 1997); David P. Currie, The Constitution in Congress: The Federalist Period, 1789-1801 (Chicago: University of Chicago Press, 1997); Stanley Elkins and Eric McKitrick, The Age of Federalism: The Early American Republic, 1788-1800 (New York: Oxford University Press, 1993); and Keith E. Whittington, Constitutional Construction: Divided Powers and Constitutional Meaning (Cambridge: Harvard University Press, 1999).

[9] David P. Currie, "Prolegomena for a Sampler: Extrajudicial Interpretation of the Constitution, 1789-1861," in Congress and the Constitution, 21, citing Currie, The Constitution in Congress: The Federalist Period, 1789-1801 (Chicago: University of Chicago Press, 1997).

[10] Mark Tushnet, "Evaluating Congressional Constitutional Interpretation," 9; citing, David P. Currie, "Prolegomena for a Sampler," in Congress and the

sometimes, according to Currie, Congress "d[id] a better job of considering constitutional issues than the Supreme Court."[11]

For example, the debate in 1789 over the President's removal power occupies several hundred pages of the Annals of Congress and, in the eyes of one scholar, constitutes an excellent analysis of the doctrine of implied powers.[12] In 1811, Representative Peter Porter of New York observed that "every member has a printed Constitution on his table before him – a Constitution drawn up with the greatest care and deliberation" – "the injunctions of which, as we in our best judgments shall understand them and not as they shall be interpreted to us by others, we are solemnly bound, by our oaths, to obey."[13] That same year Henry Clay declared members should "make that Constitution, which we have sworn to support, our invariable guide."[14]

Constitution, eds. Neal Devins and Keith E. Whittington (Durham: Duke University Press, 2005), 20 (quoting Rep. Theodore Sedgwick of Massachusetts).

[11] Tushnet, "Evaluating Congressional Constitutional Interpretation," 9. Tushnet is referring to Currie's example of the secession debate before the Civil War. Currie adds, "The congressional and executive records sparkle with brilliant insights about the meaning of constitutional provisions. . . . Both the president and members of Congress addressed themselves seriously to the merits of the constitutional question. They did so long before that question ever came up in court. The arguments were of high quality, and the best of them were made by people largely forgotten today. Finally, when the Supreme Court ultimately got around to resolving the question, it had far less to say about it than had already been said by Congress, or even the president." David P. Currie, "Prolegomena for a Sampler: Extrajudicial Interpretation of the Constitution, 1789-1861," in Congress and the Constitution, 24, 32-33.

[12] Louis Fisher, "Constitutional Interpretation by Members of Congress," North Carolina Law Review 63 (April 1985): 709; see Louis Fisher, Constitutional Conflicts Between Congress and the President (Lawrence: University Press of Kansas, 1985), 60-66.

[13] Annals of Congress, 11th Cong., 3rd sess., [H]642-64 (18 Jan. 1811).

[14] Annals of Congress, 11th Cong., 3rd sess., [S]216-218 (13 Feb. 1811).

During the early Republic, not only was "[p]olicy leadership . . . often (though not exclusively) Congress-dominated,"[15] but "constitutional analysis was by necessity dominated by Congress and the President."[16] During the First Congress

> [r]espect for the Constitution . . . went far beyond ritualistic acknowledgement of its authority; a remarkable proportion of the debate centered on the task of determining its meaning. At the outset Madison admonished the House, as Washington had admonished him, that constitutional issues should be given

---

[15] Charles Stewart III, "Congress and the Constitutional System," in The Legislative Branch, eds. Paul J. Quirk and Sarah A. Binder (Oxford: Oxford University Press, 2005), 29. Stewart adds, "now it rarely is."

[16] David P. Currie, "The Constitution in Congress: The Most Endangered Branch, 1801-1805," Wake Forest Law Review 33 (1998): 220, quoted in Louis Fisher and David Gray Adler, American Constitutional Law, Vol. 1 Constitutional Structures: Separated Powers and Federalism, 7th edition (Carolina Academic Press: Durham, North Carolina, 2007), 22. In fact, "the early period of the Virginia Dynasty, forged in the presidencies of George Washington, Thomas Jefferson, James Madison and James Monroe, represented 'a defining period in American constitutional history. The best minds in the country grappled with practical questions of applying the generalities of the Constitution to concrete and often unforeseen circumstances and with the fundamental issue of what sort of nation the Constitution had created. It was a time of great events that engendered great controversy: the Louisiana Purchase, the Burr conspiracy, the War of 1812, the Cumberland Road, the Missouri Compromise, the Monroe Doctrine. All of these controversies, and many others of the time, became, in part, constitutional controversies. And they were fought out almost exclusively in the legislative and executive branches, not in the courts." Also see Mark Tushnet, "Constitutional Interpretation outside the Courts," review of The Constitution [in] Congress: The Federalist Period, 1789-1801; The Constitution [in] Congress: The Jeffersonians, 1801-1829; The Constitution [in] Congress: Democrats and Whigs, 1829-1861; The Constitution [in] Congress: Descent into the Maelstrom, 1829-1861, by David P. Currie, Journal of Interdisciplinary History XXXVII: 3 (winter, 2007).

> 'careful investigation and full discussion' because '[t]he decision that is at this time made, will become the permanent exposition of the [C]onstitution.'[17] Constitutional questions cropped up in the House and Senate every time somebody sneezed, and one proposal after another was subjected to intensive debate to determine its compatibility with relevant constitutional provisions. Members of Congress plainly thought it necessary to demonstrate that the Constitution supported their actions, and thus everything they did as well as everything they said helps to inform our understanding of particular constitutional provisions.[18]

In addition, "[n]ot only did the early Congress almost always interpret the Constitution before the courts did, and not only did it often do a better job; in many cases congressional debates provide our *only* official discussion of constitutional issues, for many crucial constitutional controversies have never been judicially resolved."[19]

---

[17] Annals of Congress, 1st Cong., 1st sess., H514 (17 June 1789).

[18] David P. Currie, The Constitution in Congress: The Federalist Period 1789-1801 (Chicago: The University of Chicago Press, 1997), 116-117.

[19] David P. Currie, "Prolegomena for a Sampler: Extrajudicial Interpretation of the Constitution, 1789-1861," in Congress and the Constitution, 22. George Thomas writes, "[e]arly debates on the nature and meaning of the Constitution occur[ed] primarily between the executive and the legislature as well as within these branches. The debates over the president's removal power and the establishment of the national bank touch on central issues of constitutional interpretation and development, but in no way center on judicial interpretation and exposition. In these pivotal 'Madisonian Moments' of constitutional development, the judiciary was essentially silent." George Thomas, "Recovering the Political Constitution: The Madisonian Vision," The Review of Politics 66, no. 2 (Spring 2004): 245. As Fisher observes, "[t]he historical record . . . demonstrates that Congress deliberated for years on such constitutional issues as judicial review, the Bank of the United States, congressional investigative power, slavery, internal improvements, federalism, the war-making power, treaties and foreign relations, interstate commerce, the removal power, and the legislative veto long before those issues entered the courts." Fisher adds,

Thus, constitutional questions were central to the early and later political life of the Republic.[20] Vice-President Jefferson believed the

---

"[c]ongressional debate was intense, informed, and diligent. Indeed, it had to be, given the paucity of direction at that time from the Supreme Court and the lower courts." Louis Fisher, "Constitutional Interpretation by Members of Congress," North Carolina Law Review 63 (April 1985): 708-9, citing W. Andrews, Coordinate Magistrates: Constitutional Law By Congress and the President, (1969), 1-20 (judicial review), 21-43 (Bank), 44-64 (slavery), 65-95 (interstate commerce), 109-30 (removal power), 131-44 (war powers). For early debate on internal improvements, see W. Letwin, ed. A Documentary History of American Economic Policy Since 1789 (1961), 53-84. See also J. Hart, The American Presidency in Action (1948), 78-111 (treaties and foreign relations), 152-248 (removal power); C. Miller, The Supreme Court and the Uses of History (1969), 52-70, 205-210 (removal power); Donald Morgan, Congress and the Constitution (1966), 49-57 (removal power), 101-118 (investigative power), 140-59 (interstate commerce), 184-203 (legislative veto); Abraham D. Sofaer, War, Foreign Affairs and Constitutional Power (1976) (discussing constitutional deliberations by Congress from 1789-1829). See also David P. Currie, The Constitution in Congress, Volumes I-IV.

20 "It is difficult to imagine what could be said about the constitutionality of internal improvements or about the conditional admission of states that was not said by someone in Congress or in the executive branch during the period of this study. The same is true of scores of other constitutional issues, great and small, ventilated in the pitiless glare of political debate during the same time. Would you know about the reach of congressional authority or the relations between the executive and legislative departments? Look not to the judges, who, like blossoms at the whim of the capricious butterfly, pollinate the constitutional fields now and then according to the vagaries of litigation. Go to school rather with Presidents, with Cabinet ministers, with Members of Congress, who grapple with constitutional conundrums every day, in every action they contemplate, in every exercise of their official functions. . . . They will not always give you answers. Constitutional questions that are worth disputing have no answers. Look rather for insights, for wisdom, for guidance, for the raw materials that inform judgment, and you will not be disappointed. For constitutional interpretation is a matter of informed

Sedition Act of 1798 was unconstitutional.[21] Jefferson and Justice Marshall sparred over the proper allocation of judicial power.[22] Many Jacksonians thought the Whig and Henry Clay-inspired American System was unconstitutional.[23] President Jackson believed "[e]very public officer . . . took an oath to support the Constitution 'as he understands it, and not as it is understood by others.' The opinion of judges 'has no more authority over Congress than the opinion of

---

judgment, and there is nothing like the extrajudicial debates of the early years to inform our judgment as to what the Constitution means." The Constitution in Congress: The Jeffersonians 1801-1829 (Chicago: The University of Chicago Press, 2001), 344-345. During the period from the Constitutional Convention to the Civil War, "Congress took a leading part in settlement of constitutional questions, narrow and broad, interpretive and implementational." Donald G. Morgan, Congress and the Constitution: A Study in Responsibility 120 (Belknap, 1966).

[21] Mark Tushnet, "Constitutional Interpretation outside the Courts," Journal of Interdisciplinary History XXXVII: 3 (winter, 2007): 416, ft. 2.

[22] In fact, "[b]y the close of Marshall's chief justiceship, almost all of the basic measures to curb the Court had been seriously suggested or actually tried: impeachment, reduction of jurisdiction, congressional review of decisions, limited tenure, requirement for an extraordinary majority to invalidate a statute, Court-packing, presidential refusal to enforce a decision, and (at the state level) nullification and even resort to force." Walter F. Murphy, Congress and the Court: A Case Study in the American Political Process (Chicago: The University of Chicago Press, Phoenix Books, 1965), 63.

[23] Mark Tushnet, "Constitutional Interpretation outside the Courts," Journal of Interdisciplinary History XXXVII: 3 (winter, 2007): 417. "[T]he dismantling of the American System was not simply the result of the Democrats' ideological opposition to, or policy disagreements with, the Whigs and other nationalists – although those were surely at the root of the matter. Rather, the Jacksonian opposition was articulated in terms of constitutional principles and hence structured by the language of various constitutional provisions. In short, the Jacksonian Democrats articulated their opposition to the American System and Whiggish nationalism as part of a constitutional vision." J. Mitchell Pickerill, review of The Constitution in Congress: Democrats and Whigs, 1829-1861, by David P. Currie, Law & Politics Book Review 15, no. 11 (Nov. 2005): 954-958.

Congress has over the judges, and on that point the President is independent of both.'"[24] Congress was immersed in constitutional issues during the antebellum,[25] Civil War, and Reconstruction eras.[26] Later, it debated the Child Labor Act for a full decade, shifting its constitutional rationale several times. From the turn of the nineteenth-century until the beginning of World War II Congress was in dialogue with the "Lochner Court."[27]

---

[24] Richard P. Longaker, "Andrew Jackson and the Judiciary," Political Science Quarterly 71, no. 3 (Sept. 1956): 341, 358-61; quoted in Fisher and Adler, American Constitutional Law, Vol. 1 Constitutional Structures: Separated Powers and Federalism, 23-24.

[25] "[D]ebates about the nature of the constitutional compact, constitutional rights, natural rights, federal powers, and the meaning of democracy, were at the core of what Americans cared about most, and constitutional argument was taken extraordinarily seriously." Ken I. Kersch, Review of The Constitution in Congress: Descent into the Maelstrom, 1829-1861, by David P. Currie, Law & Politics Book Review 16, no. 6 (June 2006): 466.

[26] For two such in-depth excellent treatments of this era, see David P. Currie, "The Civil War Congress," The University of Chicago Law Review 73, no. 4 (autumn 2006): 1131-1226; and "The Reconstruction Congress," The University of Chicago Law Review 75, no. 1 (winter 2008): 383-495. In the former Currie writes, "there were numerous instances in which the quality of constitutional debate was high." In the preceding sentence Currie quotes a scholar referring specifically to the Thirty-seventh Congress, but this particular quote seems intended (by Currie) to be applicable to the entire "Civil War Congress." 1132.

[27] For the full timeline, see J. Mitchell Pickerill, Constitutional Deliberation in Congress: The Impact of Judicial Review in a Separated System, 76-77. The Court invalidated Congress' initial efforts. Congress shifted from a commerce power to a taxing power rationale. The Court again ruled against Congress. By 1938, Congress shifted back to a commerce power justification. A unanimous Court now agreed. *United States v. Darby*, 312 U.S. 100 (1941). See Louis Fisher and David Gray Adler, American Constitutional Law, Vol. 2 Constitutional Rights: Civil Rights and Civil Liberties, 1056-57. See also Keith E. Whittington, "Congress Before the Lochner Court," Boston University Law Review 85, no. 3 (summer 2005):

Finally, by way of historical example, the issue of war powers has also demonstrated Congress' role in constitutional deliberation. In 1801, Chief Justice Marshall wrote that "[t]he whole powers of war being, by the [C]onstitution of the United States, vested in [C]ongress, the acts of that body can alone be resorted to as our guides in this enquiry."[28] Three years later, Marshall penned the Court opinion arguing that when a presidential proclamation in a time of war conflicted with a congressional statute, the statute prevailed.[29] Fifty-nine years later, in the middle of the Civil War, the Court upheld President Lincoln's power to institute a blockade of Southern ports.[30] Nevertheless, Justice Robert Grier stated, "[b]y the Constitution, Congress alone has the power to declare a national or foreign war." Richard Henry Dana Jr., Lincoln's advocate during oral arguments, admitted that the president does not have the "the right to initiate a war, as a voluntary act of sovereignty. That is vested only in Congress."[31]

During the Korean conflict

> [f]or *three months* . . . the Senate engaged in the 'Great Debate' on the relative prerogatives of Congress and the President in exercising the war power. [Sen.] Taft believed

---

821-858. As is well-known, "'[t]he Lochner era' refers to a period of judicial decision making dating roughly from the turn of the century through 1937 and typified by the 1905 Supreme Court decision *Lochner v. New York*. This period, during which the Court overturned many legislative efforts that sought to regulate economic activity – including components of President Franklin D. Roosevelt's New Deal – is often characterized as one of judicial activism that favored business interests and laissez-faire ideology." Helena Silverstein, review of Legislative Deferrals: Statutory Ambiguity, Judicial Power & American Democracy, by George I. Lovell, Journal of Interdisciplinary History, 36, no. 1 (summer 2005): 113.

[28] *Talbot v. Seeman*, 5 U.S. 1 (1801).

[29] *Little v. Barreme*, 6 U.S. 170 (1804).

[30] *The Prize Cases*, 67 U.S. 635 (1863).

[31] Louis Fisher, "When the Shooting Starts," Legal Times XXXI, no. 30 (week of 28 Jul. 2008).

> that Congress had the power to prevent the President from sending troops anywhere in the world to involve the United States in war. In what could be read as a precursor to the War Powers Resolution, he urged Congress to assert its power in the form of a joint resolution.[32] . . . Senator John McClellan offered an amendment requiring congressional approval of future plans to send troops abroad. Although the amendment was initially rejected, 44 to 46, it was later accepted. The Senate passed the resolution by a vote of 69 to 21, expressing its approval of Truman's sending four divisions to Europe but stating that 'in the interests of sound constitutional processes, and of national unity and understanding, congressional approval should be obtained of any policy requiring the assignment of American troops abroad when such assignment is in implementation of article 3 of the North Atlantic Treaty' and that no ground troops in addition to the four divisions should be sent 'without further congressional approval.'[33]

---

[32] Congressional Record 55, 2987 (1951).

[33] Louis Fisher, Constitutional Conflicts Between Congress and the President, 4th ed. (Lawrence: University of Kansas Press, 1997), 276-277; 97 Congressional Record 55, 2987, 3082-83, 3096, 3283 (para. 6) (1951). Emphasis added. Fisher also writes: "[f]rom 1789 to 1950, lawmakers, the courts, and the executive branch understood that only Congress could initiate offensive actions against other nations. This period is faithful to the intentions of the framers, who rejected the monarchical model of Britain and granted Congress the sole authority to take the country from a state of peace to a state of war. They left the president with certain defensive powers 'to repel sudden attacks." Louis Fisher, "War Power," in The American Congress: The Building of Democracy, ed. Julian E. Zelizer (Boston: Houghton Mifflin Company, 2004), 688. "Members of Congress can point to specific language in the Constitution for their authority to declare war and provide armed forces. More difficult to locate are the legal sources for presidential authority to initiate military operations. Yet over the last half century, Presidents have been able to make war before Congress has had a chance to act. Particularly in the period since World War II, executive war-making power has increased dramatically as Presidents seek 'authority' from

Similarly, in *Youngstown Co. v. Sawyer* Justice Jackson wrote, "[a] seizure executed by the president pursuant to an act of Congress would be supported by the strongest of presumptions and the widest latitude of judicial interpretations." In addition, there is a "zone of twilight in which he and Congress may have concurrent authority or in which its distribution is uncertain. Therefore, congressional inertia, indifference or quiescence may sometimes, at least as a practical matter, enable, if not invite, measures on independent presidential responsibility."[34] In 1973, Congress overruled President Nixon's veto and passed the still-contentious War Powers Resolution.[35] According to one critic, "[t]he

---

the United Nations and the North Atlantic Treaty Organization (NATO) rather than from Congress. . . . For constitutional as well as practical reasons, the two branches are supposed to work in concert. The President commands the troops, but only Congress can provide them. Congress declares or authorizes war but depends on the President to wage it. An associate of President Cleveland was present when a delegation from Congress arrived at the White House with this announcement: 'We have about decided to declare war against Spain over the Cuban question. Conditions are intolerable.' Cleveland responded in blunt terms: 'There will be no war with Spain over Cuba while I am President.' A member of Congress protested that the Constitution gave Congress the right to declare war, but Cleveland countered that the Constitution also made him Commander in Chief. 'I will not mobilize the army,' he told the legislators. 'I happen to know that we can buy the Island of Cuba from Spain for $100,000,000 and a war will cost vastly more than that and will entail another long list of pensioners. It would be an outrage to declare war.'" Louis Fisher, Constitutional Conflicts Between Congress and the President, 5th ed., rev. (Lawrence, KS: University of Kansas Press, 2007), 249, quoting from Robert McElroy, Grover Cleveland: The Man and the Statesman 2 vols. (New York: Harper & Brothers Publishers, 1923), 2:249-50.

[34] 343 U.S. 579 (1952). Jackson added, "I should indulge the widest latitude of interpretation to sustain his exclusive function to command the instruments of national force, at least when turned against the outside world for the security of our society. But, when it is turned inward, not because of rebellion but because of a lawful economic struggle between industry and labor, it should have no such indulgence." 645.

[35] P.L. 93-148.

statute . . . shifted greater power to the president and gave Congress the illusion that its constitutional prerogatives would be protected by statutory procedures."[36] Three years later, Congress passed the National Emergencies Act.[37] Congressional constitutional prerogative in relation to war powers has remained deeply controversial.

These varied and brief historical examples and the contemporary case studies examined in the following chapters highlight "the centrality of Congress in constitutional affairs."[38]

---

[36] Louis Fisher, "War Power," in The American Congress: The Building of Democracy, ed. Julian E. Zelizer (Boston: Houghton Mifflin Company, 2004), 687.

[37] 50 U.S.C. 1601-1651. The Act "set up procedures for declaring emergencies and established automatic deadlines for the expiration of such declarations. At the time, several states of emergency dating to the 1930s technically were still in effect. The law requires that if the president declares a state of emergency he must cite which law or part of the Constitution gives him the power to do so. The administration must keep records of rules, regulations, expenditures and other activities carried out under the declaration. The law also set up a timetable for expiration of the emergency declaration, requiring Congress to consider ending it every six months until it is terminated. The president can also unilaterally terminate the state of emergency." Elizabeth A. Palmer, "Executive Powers in Crises Are Shaped By Precedent, Personality, Public Opinion," CQ Weekly Online (15 Sept. 2001): 2122, available at library.cqpress.com/cqweekly/ weeklyreport107-000000309054 (accessed October 20, 2008), citing CQ Almanac (1976): 521.

[38] "There is no shortage of prominent recent events that invite a widespread discussion about the appropriate place of constitutional values and constraints in our public life. Many of these controversies, including the conflict with Iraq, the Bush administration's response to the September 11 terrorism attacks, ongoing disputes with the White House about executive privilege and other presidential powers, and the impeachment trial of Bill Clinton, illustrate the centrality of Congress in constitutional affairs." Bruce G. Peabody, "Congressional Attitudes toward Constitutional Interpretation," in Congress and the Constitution, 61.

THE INSTITUTION

In addition to this historical context and these important historical antecedents of constitutional deliberation in Congress, the U.S. House of Representatives and U.S. Senate themselves are important. As Devins and Whittington point out, Congress:

> is the first branch of government established by the Constitution. Its priority within the constitutional text reflects the substantive importance that the Founders expected the legislature to have in the political system and its significance within their political theory. It was Congress, armed with the authority provided by popular election, that was expected to enjoy the greatest public support and to dominate national politics. It was Congress that would shoulder the task of making national policy and setting the national political agenda. It was Congress that carried the Founders' hopes for the success of the constitutional experiment, but it was also Congress and its frenetic ambitions that required the most careful attention at the constitutional convention in Philadelphia and the most detailed limitations in the constitutional text. Congress was at the center of the constitutional enterprise.[39]

---

[39] Neal Devins and Keith E. Whittington, "Introduction," in Congress and the Constitution, 1. These observations were similarly made forty years ago by James Burnham: "The primacy of the legislature in the intent of the Constitution is plain on the face of that document, as it is in the deliberations of the Philadelphia Convention. It is the Constitution's first Article that defines the structure and powers of the legislature. The legislative Congress is to be the sole source of all laws (except the clauses of the Constitution itself). In the conduct of the general government, Congress alone can authorize the getting or spending of money. It is for Congress to support, regulate and govern the Army and Navy, and to declare war. Save for the bare existence of a Supreme Court, it is for Congress to establish and regulate the judicial system. All officers of both executive and judiciary are subject to congressional impeachment; but for their own official conduct the members of Congress are answerable only to themselves." James Burnham, Congress and the American Tradition (Chicago: Henry Regnery Company,

Despite these affirming realities, there are difficulties in studying the relationship between Congress and the Constitution. Congress is a large body and often leaves an uncertain paper trail from which to decipher clear motives, beliefs, or interpretations.[40] Even more striking, critics charge that "members of Congress pay very little attention to the Constitution, have almost no understanding of what that document

---

1965), 97. Mark Brandon also writes, "[T]he allocation of interpretive authority can foster constitutional division. It attends to the authority and activity of nonjudicial actors – especially Congress - in interpreting the Constitution. It suggests that the very function of Congress and the character of congressional action in a constitutional polity make the constitutional dimensions of that function and action inescapable. In short, Congress, when it acts, is unavoidably 'interpreting' the Constitution. The functions and composition of Congress as an institution render it an interpreter with distinctive characteristics, one of which is its institutional tendency toward pragmatic accommodation and compromise. Notwithstanding this tendency, when Congress solves problems in a way that appears to be institutionally successful, it can precipitate or exploit divisions in the polity." Mark Brandon, Free in the World: American Slavery and Constitutional Failure (Princeton, New Jersey: Princeton University Press, 1998), x-xi.

[40] As one observer has remarked, "Congress is a notoriously difficult subject for legal scholars to grapple with. When Congress passes a statute, it does not issue documents like judicial opinions that provide relatively clear decisions, explain the authority of the decision-making body, and set out the reasons for the decision. Unlike the executive branch, Congress does not leave behind a trail of memoranda, briefs, or records of meetings that allows the legal scholar to reconstruct decision paths and thought processes. Congress is home to a cacophony of people, issues, arguments, reports, hearings, speeches, and events, in which it is often difficult for an outsider to determine what has happened, why it has happened, and sometimes when it happened. A legal scholar researching Congress sometimes must feel as the head of the KGB once did while gathering intelligence on the United States: when the subject under study makes so much noise, it is difficult to tell what is important and what is not." Yoo, "Lawyers in Congress," 131.

means, and seldom, if ever, engage in . . . constitutionalism."[41] Unquestionably, it is true that sometimes Congress spends very little time on the constitutionality of proposed legislation. As one member recently remarked, members consider "[p]olicy issues first, [the necessary] consensus to pass the bill, six other things, then constitutionality."[42] For example, according to Pickerill, the Gun-Free School Zones Act

> was never formally debated on the floor of either house, and there is no evidence of opposition to it. . . . Nowhere in the public record is there evidence that Congress considered the constitutional issue raised by *Lopez* – the very issue that ended up setting free a teenager who brought a gun to school for a gang war! . . . For the first time in sixty years, the Court had invoked the limits of the commerce power to strike down a federal law.[43]

Similarly

> [a] detailed legislative history and interviews with relevant policymakers involved in drafting and passing the Brady Bill show that the Tenth Amendment received virtually no attention during the decade-long debate over the legislation. Members of Congress and others either did not identify the issue or were unconcerned about it, because the Court did not seem to present a serious threat over the matter.[44]

---

[41] Eugene W. Hickok, Jr., "Congress, the Court, and the Constitution: Has Congress Abdicated Its Constitutional Responsibilities?," Heritage Foundation Lecture, 1990.

[42] Pickerill, Constitutional Deliberation in Congress, 134, citing an anonymous member.

[43] Pickerill, Constitutional Deliberation in Congress, 1-2.

[44] Pickerill, Constitutional Deliberation in Congress, 8.

Furthermore, Congress operates within "a collective institutional structure"[45] and may be in a difficult position in relation to interacting with the Constitution.[46] Elizabeth Garrett and Adrian Vermeule "[contend] that Congress's 'constitutional performance' is lacking because Congress as an institution is designed to achieve legislative goals other than constitutional deliberation."[47]

When Congress does engage the Constitution on a substantive basis, some criticism only heightens. In a pointed 1983 critique, Judge Abner Mikva found constitutional debate by members of Congress "superficial and . . . self-serving."[48] He wrote that "legislative debate, for the most part, does not explore the constitutional implications of pending legislation; and, at best, Congress does an uneven job of

---

[45] Elizabeth Garrett and Adrian Vermeule, "Institutional Design of a Thayerian Congress," in Congress and the Constitution, 244.

[46] Mikva cautioned in 1983, "both houses are large, making the process of engaging in complex arguments during a floor debate difficult. For the most part, the speeches made on the floor are designed to get a member's position on the record rather than to initiate a dialogue. Because of the volume of legislation, the time spent with constituents, and the technical knowledge required to understand the background of every piece of legislation, it is infrequent that a member considers the individual merits of a particular bill. Often a vote is determined by a thumbs up-or-down sign by the party leader, or by a political debt that needs to be repaid. While it is true . . . that a majority of the members of Congress are lawyers, they have not kept up-to-date on recent legal developments. In fact, most Supreme Court opinions never come to the attention of Congress. Unlike judges, the Representatives and Senators are almost totally dependent on the recommendations of others in making constitutional judgments." Abner J. Mikva, "How Well Does Congress Support and Defend the Constitution?," North Carolina Law Review 61 (1983): 609.

[47] Elizabeth Garrett and Adrian Vermeule, "Institutional Design of a Thayerian Congress," Duke Law Journal 50 (2001): 1277-1333.

[48] Mikva, "How Well Does Congress Support and Defend the Constitution?," 610.

considering the constitutionality of the statutes it adopts."[49] He criticized Congress for "pass[ing] over the constitutional questions, leaving the hard questions to the courts" and stated constitutional issues become "subsidiary to the desire to crack down on crime or bring administrative agencies under control."[50] Fisher himself has admitted that "congressional decisions often turn more on matters of politics, partisanship, and personality than legal analysis."[51]

Whether better described as substantive or superficial, Congress has had, as briefly discussed, an important relationship with the Constitution. Given this relationship and the fact that as the legislative body operating under our constitutional system, legislation and legislative action always fall somewhere in the milieu of its various understood and accepted (or contested) powers and limitations, attention to it is warranted. Devins and Whittington

> [c]onclude[] that Congress is institutionally well equipped to interpret the Constitution. . . . lawmakers seek to enact good public policy and . . . the legislative process promotes fact finding and deliberation. And while constitutional issues may not be front and center in these legislative deliberations, Congress is still better positioned than the Court to set the

---

[49] Fisher, "Constitutional Interpretation by Members of Congress," 707; citing Abner J. Mikva, "How Well Does Congress Support and Defend the Constitution?," 587.

[50] Mikva, "How Well Does Congress Support and Defend the Constitution?," 609. Incidentally, Mikva disagrees with the assessments of Currie and Fisher. Mikva writes, "from the earliest years of the Republic the Congressional Record casts little light on the great constitutional debates that have periodically divided the country." Mikva, "How Well Does Congress Support and Defend the Constitution?," 611.

[51] Louis Fisher, "Analysis by Congressional Staff Agencies," in Devins and Whittington, eds., Congress and the Constitution, 81. In contrast, elsewhere Fisher has written that Congress "makes significant contributions by participating in that constitutional dialogue." Louis Fisher, "Constitutional Interpretation by Members of Congress," 708.

national agenda on issues implicating federalism and the separation of powers.[52]

However, any analysis involving the contemporary Congress has to take into consideration numerous contextual and structural issues. For example, "[c]ongressional reforms in the 1970s (including . . . efforts to shift power away from committee chairs and provide new mechanisms for confronting the 'imperial presidency'), new electoral and institutional pressures (such as the rise of constituents' expectations and the emergence of the 'permanent campaign'), and altered, often hostile, relations with the presidency, are all plausible influences on Congress's formation and enforcement of its constitutional understandings."[53] Unfortunately, "Congress has not enjoyed great public esteem and is more likely to be seen as a threat to constitutional values than an embodiment of them. . . . Scholars and citizens alike perceive Congress as an arena of partisan conflict and electoral pandering, hardly as a bulwark of constitutional principles."[54] As noted earlier by Judge Mikva, in conjunction with greater party polarization, we also know that "[t]he relentless demands of constituents, lobbyists, and campaigns are likely to crowd out or at least diminish the amount of time that lawmakers devote to reflecting on constitutional affairs."[55]

---

[52] Neal Devins and Keith E. Whittington, "Introduction," in Congress and the Constitution, 13.

[53] Bruce G. Peabody, "Congressional Attitudes toward Constitutional Interpretation," in Congress and the Constitution, 46. Peabody cites, Richard L. Hall, Participation in Congress (New Haven: Yale University Press, 1996), 21-24; Barbara Sinclair, Legislators, Leaders, and Lawmaking: The U.S. House of Representatives in the Postreform Era (Baltimore: Johns Hopkins University Press, 1995); David W. Rohde, Parties and Leaders in the Postreform House (Chicago: University of Chicago Press, 1991).

[54] Neal Devins and Keith E. Whittington, "Introduction," in Congress and the Constitution, 1.

[55] For example, see Sean M. Theriault, Party Polarization in Congress (Cambridge: Cambridge University Press, 2008) and Colton C. Campbell and Nicol C. Rae, The Contentious Senate: Partisanship, Ideology, and the Myth of Cool Judgment (Lanham, MD: Rowman & Littlefield, 2001). The

While many would agree that individuals like members of Congress are not reductionistic "gases or pistons,"[56] congressional scholarship has noted the presence of the "electoral connection,"[57] the multiplicity of goals pursued by legislators,[58] their "severely constricted agenda[s],"[59] as well as the importance of "veto points."[60] As

---

quote comes from Bruce G. Peabody, "Congressional Attitudes toward Constitutional Interpretation," in Congress and the Constitution, 50. Louis Fisher states, "Well I came to CRS in the 1970s and I worked with a lot of members and committees that cared a lot about separation of powers and legislative prerogatives. There are very few people that I know today that take that as an interest. There are a lot of reasons for that. . . . So I think what we've had is five decades of continued presidential dominance, less involvement, often no involvement by the courts and less understanding by members of Congress on what their legislative prerogatives are and how the structure of government is meant to protect individual rights and liberties. That was all supposed to come out of a rejection of monarchy an acceptance of small r, republican form of government." Interview with Louis Fisher conducted by Alison Rostankowski, "TOPIC: USA Patriot Act", (2004), available at www.duncanentertainment.com/interview_fisher.php (accessed December 15, 2008).

[56] John Lewis Gaddis, The Landscape of History: How Historians Map the Past (Oxford: Oxford University Press, 2002), 38, citing, Stanley Hoffmann, "International Relations: The Long Road to Theory," in International Relations and Foreign Policy: A Reader in Research and Theory, ed. James N. Rosenau (New York: Free Press, 1961), 429.

[57] David Mayhew, Congress: The Electoral Connection (New Haven: Yale University Press, 1974).

[58] Elizabeth Garrett and Adrian Vermeule, "Institutional Design of a Thayerian Congress," in Congress and the Constitution, 246, citing, Richard F. Fenno's classic, Congressmen in Committees (Boston: Little, Brown, 1973); John W. Kingdon, "Models of Legislative Voting," 39 Journal of Politics 563 (1977): 569-70; John W. Kingdon, Congressmen's Voting Decisions, 3rd ed. (Ann Arbor: University of Michigan Press, 1989).

[59] Elizabeth Garrett and Adrian Vermeule, "Institutional Design of a Thayerian Congress," in Congress and the Constitution, 248.

previously mentioned, the sheer number of members often inhibits precision in delineating congressional action or inaction. As one scholar has asked, "[d]oes Congress have a collective mind? Is there a congressional psyche to be analyzed? Or are there simply 535

---

[60] "Perhaps, however, irresponsibility is structural. Political scientists have noted how many veto points there are in the legislative process. That is, for Congress to take what I have called a completed action, many individual members of Congress, acting on their own rather than through some version of majority rule, must refuse to exercise a power to halt the action's advance. Consider the meaning of a failure to exercise an effective veto by a member situated at a veto point and empowered by his or her constituents to act according to the member's sense of constitutional responsibility. When the action proceeds through the veto point, it receives real constitutional consideration and thereby gains some constitutional respectability. With many veto points and some members of Congress free to act on their sense of constitutional responsibility, completed actions may frequently be constitutionally responsible as well. . . . When members exercise their vetoes sequentially, though, a problem of irresponsibility may arise. The difficulty is that the completed *action* we are looking for turns out to be *inaction* as soon as a veto is exercised, even by a member who is personally acting in a constitutionally responsible manner. Were the Constitution to require action on some matter, inaction as an outcome would be irresponsible. Yet the occasions on which the Constitution uncontroversially requires action are rare indeed – although exercising the power to declare war may be one of them. And yet, of course, precisely *when* the Constitution requires a declaration of war as a predicate for military action is itself a matter of substantial constitutional controversy. . . . More problematically, the presence of many veto points at which individual members can act according to their own views of the Constitution may skew outcomes *against* action." Mark Tushnet, "Evaluating Congressional Constitutional Interpretation: Some Criteria and Two Informal Case Studies," in Congress and the Constitution, 287. Emphasis in original.

individual politicians, with conflicting values and interests, inclined to vote them, but not always doing so in a consistent fashion?"[61]

Reflecting on the popularity of a particular measure might lead some members to neglect constitutional dimensions,[62] an overabundance of information given limited time constraints often hinders members,[63] and the place of members of Congress within social science itself has often made the modern Congress difficult to study.[64]

---

[61] Paul L. Rosen, review of Contest for Constitutional Authority: The Abortion and War Powers Debates, by Susan R. Burgess, Canadian Journal of Political Science 26, no. 3 (Sep. 1993): 598.

[62] As Pickerill writes, "the level of public and congressional support for a policy might be so strong that policy makers are simply unaware of a potential constitutional issue. The goal is to get consensus in Congress, pass the legislation, and satisfy voters. Strong consensus for a public policy, and for relevant legislation, means that supporters simply do not look for potentially damaging aspects of a bill." Pickerill, Constitutional Deliberation, 65.

[63] Quirk and Binder write, "[a]cquiring information and deliberating intelligently is perhaps the most critical capacity of an independent legislature. Congress's difficulty in this regard is certainly not lack of information. Instead, the key challenges for Congress in achieving sound deliberation are the superabundance of information, the difficulties of assessing the validity and significance of the information it acquires, the obstacles to reflecting thoughtfully in a charged, competitive environment, and the temptation to employ facts and arguments as tools for manipulation." Paul J. Quirk and Sarah A. Binder, "Introduction: Congress and American Democracy: Institutions and Performance," in Paul J. Quirk and Sarah A. Binder, eds. The Legislative Branch (Oxford: Oxford University Press, 2005), xxvi.

[64] Mayhew writes, "the actions of members of Congress . . . do not enjoy much of a place in social science, even if they rate high with journalists, traditional historians, and alert citizens. As a theoretical matter, social scientists tend to see Congress as a place where externally determined views or interests – that is, those of the society's classes, interest groups, electorates, and the like – are *registered*. Causal arrows are aimed at Capitol Hill, and they hit. This is virtually all that happens. Also, as a conceptual matter, the making of laws tends to be the only activity worth addressing. And as an empirical matter, roll call voting in the service of lawmaking is virtually the only evidence

Despite these limitations, at least within certain parameters, many still find value in Congress' constitutional deliberations.[65]

DELIBERATION & DIALOGUES

As already highlighted, there have been many important works on congressional constitutional deliberation,[66] and as Paul J. Quirk has

---

worth examining." Mayhew adds in a citation, "[a]genda manipulation is said to make a difference. But in theory, that ordinarily takes place in a context of ready-made, exogenously determined distributions of ideal points." David R. Mayhew, "Actions in the Public Sphere," in Paul J. Quirk and Sarah A. Binder, eds. The Legislative Branch (Oxford: Oxford University Press, 2005), 69, 100. Mayhew adds, "To array members of Congress from most liberal to most conservative on a summary roll call measure, a popular simplifying device, is to say little about the substantive content of that dimension. The ingredients of the content need to be invented day after day, year after year, generation after generation, by enterprising politicians and others. They do not exist 'naturally.'" David R. Mayhew, "Actions in the Public Sphere," in Paul J. Quirk and Sarah A. Binder, eds. The Legislative Branch (Oxford: Oxford University Press, 2005), 70.

[65] "[M]y argument is that so long as members pursue good public policy and not solely reelection, they must, for purely instrumental reasons, take into account the constitutionality of the legislation they pass. Furthermore, to the extent that the congressional legislative process promotes fact finding and deliberation and thereby the making of good public policy, Congress has as good a claim as the Court to determine constitutionality in domains where its policy and political expertise are key." Barbara Sinclair, "Can Congress Be Trusted with the Constitution? The Effects of Incentives and Procedures," in Congress and the Constitution, 294.

[66] For just a few examples in chronological content order, see, Charles Hyneman and George Carey, A Second Federalist: Congress Creates a Government (1967); David P. Currie, The Constitution in Congress, 4 vols. (Chicago: University of Chicago Press, 1997-2005); William Lee Miller, Arguing About Slavery: John Quincy Adams and the Great Battle in the United States Congress (New York: Vintage Books, 1995); David P. Currie, "The Civil War Congress," The University of Chicago Law Review 73, no. 4

written, "[t]o perform effectively as a policymaking institution, Congress cannot simply identify the policy preferences of various constituencies, form coalitions among their supporters, and count up the votes. Rather, a key part of Congress's task is [to] develop alternatives, collect and evaluate information, and weigh consequences – in short to deliberate about public policy."[67] This has both beneficial and non-beneficial potential. As Fearon, Garrett and Vermeuele note:

> Deliberation also provides institutional and process benefits, however. It exploits the collective character of legislatures in ways that can in principle improve Congress's constitutional performance. Among the concrete benefits of deliberation are its tendencies to encourage the revelation of private information, to expose extreme, polarized viewpoints to the moderating effect of diverse arguments, to make outcomes more legitimate by providing reasons to defeated parties, and to require the articulation of public-spirited justifications for votes.[68]
>
> To be sure, deliberation also suffers pathologies, quite apart from opportunity costs: it can reduce candor, encourage posturing, trigger herd behavior, and silence dissenters. Yet

---

(autumn 2006): 1131-1226; James Burnham, Congress and the American Tradition (Chicago: Henry Regnery Company, 1965); Walter F. Murphy, Congress and the Court: A Case Study in the American Political Process (Chicago: The University of Chicago Press, 1962).

[67] Paul J. Quirk, "Deliberation and Decision Making," in The Legislative Branch, eds. Paul J. Quirk and Sarah A. Binder (Oxford: Oxford University Press, 2005), 314. Quirk adds in a footnote what he considers the "pioneering studies of Congress as a deliberative institution." They are Arthur Maass, Congress and the Common Good (New York: Basic Books, 1983); Joseph M. Bessette, The Mild Voice of Reason: Deliberative Democracy and American National Government (Chicago: University of Chicago Press, 1994); and Keith Krehbiel, Information and Legislative Organization (Ann Arbor: The University of Michigan Press, 1991).

[68] James D. Fearon, "Deliberation as Discussion," in Deliberative Democracy, ed. Jon Elster (New York: Cambridge University Press, 1998), 44, 53-56, 63-64.

> the alternative to deliberation is simply voting without discussion, a procedure that no modern legislature, and few if any collective bodies generally, would ever adopt. It seems indisputable that on balance, some congressional deliberation on constitutional questions is better than none at all.[69]

In seeking definitional specificity, "deliberation" can be elusive. Is it merely constitutional "discourse" in Congress: the rhetoric, language, arguments, assertions, and interpretations of and about the Constitution used by members of Congress? Is it the mere vote tallies on constitutional amendments or resolutions and bills that are clearly constitutional in nature? Pickerill correlates "'deliberation' with 'reflection' and debate over the scope of federal powers under the Constitution in the context of legislation"[70] and argues that "deliberation motivated by the threat of judicial review is better than no deliberation, or deliberation motivated only by public policy or public opinion."[71]

As has been mentioned, members of Congress often have competing and more importantly, self-serving goals. For example, "granting the courts' power over constitutional questions often serves legislative interests by allowing lawmakers to cede divisive, volatile political issues to another branch."[72] Furthermore, "we might speculate that members of Congress, whether generally favoring deferential or

---

[69] Elizabeth Garrett and Adrian Vermeule, "Institutional Design of a Thayerian Congress," in Congress and the Constitution, 248.

[70] Whittington comments that "'reflection' and 'debate' seem a bit strong given the evidence presented." Keith E. Whittington, "Review: James Madison Has Left the Building," Review of Constitutional Deliberation in Congress: The Impact of Judicial Review in a Separated System by J. Mitchell Pickerill University of Chicago Law Review 72 (summer 2005): 1156; citing Pickerill, Constitutional Deliberation, 11.

[71] J. Mitchell Pickerill, Constitutional Deliberation in Congress, 130.

[72] Bruce G. Peabody, "Congressional Attitudes toward Constitutional Interpretation," in Congress and the Constitution, 42. See, Mark Graber, "The Non-Majoritarian Problem: Legislative Deference to the Judiciary," Studies in American Political Development 7 (1993): 35-73.

independent attitudes, would express the greatest interest in constitutional issues likely to affect their constituents' or their institutional interests directly, such as constitutional questions related to the scope of congressional authority or the balance of power between the legislative and executive branches."[73] Tushnet argues that deliberation has to be something Congress as an institution does, not the action or actions of individual members.[74]

> It is trivially easy to compile a list of constitutionally irresponsible or thoughtless proposals made by members of Congress. A member will shoot out a press release responding to some local outrage, or put a bill in the hopper without taking any time to consider its constitutionality. Often these proposals result from the member's desire to grandstand, to do something that gets his or her name in the nightly news in the district.[75] They are not serious proposals for legislation, and the member has no real expectation that they will be enacted. . . . Noting grandstanding actions of this sort provides no basis for evaluating Congress's behavior. What we need to examine are institutional actions, those that represent the outcome of a completed congressional process. Institutional actions can of course be inaction as well. Grandstanding proposals may count against assertions that members of Congress act in a constitutionally responsible manner, but the failure of such proposals to move through the legislative process should count in favor of such assertions. Institutional actions have proceeded through a complex set of organization structures. Those structures, designed for other purposes, may sometimes serve (imperfectly and as a byproduct) to screen out constitutionally irresponsible actions. . . . Judges write opinions when they decide what the Constitution means. Congress does not. Enacted statutes typically become effective

---

[73] Bruce G. Peabody, "Congressional Attitudes toward Constitutional Interpretation," in Congress and the Constitution, 43.

[74] Tushnet, "Evaluating Congressional Constitutional Interpretation," 270-271.

[75] See, e.g., David Mayhew, Congress: The Electoral Connection (New Haven: Yale University Press, 1974), 61.

> without an accompanying statement of the constitutional rationale on which Congress relied. . . . Determining the constitutional basis for a completed action by Congress requires us to examine a range of materials, such as committee reports, floor debate, and even newspaper stories, from which we can infer the constitutional basis on which Congress acted. Inferences of this sort will inevitably be open to question."[76]

In relation to those collective enterprises, given the curtness of much floor debate and the brevity of newspaper and journalistic stories, committee hearings often provide the most content with which to work. In fact, "[m]uch of the important work of Congress is done in committees."[77] Nevertheless, "[c]ongressional committees are nonetheless largely unchartered territory for constitutional scholars. The new scholarly interest in extrajudicial constitutional interpretation has been more likely to focus on floor debates or committee activities of extraordinary interest, such as the hearings of the Senate Judiciary Committee on the nomination of Robert Bork to the Supreme Court, than on the congressional committee system generally and its routine work."[78] Be that as it may, if "the Constitution is broadly relevant to American governance, it might be hoped that the Constitution would make an appearance before a variety of committees with a variety of policy concerns."[79] Given his findings after analyzing only hearing titles, Whittington states that "[t]hose interested in the 'Constitution outside the courts' should look to committee hearings to gain an understanding of how the Constitution is used in legislative and electoral politics. It now seems clear that the Constitution often makes an appearance in congressional deliberations."[80]

---

[76] Tushnet, "Evaluating Congressional Constitutional Interpretation," 270-71. Emphasis added.

[77] Whittington, "Hearing about the Constitution," 87.

[78] Whittington, "Hearing about the Constitution," 87. Emphasis added.

[79] Whittington, "Hearing about the Constitution," 96.

[80] Whittington analyzes committee hearings in the U.S. House of Representatives and the U.S. Senate from 1991 to 2001. Utilizing the Congressional Information Service and its coding mechanisms, Whittington

Drawing off of Whittington's delineation of deliberation in committees and Tushnet's delineation of deliberation in Congress, deliberation was defined as legislative action, engaged in by Congress, considered as an institution, that has "proceeded through [the] complex set of organization structures" within Congress which make "substantive reference to the U.S. Constitution" as well as floor statements and interviews which are also substantive, not ones that are merely perfunctory.[81] In the three cases before us, the three cases and all legislative action related to them cannot help but meet such criteria because there are constitutional, and not merely statutory, issues at stake in each respective piece of legislative, two of which are now public laws.

---

found 406 hearings in the House and Senate from 1991 to 2001 that mentioned "constitutional" in a prominent manner. Whittington catalogued when such hearings were held, by whom, in which issue areas, and the extent to which they were driven by the action of the other branches of government. He found that elections were important, judiciary committees did not monopolize constitutional deliberation in congressional committees, structural matters received as much attention as individual rights, the courts may not be as important as is generally thought, and the executive branch may be more important than originally thought. More specifically in terms of this overall literature, in relation to the statement that the courts may not be as important as generally thought, contra Pickerill, Whittington found that the Congress held fewer hearings discussing constitutional issues after the Court announced its increased scrutiny of federal legislation. Whittington, "Hearings about the Constitution," 87-109.

[81] Mark Tushnet, "Evaluating Congressional Constitutional Interpretation," 270-71. Whittington, "Hearing about the Constitution," 92. Pickerill, too, nicely provides a working and useful definition as "constitutional debate among members or other relevant policy-makers and lawmakers, committee hearings that focus at some length on constitutional issues, language in a bill or a statute that reflects constitutional principles or judicial doctrines, or some other indication that constitutional issues played an important part when the legislation in question was considered." J. Mitchell Pickerill, Constitutional Deliberation in Congress: The Impact of Judicial Review in a Separated System, 64

The relationship among the branches of government is also an important part of this discussion and should not be ignored. In 1962, Walter F. Murphy wrote that "[t]he observation that Supreme Court decisions are political in effect is commonplace, yet there is relatively little literature which actually explores the reactions of other branches of government to Court decisions."[82] Congress cannot help but have interaction with the other branches of our government. In his seminal work, The Least Dangerous Branch, Alexander Bickel referred to a "continuing colloquy" between the Supreme Court, political institutions, and society at large.[83] Donald G. Morgan found that since 1890, there had been "an alarming increase in congressional abdication of its proper role in such matters, coupled with a proportionate increase in legislative acquiescence in judicial determination."[84] Pickerill posits eras of "judicial dualism" and "judicial deference," where the Court has oscillated between having a mixed view of federalism in relation to Congress and a view that completely defers to Congress in matters involving federalism.[85] C. Herman Pritchett concluded in his study of

---

[82] Walter F. Murphy, Congress and the Court: A Case Study in the American Political Process (Chicago: The University of Chicago Press, 1962), vii.

[83] Alexander Bickel, The Least Dangerous Branch: The Supreme Court at the Bar of Politics (New York: The Bobbs-Merrill Co., 1962), 240.

[84] Stanley I. Kutler, review of Congress and the Constitution: A Study of Responsibility, by Donald G. Morgan, The American Historical Review 73, no. 3 (Feb. 1968): 904. On a side note, Kutler noted the lack of consistency in American political thought. "Few men in American political life (and especially congressmen) have had a consistent attitude toward the problem. Thus Jefferson favored judicial review in the 1790's and opposed it after he became President; William Howard Taft berated Congress in 1913 for 'passing the buck' on prohibition to the Court, but eight years later as Chief Justice, of course, he insisted that he judiciary had primary responsibility for determining constitutionality; and . . . southern congressmen . . . insisted that *Brown v. Board of Education* determined nothing, while urging submission to the *Civil Rights Cases* (1883) and *Plessy v. Ferguson* (1896) as proper readings of the Fourteenth Amendment and therefore the 'law of the land.'" 904.

[85] J. Mitchell Pickerill, Constitutional Deliberation in Congress: The Impact of Judicial Review in a Separated System (Durham: Duke University Press,

Congress's reaction to the Supreme Court's decisions in the late 1950s in the area of freedom of speech and association, "[i]n essence, all that the Court can do with its great power is to enforce a waiting period during which its doctrines are subject to popular consideration."[86]

SCHOLARLY ANTECEDENTS

This research builds on the literature mentioned previously discussing the interaction between Congress and the Constitution. However, as Devins and Whittington have recently stated, "the engagement of political actors with the constitutional text is largely terra incognita. Scholars have only begun to explore the nature, extent, and consequence of constitutional discourse beyond the courtroom."[87] Bruce Peabody writes, "[f]or those interested in the relationship between Congress and the Constitution and, more specifically, the suitability and feasibility of greater legislative participation in constitutional lawmaking, current scholarship largely overlooks vital questions about lawmakers' subjective understanding of our supreme law."[88]

Given "the fact that the study of Congress and the Constitution is still nascent," they thus describe recent work as "more a wake-up call than a definitive statement."[89] They write

> [t]here has been little sustained attention to congressional treatment of the Constitution and constitutional issues. It has

---

2004), 7; the first phrase comes from constitutional historian Robert G. McCloskey, The American Supreme Court (Chicago: University of Chicago Press, 1960).

[86] C. Herman Pritchett, Congress versus the Supreme Court, 1957-1960 (Minneapolis: University of Minnesota Press, 1961), 133.

[87] Neal Devins and Keith E. Whittington, "Introduction," in Congress and the Constitution, 5.

[88] Bruce G. Peabody, "Congressional Attitudes toward Constitutional Interpretation," in Congress and the Constitution, 39.

[89] Neal Devins and Keith E. Whittington, "Introduction," in Congress and the Constitution, 5.

> simply not been part of the research agenda of congressional scholars, who unsurprisingly have been preoccupied with other concerns that are perceived to be closer to the heart of legislative politics and more amenable to systemic study. Constitutional scholars have generally turned a blind eye to Congress as well. The study of the Constitution has largely been defined within the academy as the study of constitutional law as produced by the courts. From this perspective, Congress is a target of constitutional law, not a producer of it. . . . After long neglect, the time is ripe for more sustained study of Congress as a constitutional interpreter and responsible constitutional agent. Recent Supreme Court decisions have focused attention on the constitutional powers and responsibilities of Congress, and the sustained judicial inquiry into the relationship between Congress and the Constitution has encouraged a heightened awareness of Congress in constitutional scholars as well. At the same time, a somewhat independent scholarly turn to the 'Constitution outside the courts' has opened up space for considering extrajudicial constitutional interpretation and the relationship between nonjudicial political actors and the Constitution. Now that constitutional scholars have begun to look beyond the courts, we believe a more careful examination of the Congress as an institution and a political entity will be needed in order to fully understand, appreciate, and evaluate congressional engagement with the Constitution.[90]

---

[90] Neal Devins and Keith E. Whittington, "Introduction," in Congress and the Constitution, 2. Likewise, Richard Pildes writes, "American political culture has long been characterized by a unique paradox: although it is the country with the most deeply penetrating democratic sensibility, the US also has the most robust tradition of judicially enforced constitutional constraints on political power. The formal institutional site at which this tension is most acutely sharpened is the interchange between Congress (and, to a lesser extent, the executive branch) and the Supreme Court over the meaning of the Constitution itself. Congress engages the Court in various ways: by deciding how to respond to Court decisions holding laws unconstitutional; by taking (or not taking) constitutional doctrine into account when legislating; by

Despite an apparent lack of specialization, this "recent literature has important antecedents, produced by political scientists, which often did focus on Congress as a constitutional interpreter."[91] For example, as mentioned, Donald Morgan "examin[ed] a wide range of cases that traced congressional responsibility for constitutional interpretation over the course of American history." He argued that Congress changed during the New Deal and he was "particularly distressed to find a decline in the acceptance of such congressional responsibility and the rise of 'judicial monopolism' by which the 'legislative function could receive definition solely in relation to policy' while the Constitution was understood to be 'technical, and too abstruse for any but lawyers in the courtroom and judges on the bench to discuss with sense.'"[92]

More recently, Pickerill has "investigate[d] how Congress reacts to the judicial invalidation of federal statutes" by analyzing all federal legislation related to federalism declared unconstitutional from 1953 through the 1996-97 term of the Rehnquist Court.[93] He found that "members of Congress do sometimes engage in constitutional deliberation, but that deliberation is often motivated and shaped by the

---

seeking to influence the Court's constitutional approach through the confirmation process. Yet, this particular congressional role has received only limited academic analysis, the focus of which has been mostly limited to the 19th century." Richard H. Pildes, review of Congress and the Constitution, by Neal Devins and Keith E. Whittington, eds. Journal of Politics 69, no. 1 (2007): 268.

[91] Tushnet, "Evaluating Congressional Constitutional Interpretation," 5; citing, Donald G. Morgan, Congress and the Constitution, (Cambridge: Harvard University Press, 1966), 334-35.

[92] Neal Devins and Keith E. Whittington, "Introduction," in Congress and the Constitution, eds. Neal Devins and Keith E. Whittington (Durham: Duke University Press, 2005), 5, citing, Donald G. Morgan, Congress and the Constitution (Cambridge: Harvard University Press, 1966), 334-35.

[93] Keith E. Whittington, "Review: James Madison Has Left the Building," Review of Constitutional Deliberation in Congress: The Impact of Judicial Review in a Separated System by J. Mitchell Pickerill University of Chicago Law Review 72 (summer 2005): 1137-1158.

Court's judicial review decisions."[94] Congress is occasionally motivated by Supreme Court opinions when writing legislation, but usually legislators are inattentive to such matters preferring to focus on public policy results and constituent demands. While many believe when the Court wields the judicial veto, Congress is thwarted outright, Pickerill found that "while judicial review can be a roadblock to legislation, it is often more of a speed bump or detour."[95]

---

[94] Pickerill, Constitutional Deliberation, 3. More thoroughly, he states, "that the Court's judicial review decisions help to create conditions under which constitutional deliberation in Congress is more likely, and that the language of the Court's opinions and doctrines is likely to influence the content of legislation and constitutional deliberation in Congress. . . . there is legislative life after judicial review. The data suggest that Congress is highly responsive to Supreme Court decisions striking down federal statutes; that is, Congress usually responds formally to the Supreme Court by repassing the statute in modified form, amending the Constitution, or taking other official action. Often, Court decisions forbid Congress to use particular means to achieve policy goals, and the challenge for Congress is to find permissible means to achieve the same or substantially similar goals. . . . Congress is more likely to amend legislation in a manner that reflects deference to or compliance with the Court's interpretations and doctrines. . . . members of Congress and other lawmakers frequently consider constitutional arguments in an instrumental and strategic manner, the main objective being to pass or sustain popular public policies. This does not mean that those in Congress are hostile to constitutional deliberation, but it does mean that constitutional issues are not generally institutional priorities in Congress. Constitutional debates in Congress are frequently conducted in reaction to and in anticipation of the Court's exercise of judicial review. . . . judicial review is a crucial mechanism in the lawmaking process, as important for federalism as for other areas of the Constitution."" 6-9.

[95] Pickerill, Constitutional Deliberation in Congress, 31. Pickerill "looked at any law that established, amended, or repealed the provisions of the statute reviewed by the Court and coded them as no response, a repeal, an amended statute, a repeal combined with the passage of a new law, or a constitutional amendment. He found that the median time between the passage of a statute and its nullification by the Court was just under ten years, while Congress

In addition, Pickerill found that Congress amends "legislation in a manner that makes clear concessions to the Court's decision."[96] Generally speaking, Congress and the Supreme Court operate on different policy dimensions, constitutional policy and public policy, the fact of which allows a "win-win" situation to take place.[97] The "Court is able to announce the constitutional law it wants, but Congress is usually able to work within those doctrinal constraints to achieve most of the public policy results it wants."[98] He "posits that congressional deliberation on constitutional issues will be more likely when the Court is relatively active in reviewing the legislature's handiwork and when the bill is controversial enough that there will be a mobilized opposition to raise constitutional objections."[99] Given the incentives facing legislators, "constitutional issues are not an automatic item on the legislator's checklist when drafting and considering bills"[100] and in terms of "low-salience bills that generate little controversy, no one on Capitol Hill is likely to take the time to vet their constitutionality."[101]

Furthermore, Pickerill adds

> constitutional issues are not priorities in Congress. Politics and policy dominate congressional decision making, and members of Congress do not systematically consider the constitutional

---

took a median of nearly four years to respond (when it did respond) to the judicial invalidation. Overall, Congress neglected to respond or decided to simply repeal the affected policy in just over half the cases in the overall sample and when the Court struck down a federal law, Congress's most common response was simply to amend the statute to work around the constitutional obstacle." Pickerill, Constitutional Deliberation in Congress, 42-43.

[96] Pickerill, Constitutional Deliberation in Congress, 49.

[97] Pickerill, Constitutional Deliberation in Congress, 36-37.

[98] Whittington, "Review: James Madison Has Left the Building," 1146.

[99] Whittington, "Review: James Madison Has Left the Building," 1151; citing Pickerill, 64-67.

[100] Pickerill, Constitutional Deliberation in Congress, 67.

[101] Whittington, "Review: James Madison Has Left the Building," 1151.

authority for their actions. Much of the time, there is no need to consider constitutional issues, but there is always a need to consider the policy and political implications of proposed legislation.[102] . . . The constitutional deliberation that does take place can do so on two dimensions: a more philosophical one over specific constitutional values or principles, or a more instrumental one over satisfying the Supreme Court's doctrine in a given area.[103] . . . At best, judicial review forces Congress to craft constitutional statutes, and at a minimum, the Court reminds Congress that it operates within a constitutional framework.[104]

---

[102] J. Mitchell Pickerill, Constitutional Deliberation in Congress: The Impact of Judicial Review in a Separated System (Durham: Duke University Press, 2004), 144.

[103] J. Mitchell Pickerill, Constitutional Deliberation in Congress: The Impact of Judicial Review in a Separated System (Durham: Duke University Press, 2004), 145.

[104] J. Mitchell Pickerill, Constitutional Deliberation in Congress: The Impact of Judicial Review in a Separated System (Durham: Duke University Press, 2004), 147, quoting a then-current Supreme Court Justice. "[M]uch of the constitutional deliberation in Congress takes place, or is perceived to take place, in the context of well-known Supreme Court caselaw. Some of the time, a Court decision must be addressed because it is very recent or otherwise famous. At the same time, however, it also became evident that the perceived need to address the Court's caselaw was part of the politics of the bill, especially the political opposition to a policy or proposed legislation. . . . Thus, I believe that the Rehnquist Court's decisions should be viewed as a reinitiation of dialogues and negotiations with Congress that remained dormant for decades, and that this is an appropriate role for the Court and judicial review. The Court is neither an insurmountable obstacle for the legislative majority nor a savior of the people from unwanted government. And to eliminate the Court from the debate would disrupt inter-institutional lawmaking, in which each unique institution of government makes unique contributions to ever-changing laws. Most importantly, the justices bring unique perspectives on – and methods for- constitutional interpretation. . . . If we take the notion of constitutionalism seriously, it is desirable to have an

Keith Whittington has hypothesized that in the 1990s Congress choose not to respond more aggressively to Supreme Court invalidations of congressional statutes simply because the majority power in Congress was not opposed to such limitations upon federal power.[105] Whittington found Congress responds not to Supreme Court decisions that challenge the abstract institutional power of Congress, but to those of substantive concern to the current Congress. Committees did hold hearings about several Court decisions on matters of constitutional power in the 1990s, such as those involving religious liberty and local control over waste disposal, but did not question the rulings which were more focused on limiting national power. Tushnet found Congress has been "responsible" in interpreting the Constitution in areas where the court is reluctant to intervene, such as impeachment and war powers.[106]

---

institution empowered to make the primary determinations about constitutional meaning, for many of the reasons put forth by Larry Alexander and Frederick Schauer in defense of judicial supremacy (1997). Likewise, if we take the notion of democratic and representative lawmaking seriously, it is desirable to entrust that power to democratic and republican institutions. On the other hand, it would be dangerous to exonerate Congress from any responsibility over constitutional interpretation. While constitutional interpretation may be a secondary responsibility for Congress, the Court's constitutional interpretations should not go unchecked, and there may be times when alternative political venues are needed for airing constitutional claims. We should expect the Court's exercise of judicial review to naturally result in a relationship with Congress characterized by interaction and reaction, by negotiation and anticipation. In a sense, then, the true role of judicial review in our system is something in between judicial supremacy and an egalitarian view of coordinate construction." 142; 149; 153.

105 Whittington, "Hearings about the Constitution in Congressional Interpretation," 87-109.

106 Tushnet, "Evaluating Congressional Constitutional Interpretation," 269-292. Most of Tushnet's chapter is a discussion of criteria he suggests to study actual constitutional deliberation in Congress. He does not engage in a lengthy discussion of the constitutional arguments over Clinton's impeachment and he only uses the case of Kosovo as evidence for "responsible" discussions over war powers.

More importantly, while keeping our definition of constitutional deliberation in mind,[107] modes of analysis centered on "political time" and "political regimes" provide the best means by which to understand these cases. The notion of political regimes "incorporates not only electorally dominant partisan coalitions, but also a set of dominant policy concerns and legitimating ideologies. A regime in this sense overarches contending policy orientations at lower levels such that even electorally successful oppositional figures can be forced to sustain the commitments of the dominant regime."[108] Within this framework, the Court plays an important part and "[f]or at least fifty years, prominent political scientists have traced the decisions of the U.S. Supreme Court to the policy and political commitments of governing partisan regimes." They have found that "justices have almost always acted in alliance with the governing coalition of which they themselves are generally members."[109] During these "ordinary" times, as Pickerill and

---

[107] Legislative action, engaged in by Congress, considered as an institution, that has "proceeded through [the] complex set of organization structures" within Congress which make "substantive reference to the U.S. Constitution" as well as floor statements and interviews which are also substantive, not ones that are merely perfunctory. In addition, "constitutional debate among members or other relevant policy-makers and lawmakers, committee hearings that focus at some length on constitutional issues, language in a bill or a statute that reflects constitutional principles or judicial doctrines, or some other indication that constitutional issues played an important part when the legislation in question was considered." See footnote 81.

[108] Keith E. Whittington, "The Political Foundations of Judicial Supremacy," 264-265, in Sotirios A. Barber and Robert P. George, eds., Constitutional Politics: Essays on Constitution Making, Maintenance, and Change (Princeton: Princeton University Press, 2001), citing Stephen Skowronek, The Politics Presidents Make (Cambridge: Harvard University Press, 1993).

[109] Thomas M. Keck, "Party Politics or Judicial Independence? The Regime Politics Literature Hits the Law Schools," review of From Jim Crow to Civil Rights: The Supreme Court and the Struggle for Racial Equality, by Michael J. Klarman, The Most Democratic Branch? How the Courts Serve America, by Jeffrey Rosen, and A Court Divided: The Rehnquist Court and the Future of Constitutional Law, by Mark Tushnet, Law & Social Inquiry 32, no. 2

Clayton write, "one expects the Court's decisions to reflect broader regime values,"[110] while, "[u]nder some circumstances, the Court may stray quite far from some of the dominant regime's values, as long as it does not challenge core values and constituencies."[111]

Furthermore, while in 1957 Dahl "argued that the Court rarely exercises the power of judicial review in a way that is contrary to the interests of the governing coalition in the national political system,"[112] the era encompassing these three cases has been dominated by a relatively divided, or competing, governing coalition(s) and partisan environment.[113] This is evident in the partisan compositions of

---

(spring 2007): 511-12. Dahl wrote, "[t]he fact is, then, that the policy views dominant on the Court are never for long out of line with the policy views dominant among the lawmaking majorities of the United States." 285. Robert A. Dahl, "Decision-Making in a Democracy: The Supreme Court as a National Policy-Maker," Journal of Public Law 6 (1957): 279-295.

[110] J. Mitchell Pickerill and Cornell W. Clayton. "The Rehnquist Court and the Political Dynamics of Federalism." Perspectives on Politics 2, no. 2 (June 2004): 236.

[111] J. Mitchell Pickerill and Cornell W. Clayton, "The Rehnquist Court and the Political Dynamics of Federalism." Perspectives on Politics 2, no. 2 (June 2004): 236, citing, Neal Devins, "The Federal-Rights Nexus: Explaining why Senate Democrats Tolerate Rehnquist Court Decision Making but not the Rehnquist Court," University of Colorado Law Review 73, no. 4 (2002): 1307-36, and Keith E. Whittington, "Taking What They Give Us: Explaining the Court's Federalism Offensive," Duke Law Journal 51, no. 1 (2001): 477-520. As Pickerill and Clayton wrote regarding the Rehnquist Court's federalism decisions, "[y]et the Court's decisions show little sign of challenging the core political values of the national governing regime." 240. As Fisher writes, "[t]he Court has the 'power' to declare presidential and congressional acts unconstitutional, but it can exercise that power effectively only by acknowledging its place within the political system." Louis Fisher, Constitutional Dialogues: Interpretation as Political Process (Princeton: Princeton University Press, 1988), 221.

[112] Cornell Clayton and David A. May, "A Political Regimes Approach to the Analysis of Legal Decisions," Polity 32, no. 2 (Winter 1999): 242.

[113] As opposed to an era of realignment, as described by Fisher: "The judiciary is most likely to be out of step with Congress or the President during periods

Congress over the past twenty to thirty years in which these cases and their antecedents inhabit.[114] During times of divided government:

> 'regime' values will be less stable and more conflicted, since neither party enjoys consistent control over legislative institutions. It is true that even when a single party dominates the electoral system, regime values may conflict, as for instance in the conflict between blue-collar labor interests and the civil rights movement within the Democratic coalition of the 1960s. But such conflicts are more prevalent when the regime lacks a unifying party structure to harmonize those competing interests. Even modest alterations to existing legal doctrines may induce dire warnings from politicians as the parties become ideologically more polarized and face a growing incentive to exaggerate the importance of change in an effort to lure independent voters. Third, the electorate is unlikely to mobilize against the Court's positions. To some extent, the polarization within the elected branches reflects

---

of electoral and partisan realignment, when the country is undergoing sharp shifts in political directions while the courts retain the orientation of an age gone by." Louis Fisher, Constitutional Dialogues: Interpretation as Political Process (Princeton: Princeton University Press, 1988), 201, citing, Richard Funston, "The Supreme Court and Critical Elections," American Political Science Review 69, no. 3 (1975): 795-811, and David Adamany, "Legitimacy, Realigning Elections, and the Supreme Court," Wisconsin Law Review 1973, no. 3 (1973): 790-846.

[114] In the Senate, Democrats controlled the chamber during the 96th (58-41-1), 100th (55-45), 101st (55-45), 102nd (56-44), 103rd (57-43), 110th (49-49-2), and the 111th Congress (57-41-2). Republicans were in control of the 97th (53-46-1), 98th (55-45), 99th (53-47), 104th (52-48), 105th (55-45), 106th (55-45), 108th (51-48-1), and 109th (55-44-1). The 107th Senate was evenly divided. In the House, Democrats controlled the 96th (277-158), 97th (242-192-1), 98th (269-166), 99th (253-182), 100th (258-177), 101st (260-175), 102nd (267-167-1), 103rd (258-176-1), 110th (233-202), and the 111th (257-178). Republicans controlled the 104th (230-204-1), 105th (228-206-1), 106th (223-211-1), 107th (221-212-2), 108th (229-205-1), and 109th (232-202-1).

> polarization within the electorate itself. Indeed, the 2000 election saw the highest level of straight party voting in fifty years of National Elections Studies surveys, and, according to public opinion polls, marked the high point of a thirty-year trend of partisan and ideological polarization. During such periods of division, the Court's decisions will always enjoy support from a significant portion of the public.[115]

Thus, due to the divided nature of the regime, the Court has more latitude to rule independently, possibly even on issues they would have not ruled on otherwise. As Dahl wrote, "[i]t is to be expected, then, that the Court is least likely to be successful in blocking a determined and persistent lawmaking majority on a major policy and most likely to succeed against a 'weak' majority; e.g., a dead one, a transient one, a fragile one, or one weakly united upon a policy of subordinate importance."[116] While it may be true that, "[t]he influence of regime politics ensures that federal judges, especially at the top of the judicial hierarchy, will have concerns and preferences that are usually in sync

---

[115] J. Mitchell Pickerill and Cornell W. Clayton, "The Rehnquist Court and the Political Dynamics of Federalism," Perspectives on Politics 2, no. 2 (June 2004): 242. Citations omitted. As Keck adds, "the governing coalition is so often divided on important matters that the justices will have multiple acceptable alternatives in most cases. The Court's decision in a given case may be supported by some members of the governing coalition, but if the opposite decision would have been supported by other members of the coalition, then the justices may well have significant room for independent action." Thomas M. Keck, "Party Politics or Judicial Independence? The Regime Politics Literature Hits the Law Schools," review of From Jim Crow to Civil Rights: The Supreme Court and the Struggle for Racial Equality, by Michael J. Klarman, The Most Democratic Branch? How the Courts Serve America, by Jeffrey Rosen, and A Court Divided: The Rehnquist Court and the Future of Constitutional Law, by Mark Tushnet, Law & Social Inquiry 32, no. 2 (spring 2007): 517.

[116] Robert A. Dahl, "Decision-Making in a Democracy: The Supreme Court as a National Policy-Maker," Journal of Public Law 6 (1957): 286.

with other national power holders,"[117] if those other national power holders are divided, so may be the Court, which even among the "conservative" bloc of justices, is what we have seen.[118]

It is important to keep in mind, that this correlation says nothing about the very personal nature of judicial decision-making and its relationship to institutional, legal, and normative commitments.[119] As

---

[117] Howard Gillman, "Regime Politics, Jurisprudential Regimes, and Unenumerated Rights," University of Pennsylvania Journal of Constitutional Law 9, no. 1 (2006): 108.

[118] See Mark Tushnet, A Court Divided: The Rehnquist Court and the Future of Constitutional Law (W.W. Norton, 2005).

[119] As Clayton and May write, "[t]hus, the mere fact that judges decide cases in line with the views of the dominant governing coalition, or the fact that the Court 'follows the election returns,' does not necessitate the conclusion that judges are deciding cases on the basis of personal policy preferences or strategic calculations about their power relative to the other branches. Legal doctrines and standards such as those described above recognize the political contingency of law and require any authentic commitment to law to be responsive to the views held by important political actors such as Congress, the president, states and interest groups. Thus, a justice could be truly committed to law and yet sensitive to the dominant values of the political regime." Cornell Clayton and David A. May, "A Political Regimes Approach to the Analysis of Legal Decisions," Polity 32, no. 2 (Winter 1999): 244-245. Keck writes, "[j]ustices are also influenced by norms of their profession, institutional duty, and perceived fidelity to the law. As Keck writes, "The regime politics literature may well be the best starting point for this effort, but only if its proponents acknowledge more clearly that partisan coalitions do not always dictate the Court's decisions. The fundamental empirical question here is whether—or to what degree, or under what conditions—judges are likely to act independently of the wishes of other power holders. Rather than exerting so much energy in showing that the Court's decisions are influenced by external forces, then, it seems worthwhile at this point to take that fact as given and to explore the variety of ways in which these external forces interact with other influences on the justices. The justices are political people with political preferences, placed on the bench for political reasons. But they are also—most of them—legal

Keck rightly points out, "[f]rom Dahl forward, the chief weakness in the regime politics literature has been a tendency to overstate the influence of external political pressure in a way that implies that the justices' actual decisions were inevitable and neglects the possibility of relatively independent institutional action by the Court."[120] After all, "legal institutions and political values cannot be conceptually separated, and the 'political regimes' insight that the values and attitudes found within the judiciary are shaped by (but in turn can also shape) the existing configuration of political institutions and power across the regime"[121] should not be forgotten. As Clayton and May posit, there are simultaneous interactions and interdependent relationships taking place between changing social values and attitudes, elections, legal positions by key actors, litigation, Court decisions and articulations of the law, as well as applications of the law.[122]

These cases will affirm that members of Congress operate in an extremely political environment. They often "only have fifteen minutes

---

professionals, committed to maintaining the Court's independence and autonomy. Thus, they will ever be pulled in two directions." Thomas M. Keck, "Party Politics or Judicial Independence? The Regime Politics Literature Hits the Law Schools," review of From Jim Crow to Civil Rights The Supreme Court and the Struggle for Racial Equality, by Michael J. Klarman, The Most Democratic Branch? How the Courts Serve America, by Jeffrey Rosen, and A Court Divided: The Rehnquist Court and the Future of Constitutional Law, by Mark Tushnet, Law & Social Inquiry 32, no. 2 (spring 2007): 540-541.

[120] Thomas M. Keck, "Party Politics or Judicial Independence? The Regime Politics Literature Hits the Law Schools," review of From Jim Crow to Civil Rights: The Supreme Court and the Struggle for Racial Equality, by Michael J. Klarman, The Most Democratic Branch? How the Courts Serve America, by Jeffrey Rosen, and A Court Divided: The Rehnquist Court and the Future of Constitutional Law, by Mark Tushnet, Law & Social Inquiry 32, no. 2 (spring 2007): 513.

[121] Cornell Clayton and David A. May, "A Political Regimes Approach to the Analysis of Legal Decisions," Polity 32, no. 2 (Winter 1999): 246.

[122] Cornell Clayton and David A. May, "A Political Regimes Approach to the Analysis of Legal Decisions," Polity 32, no. 2 (Winter 1999): 249.

to decide an issue"[123] and it is important to keep in mind what we already understand about members of Congress from previous studies. As Pickerill reminds us:

> [w]e should not expect members of Congress to routinely or systematically consider, of their own volition, constitutional issues raised by legislation. . . . [M]embers of Congress are primarily motivated by the 'electoral connection,' notions of representation, and the desire to make good public policy, and the institution of Congress is designed to help achieve these goals efficiently. However, Congress does not operate in a vacuum, and it may sometimes need to consider the actions of the judiciary, the presidency, or other institutions. Likewise, the Court's actions may be viewed as having important effects on other institutions of government and on the broader lawmaking process. . . . Constitutional issues must compete with other factors that influence congressional decision making.[124]

---

[123] Staff Interview, 2008.

[124] J. Mitchell Pickerill, Constitutional Deliberation, 3, 21-22; citing Douglass Arnold, The Logic of Congressional Action (New Haven: Yale University Press, 1990); Richard Fenno, "U.S. House Members in Their Constituencies: An Exploration," American Political Science Review 71 (1977): 883-917; Elizabeth Garrett and Adrian Vermeule, "Institutional Design of a Thayerian Congress," Duke Law Journal 50 (2001): 1277-1333; John Kingdon, Congressmen's Voting Decisions (Ann Arbor: University of Michigan Press, 1989); David R. Mayhew, Congress: The Electoral Connection (New Haven: Yale University Press, 1974); Kenneth A. Shepsle and Barry R. Weingast, eds. Positive Theories of Congressional Institutions (Ann Arbor: University of Michigan Press, 1995); Charles M. Cameron, Veto Bargaining: Presidents and the Politics of Negative Power (Cambridge: Cambridge University Press, 2000); William N. Eskridge, Jr., "The Judicial Review Game," Northwestern University Law Review 88 (1993): 382-95; Charles O. Jones, The Presidency in a Separated System (Washington: Brookings Institution, 1994); Mark A. Peterson, Legislating Together: The White House and Capitol Hill from Eisenhower to Reagan (Cambridge: Harvard University Press, 1990); Charles R. Shipan, Designing Judicial Review: Interest Groups,

Given the increase in party polarization and the divided nature of the national governing majority and the characteristics it brings, within a regime structure of fundamental and secondary, of settled and unsettled values,_ we would expect the deliberations to elicit predictable partisan divisions and responses.

Again, these divisions highlight the presence of and the importance thereto of dueling governing coalitions that have been battling over the definition of the regime. Instead of one national governing coalition being dominant, there have been competing coalitions, and while at various times and in various circumstances each has been successful to

---

Congress and Communications Policy (Ann Arbor: University of Michigan Press, 1997); Bradley C. Canon and Charles A. Johnson, Judicial Policies: Implementation and Impact, 2d ed. (Washington: CQ Press, 1999); Louis Fisher, Constitutional Dialogues: Interpretation as Political Process (Princeton: Princeton University Press, 1988); Charles O. Jones, "A Way of Life and Law: Presidential Address, American Political Science Association," American Political Science Review 89 (1994): 1-9; Richard Fenno, Home Style: House Members in Their Districts (Boston: Little, Brown, 1978); Congressmen in Committees (Boston: Little, Brown, 1973); John E. Jackson and John Kingdon, "Ideology, Interest Group Scores, and Legislative Votes," American Journal of Political Science 36 (1992): 805-823; John Kingdon, Agendas, Alternatives and Public Policies, 2nd ed. (New York: Longman, 1995); Keith Krehbiel, Information and Legislative Organization (Ann Arbor: University of Michigan Press, 1991); Kenneth Shepsle, "Institutional Arrangements and Equilibrium in Multidimensional Voting Models," American Journal of Political Science 23 (1979): 27-59; Barry Weingast, "A Rational Choice Perspective on Congressional Norms," American Journal of Political Science 23 (1979): 245-62; Robert A. Katzmann, ed., Judges and Legislators: Toward Institutional Comity (Washington: Brookings Institution, 1988), 7. Although this former member downplayed the role of re-election. "Almost all members base their votes on principle and their own careful analysis, drawing on staff research, testimony, scholarly data, anecdotal testimony from constituents and a variety of other sources. The belief that most members base their votes on a re-election calculus is poli sci nonsense – constituent concerns and preferences are included, properly, in the decision[-]making process, among a great number of factors." (Former Member of Congress, Interview, 2008).

some extent, one has not been able to dominate the political landscape. Thus, as Pickerill and Clayton describe:

> [w]ithout taking a position in this debate, we simply note that in contrast to earlier periods of American history and previous constitutional regimes, the post-1960s American political system has been characterized by electoral dealignment, divided government, and a rise in partisan polarization. [] Indeed, divided government has become the norm during this period; between 1968 and 2002, the same party controlled both the White House and both houses of Congress during only seven years. . . . The consequences of this political system for the role of the Court and judicial review are at least threefold. First, during extended periods of divided government,_ a stronger form of judicial review becomes possible. Without a stable coalition controlling the elected branches, both parties have an incentive to turn to the courts to resolve political issues, while judges are less afraid of institutional retaliation if they make unpopular decisions. Unlike under unified government, presidents and legislators are unwilling or unable to coordinate an assault on judicial independence, and each party will fiercely defend the judiciary from encroachments by the other party.[125]

In conjunction with the political regime underlying the political environment, particularly one marked by divided government or divided national coalitions, the entire era of these case studies can best be understood in "political time" as an affiliated era, encompassed by "affiliated" presidents.[126] If "reconstructive" presidents are able to

---

[125] J. Mitchell Pickerill and Cornell W. Clayton, "The Rehnquist Court and the Political Dynamic of Federalism," Perspectives on Politics 2, no. 2 (June 2004): 240-241.

[126] "Stephen Skowronek has labeled this cyclical feature of presidential leadership, 'political time.' . . . The idea of a political regime incorporates not only electorally dominant partisan coalitions, but also a set of dominant policy concerns and legitimating ideologies. A regime in this sense

fundamentally re-set long-standing assumptions and norms in the nation's political life, then "affiliated" presidents "arise during a period of regime stability and are in concert with those dominant commitments. Their mandate is to extend and consolidate what they have inherited."[127]

---

overarches contending policy orientations at lower levels such that even electorally successful oppositional figures can be forced to sustain the commitments of the dominant regime. A strong regime transcends partisanship." Keith E. Whittington, "The Political Foundations of Judicial Supremacy," in Sotirios A. Barber and Robert P. George, eds., Constitutional Politics: Essays on Constitution Making, Maintenance, and Change (Princeton: Princeton University Press, 2001), 264-265, citing, Stephen Skowronek, The Politics Presidents Make (Cambridge: Harvard University Press, 1993), 38-39. Skowronek elaborates, "[p]olitical time is the medium through which presidents encounter received commitments of ideology and interest and claim authority to intervene in their development. Political time has a narrative structure: Presidents bid for authority by reckoning with the work of their predecessors, locating their rise to power within the recent course of political events, and addressing the political expectations that attend their intervention in these affairs." Stephen Skowronek, Presidential Leadership in Political Time: Reprise and Reappraisal (2nd ed, revised and expanded) (Lawrence, KS: University Press of Kansas, 2011), 18.

[127] Keith E. Whittington, "The Political Foundations of Judicial Supremacy," in Sotirios A. Barber and Robert P. George, eds., Constitutional Politics: Essays on Constitution Making, Maintenance, and Change (Princeton: Princeton University Press, 2001), 265-266. While it is true that "[a]ll presidents disrupt the status quo and change their political environments to some extent. Not all presidents, however, have the authority to explain and legitimate those changes. Not all presidents have the ability to lead. . . . Those that do have the ability to lead are usually, if not always, opposing collapsing regimes, thereby allowing them to be 'reconstructive' presidents, presidents who redefine the underlying political assumptions of the time." Other presidents, 'preemptive' presidents, "overcome the electoral bias against them usually through some unusual characteristic or circumstance such as the splintering of the dominant party." Premptive presidents "interrupt[] otherwise stable electoral and political orders." Disjunctive presidents inherit weak regimes and have little authority, other than trying to exist and attain

While "[r]econstructive presidents are relatively rare," since "[f]ew presidents have the desire or authority to challenge inherited constitutional and ideological norms and to attempt construction of a new political regime," "[f]ar more common are affiliated leaders, who rise to power within an assumed framework of goals, possibilities, and resources. . . . who are "primarily concerned with continuing, extending, or more creatively reconceptualizing the fundamental commitments made by an earlier reconstructive leader. They are second-order interpreters."[128] Affiliated leaders, by contrast, are authorized only to articulate, interpret, and apply that preexisting set of commitments.[129]

Robert Dahl has famously argued that "[e]xcept for short-lived transitional periods . . . the Supreme Court is inevitably part of the dominant national alliance,"[130] of which the affiliated president and affiliated Court will be a part. In political "time" and in a view from regime analysis, this will mean two things. First, there will be fundamental regime commitments supported by a large if not

---

minimal policy goals. Keith E. Whittington, "The Political Foundations of Judicial Supremacy," in Sotirios A. Barber and Robert P. George, eds., Constitutional Politics: Essays on Constitution Making, Maintenance, and Change (Princeton: Princeton University Press, 2001), 265.

[128] Keith E. Whittington, "The Political Foundations of Judicial Supremacy," in Sotirios A. Barber and Robert P. George, eds., Constitutional Politics: Essays on Constitution Making, Maintenance, and Change (Princeton: Princeton University Press, 2001), 275, adding, "Skowronek distinguishes between two types of affiliated leaders, those in a politics of articulation and those in a politics of disjunction. As we will see, that distinction is relevant to judicial authority as well. But I find the differences between affiliated leaders to be less important than their similarities for purposes of examining the logic of their relationship to the Court."

[129] Keith E. Whittington, "The Political Foundations of Judicial Supremacy," in Sotirios A. Barber and Robert P. George, eds., Constitutional Politics: Essays on Constitution Making, Maintenance, and Change (Princeton: Princeton University Press, 2001), 278.

[130] Robert Dahl, "Decision-Making in a Democracy: The Supreme Court as National Policy-Maker," Journal of Public Law 6 (1957): 293.

overwhelming segment of not just the political class but also the electorate at large. Thus, we would expect to see the Supreme Court supporting, upholding, affirming, and extending those fundamental regime commitments. Secondly, while, as Dahl argues, the Court may be part of the "dominant national alliance", that alliance may not be veto or opposition-proof, and thus, from issue to issue, the "dominant" aspect may range from a slim majority to temporally tenuous. It would be expected to have divided sects between partisanly nominated majority justices, as for example between the nominees of Republican presidents on the Court.[131] As Whittington writes:

> "The Court must compete with other political actors for the authority to define the terms of the Constitution. For the Court to compete successfully, other political actors must have reasons for allowing the Court to 'win.' The president, among others, must see some political value in deferring to the Court and helping to construct a space for judicial autonomy. . . . For affiliated leaders who enjoy political dominance in the government and the electorate, problems of coalitional maintenance dictate maintaining a prominent place for the Court. An unelected judiciary can independently advance regime commitments, while protecting other government officials from potential electoral fallout. An autonomous judiciary can be politically more valuable than a judicial puppet. Moreover, a general acceptance of the virtue of constitutional interpretation empowers the Court by providing it with a real political resource that does not rest on immediate electoral approval.[132]

---

[131] For example, see Mark Tushnet, A Court Divided: The Rehnquist Court and the Future of Constitutional Law (New York: W.W. Norton, 2005) which underscores the divide among the Republican justices.

[132] Keith E. Whittington, "The Political Foundations of Judicial Supremacy," in Sotirios A. Barber and Robert P. George, eds., Constitutional Politics: Essays on Constitution Making, Maintenance, and Change (Princeton: Princeton University Press, 2001), 290-292.

THE CASES

For this comparative case study on constitutional deliberation in Congress, I was trying to understand the deliberative process (what kind of deliberation goes on, by whom, when) and deliberative nature and quality of the three bills in particular as well as delineate whether certain issue domains are more likely to receive greater deliberation than others. As previously described, I operated under the following definition of constitutional deliberation:

> Legislative action, engaged in by Congress, considered as an institution, that has 'proceeded through [the] complex set of organization structures' within Congress which make 'substantive reference to the U.S. Constitution' as well as floor statements and interviews which are also substantive, not ones that are merely perfunctory.[133]
>
> [C]onstitutional debate among members or other relevant policy-makers and lawmakers, committee hearings that focus at some length on constitutional issues, language in a bill or a statute that reflects constitutional principles or judicial doctrines, or some other indication that constitutional issues played an important part when the legislation in question was considered.[134]

I examined a set of contemporaneous cases cutting across policy areas with the specific intention of describing, explaining, and assessing the scope and character of constitutional discourse in Congress. I agree with Tushnet: "[c]onducting an empirical inquiry into Congress's performance in constitutional matters is not simple, though. In particular, cases need to be selected with some care if the goal is to

---

[133] Mark Tushnet, "Evaluating Congressional Constitutional Interpretation," 270-71. Whittington, "Hearing about the Constitution," 92.

[134] J. Mitchell Pickerill, <u>Constitutional Deliberation in Congress: The Impact of Judicial Review in a Separated System</u> (Durham: Duke University Press, 2004), 64.

evaluate Congress's performance."[135] Therefore, for this approach to be viable several basic criteria had to be met.

First, while it is obvious that constitutional discourse and discussion can take place anytime in Congress, in order to understand the extended process of deliberation it was important for Congress in its legislative endeavors to have proceeded through several organizational layers (i.e. a bill has gone through hearings, floor debate, and has been passed or at least introduced on the floor).[136] While the authenticity of such member remarks and responses can always be questioned, institutionally, deliberation has to require normal institutional procedure in relation to the issue at hand. Secondly, also in the interest of understanding deliberation as an iterative and lengthy process, the Supreme Court had to have issued at least one ruling in relation to each issue. This verifies the Court and Congress have had an interactive relationship. Congress did not simply pass something the Court was able to ignore nor did the Court ruling simply guide policy behavior in the country while it was ignored in the halls of Congress. Thirdly, cases needed to be relatively contemporaneous in order to facilitate the

---

[135] Tushnet, "Evaluating Congressional Constitutional Interpretation," 269. Although I here agree with Tushnet's statement, his subsequent criteria seem much too pinched, in effect, because of their system-wide isolation, leaving only war-powers and impeachment as suitable issues for study in relation to constitutional deliberation in Congress. Tushnet's criteria are "Examine Institutional Performance, Not Individual Behavior," "Examine Institutional Actions outside the Shadow Cast by the Courts," "Avoid Examining Problems Where People Can Reasonably Disagree about the Constitution's Meaning," and "Examine Only Cases Where the Constitution Provides Answers." Tushnet, "Evaluating Congressional Constitutional Interpretation," 270-277.

[136] As when Tushnett remarks that "Congress's actions during Clinton's impeachment offer good opportunities to assess Congress's constitutional performance [because] [t]here was a completed congressional process," so these case studies also offer a completed process to analyze. Mark Tushnet, "Evaluating Congressional Constitutional Interpretation: Some Criteria and Two Informal Case Studies," in Congress and the Constitution, eds. Neal Devins and Keith E. Whittington (Durham: Duke University Press, 2005), 277.

conduction of interviews from those involved in such deliberation and interaction. Fourthly, cases had to involve important constitutional issues. Statutory issues may be involved but constitutional issues are an obvious prerequisite for studying constitutional deliberation in Congress. Finally, cases had to cut across policy domains in order to ensure acceptable variable diversification so that findings are not specific to one particular policy domain, in which case it would become impossible to employ generalization. To meet these criteria, the Civil Rights Act of 1991, the Partial-Birth Abortion Ban Act of 2003, and the Habeas Corpus Restoration Act of 2007 were chosen. They each respectively meet all the above criteria and in relation to the final two criteria situate themselves within policy and constitutional domains encompassing race, equal protection, abortion, privacy, and war-powers.[137]

SUMMARY PREVIEW

Operating within a political regime construct and in an era of divided government, these cases demonstrate that Congress is a highly political institution functioning within a highly political environment encompassing both fundamental "settled" values and secondary "unsettled" values. In the three cases studied here, despite competing governing coalitions, there were these fundamental "core" values, policy concerns, and legitimating ideologies that went unchallenged and virtually unspoken by both coalitions. They were reluctant to touch them until future elections or political factors change the regime dynamics so that the current underlying consensus is less secure or a new consensus has emerged.

Given they are operating within a political regime context, combined with the fact that they are unable and unwilling to directly address the values of the fundamental regime, we see members of Congress being very willing to try and influence their body, the other

[137] Interviews with congressional staff members and members of Congress were conducted while participating as a Congressional Fellow in the American Political Science Association's 2007-2008 Congressional Fellowship Program.

branches, and the political context by influencing perceptions, facts, and outcomes at a secondary regime value level. National coalition members are willing to fight over these secondary values. These include the demarcation between racial intents and racial effects in public policy, the exact contours of the right to privacy, and the limits of habeas corpus itself. These issues are not settled, either because of their controversial nature, or because they simply are not as well-known, as may have been the case with habeas.

Thus, Congress' deliberation is circumscribed by the political regime situated within the political time it inhabits, and is for the most part symbolic and derivative in nature, acting under an umbrella of judicial supremacy and attempting to exert influence primarily on unsettled values reflecting members' regime preferences, by which fundamental regime shifts are sought. These cases belie the notion of "settled" law and a "settled" regime, yet, despite these deviations from an undiluted "republic of reasons,"[138] Congress plays an important representational role by acting, and, further still, continues and perpetuates an ongoing dialogue with the other branches which would arguably not take place without their agency.

---

[138] J. Mitchell Pickerill, Constitutional Deliberation in Congress: The Impact of Judicial Review in a Separated System, 26, 131, citing Cass R. Sunstein, The Partial Constitution (Cambridge: Harvard University Press, 1993).

CHAPTER 2

The Civil Rights Act of 1991

If the Senator can find in Title VII . . . any language which provides that an employer will have to hire on the basis of percentage or quota related to color, race, religion, or national origin, I will start eating the pages one after another, because it is not in there. . . . Nothing contained in [Title VII] . . . shall be interpreted to require any employer to grant preferential treatment to any individual or to any group because of race . . . on account of an imbalance which may exist with respect to the total number or percentage of persons employed . . . in comparison with the available work force.[139]

The Civil Rights Act of 1991 had a contextual history dating back twenty years. In 1971, the Supreme Court upheld busing.[140] More importantly, they issued *Griggs v. Duke Power Company*,[141] initiating "disparate impact" analysis, whereby an employer would have to justify business practices shown to result in disproportional minority employment representation. The unanimous decision interpreted the 1964 Civil Rights Act to prohibit not only overt discrimination but also "practices that are fair in form, but discriminatory in operation."[142]

---

139 Sen. Hubert Humphrey (D-MN), Congressional Record, 88th Cong., 2nd sess., 1964, 110, 12723; 7420 (9 April 1964).

140 *Swann v. Charlotte-Mecklenburg Board of Education*, 402 U.S. 1 (1971).

141 401 U.S. 424 (1971).

142 401 U.S. 424, 431 (1971) (8-0 decision; Justice Brennan recused himself). This "'disparate impact analysis,' is a statistical method for determining employers' compliance with Title VII. Essentially, the court said plaintiffs in discrimination suits could use the racial composition of the surrounding

Seven years later, *University of California Regents v. Bakke* was decided, allowing race to be a factor in educational entrance requirements.[143] The Court would sanction affirmative action-related programs several more times in the immediate years.[144]

With the election of a new president in 1980, and under the leadership of new personnel in the Department of Justice, civil rights-related issues received additional scrutiny, given that the three branches were often in sharp disagreement.[145] Eight months into the new

---

community as evidence of their compliance. Opponents believe that more and more employers adopted quota policies to bring their work force into balance with the surrounding community and thus ensure Title VII compliance." Mary H. Cooper, "Racial Quotas," CQ Researcher Online 1 (17 May 1991): 277-300. library.cqpress.com/cqresearcher/cqresrre1991051700 (accessed August 22, 2008). Katherine Naff writes that "[t]he importance of this case . . . was that it recognized that discrimination could occur, even if unintentionally, and gave employers an incentive to hire underrepresented minorities so as to avoid a potential charge of disparate impact." Katherine C. Naff, "From *Bakke* to *Grutter* to *Gratz*: The Supreme Court as a Policymaking Institution," Review of Policy Research 21, no. 3 (2004): 406.

[143] 438 U.S. 265 (1978).

[144] In *United Steelworkers of America v. Weber*, 443 U.S. 193 (1979), the Court permitted an employer's voluntarily imposed and temporary affirmative action program. Also in this case, "it was explicitly argued to the Court that reverse discrimination had to be allowed under Title VII because this was precisely what *Griggs* required." Roger Clegg, "Introduction: A Brief Legislative History of the Civil Rights Act of 1991," Louisiana Law Review 54, no. 6 The Civil Rights Act of 1991: A Symposium (1993-1994): 1460, citing Brief for Petitioner, at 13-22, 49-50; Brief for the U.S. and Equal Employment Opportunity Commission, at 24-25. In *Fullilove v. Klutznick*, 448 U.S. 448 (1980), the Court again ruled that Congress could remedy past discrimination.

[145] See Raymond Wolters, Right Turn: William Bradford Reynolds, the Reagan Administration, and Black Civil Rights (New Brunswick, N.J.: Transaction, 1996); David G. Savage, Turning Right: The Making of the Rehnquist Supreme Court (John Wiley & Sons, 1992); and Neal Devins, "Reagan Redux: Civil Rights Under Bush." Notre Dame Law Review 68, no. 5 Symposium:

presidency, the Assistant Attorney General for Civil Rights told a House subcommittee the Justice Department would "no longer . . . insist upon or in any respect support the use of quotas or any other numerical or statistical formulae designed to provide to non-victims of discrimination preferential treatment based on race, sex, national origin or religion."[146] For its part, Congress "enacted [legislation] to overturn decisions of the Supreme Court misinterpreting the procedural requirements and substantive protections of federal civil rights laws and to restore interpretations of laws that had been accepted prior to such decisions."[147] In 1982, Congress' amendments to the Voting Rights Act "explicitly vitiated" *City of Mobile v. Bolden,*[148] the Civil Rights Restoration Act of 1987 overturned *Grove City College v. Bell*,[149] and in 1988 Congress amended the Fair Housing Act.

During the second half of the decade the Court would issue rulings giving inconclusive explication of appropriate affirmative action policies. In *Library of Congress v. Shaw*[150] and *Crawford Fitting Co. v.*

The Civil Rights Act of 1991: Theory and Practice (1993): 955-1001.

[146] Mary H. Cooper, "Racial Quotas," CQ Researcher Online 1 (May 17, 1991): 277-300. library.cqpress.com/cqresearcher/cqresrre1991051700 (accessed October 12, 2007).

[147] Reginald C. Govan, "Honorable Compromises and the Moral High Ground: The Conflict between the Rhetoric and the Content of the Civil Rights Act of 1991," Rutgers Law Review 46, no. 1 (fall 1993): 8.

[148] 446 U.S. 55 (1980). *City of Mobile* had limited the enforcement of the Act by requiring proof of an intent to discriminate to establish a violation of the law.

[149] 465 U.S. 455 (1984). In *Grove City*, the Court had retrenched on the enforcement of four separate civil rights laws, including Title IX of the 1972 Education Act Amendments. It did this by holding that only a "program or activity," not an entire institution, which was the recipient of federal aid was covered by the anti-bias laws. Congress overturned this by overriding President Reagan's veto. They also made clear that anti-bias provisions of three other laws applied to entire institutions if any segment or program received federal funding. The three were the Civil Rights Act of 1964, Section 504 of the 1973 Rehabilitation Act and the 1975 Age Discrimination Act.

[150] 478 U.S. 310 (1986).

J.T. Gibbons,[151] the Court restricted the reach of affirmative action programs, in *Johnson v. Transportation Agency of Santa Clara County*[152] the Court endorsed a limited affirmative action plan for women, and in *United States v. Paradise*[153] the Court upheld a temporary and "narrowly tailored" quota system to bring about job promotion for black state troopers in Alabama, where the state's affirmative action plan imposed a "one black-for-one-white" promotion quota and was deemed justifiable by the "long and shameful record of delay and resistance" to employment opportunities for African-Americans in the Alabama state police force. Two years later, the Court struck down a Richmond, Virginia affirmative-action plan whereby 30% of municipal contracts were awarded on a "racially preferential basis."[154] Thus, according to one interpretation:

> [i]n sum Congress spent the decade of the 1980s debating and resolving a wide variety of federal civil rights issues. Congress overturned no fewer than six erroneous Supreme Court interpretations of one or another federal civil rights statutes; enacted legislation strengthening the enforcement provisions of equal employment, voting rights, fair housing and equal educational opportunity statutes; and refused to consent to the appointment of numerous persons to leadership positions in federal civil rights enforcement agencies and to the federal bench because of their records on civil rights issues. Congress's ultimate response to the series of decisions during the 1988-89 Term of the Supreme Court interpreting Title VII

---

[151] 482 U.S. 437 (1987).

[152] 480 U.S. 616 (1987).

[153] 480 U.S. 149 (1987). See, "Black America Long March for Equality," CQ Researcher (November 15, 1985), available at cqpress.com.

[154] *City of Richmond v. J.A. Croson Co.*, 488 U.S. 469 (1989). Roger Clegg, "Introduction: A Brief Legislative History of the Civil Rights Act of 1991," Louisiana Law Review 54, no. 6 The Civil Rights Act of 1991: A Symposium (1993-1994): 1459, n.2. In dissent, Justice Marshall accused the majority of "constitutionalizing its wishful thinking" and "launch[ing] a grapeshot attack on race-conscious remedies." 529, 552-53. Congress chose not to respond to *City of Richmond* (a constitutional, not statutory, ruling).

> and § 1981 merely continued the struggle of the 1970s and 1980s to enact legislation to strengthen enforcement mechanisms and, when necessary, to restore the 'original' intent of federal civil rights statutes.[155]

LEGISLATIVE HISTORY

Within this civil rights milieu and context, not only was the 1991 Civil Rights Act an extremely important legislative endeavor,[156] it was also "one of the most controversial pieces of legislation in recent history."[157] Fought over for two years, the legislation was the result of numerous controversial and "stunning" Supreme Court rulings issued in less than an eight week span during the fifth and sixth months of 1989.[158] The rulings allegedly "made it harder to prove job discrimination and easier to challenge affirmative action programs."[159] Thus, some referred to

---

[155] Reginald C. Govan, "Honorable Compromises and the Moral High Ground: The Conflict between the Rhetoric and the Content of the Civil Rights Act of 1991," Rutgers Law Review 46, no. 1 (fall 1993): 16.

[156] For a sample of post-passage analysis, see California Law Review 79, no. 3 Symposium: Civil Rights Legislation in the 1990s (May 1991): 591-805; Notre Dame Law Review 68, no. 5 Symposium: The Civil Rights Act of 1991: Theory and Practice (1993): 911-1164; Louisiana Law Review 54, no. 6 The Civil Rights Act of 1991: A Symposium (1993-1994): 1459-1617; Rutgers Law Review 45, no. 4 Symposium: The Civil Rights Act of 1991: Unraveling the Controversy (summer 1993): 887-1141.

[157] "Foreword: The Civil Rights Act of 1991: Unraveling the Controversy," Rutgers Law Review 45, no. 4 Symposium: The Civil Rights Act of 1991: Unraveling the Controversy (summer 1993): 887.

[158] Louis Fisher and David Gray Adler, American Constitutional Law, Vol. 2 Constitutional Rights: Civil Rights and Civil Liberties, 810.

[159] Mary H. Cooper, "Racial Quotas," CQ Researcher Online 1 (17 May 1991): 277-300. library.cqpress.com/cqresearcher/cqresrre1991051700 (accessed October 12, 2007).

these rulings as a "fusillade"[160] or (more pejoratively) the "civil rights massacre of 1989."[161]

After the Civil War, legislative endeavors concerning civil rights involved segregation, public accommodations, and voting rights. The 1989 cases had to do with the right to hold a job and advance through promotion, as well as the responsibility of government and private employers to redress the past exclusion of blacks and other groups from large segments of the labor market. Plaintiffs included bank tellers, firemen, construction contractors, and Alaskan Filipino and Eskimo salmon cannery workers.[162]

---

[160] Charles V. Dale, "Federal Civil Rights Decisions of the U.S. Supreme Court During the 1988-89 Term," Library of Congress Congressional Research Service Report for Congress (20 July 1989), 1.

[161] Mary H. Cooper, "Racial Quotas," CQ Researcher Online 1 (17 May 1991): 277-300. library.cqpress.com/cqresearcher/cqresrre1991051700 (accessed October 12, 2007).

[162] The cases in focus were respectively, *Price Waterhouse v. Hopkins*, 490 U.S. 228 (1989) (decided May 1, 1989) (6-3 decision); *Wards Cove Packing Co. Inc. v. Atonio*, 490 U.S. 642 (1989) (decided June 5, 1989) (5-4 decision); *Martin v. Wilks*, 490 U.S. 755 (1989) (decided June 12, 1989) (5-4 decision); *Lorance v. AT&T Technologies, Inc.*, 490 U.S. 900 (1989) (decided June 12, 1989) (5-3 decision; Justice O'Connor took no part in the consideration or decision of the case); *Patterson v. McLean Credit Union*, 491 U.S. 164 (1989) (decided June 15, 1989) (5-4 decision); *Independent Federation of Flight Attendants v. Zipes*, 491 U.S. 754 (1989) (decided June 22, 1989) (6-2 decision) (Justice Stevens took no part in the consideration or decision of the case). Two other cases were eventually involved in the final bill: *West Virginia University Hospitals v. Casey*, 499 U.S. 83 (1991) (decided March 19, 1991) (6-3 decision); *Equal Employment Opportunity Commission v. Arabian American Oil Co. and Aramco Services Co.*, 499 U.S. 244 (1991) (decided March 26, 1991) (6-3 decision). Each of these cases involved statutory interpretation, which, as William Eskridge describes, "is an inherently dynamic process: the text evolves as it is interpreted." William N. Eskridge, Jr., "Reneging on History? Playing the Court/Congress/President Civil Rights Game," California Law Review 79, no. 3 Symposium: Civil Rights Legislation in the 1990s (May 1991): 616. In statutory cases, Congress has often "overruled decisions of the Court, most

The first ruling, *Price Waterhouse v. Hopkins*, was a "mixed motive" case. The Court held that Title VII of the Civil Rights Act of 1964 covering discrimination in employment was not violated even when a particular employer admits to discriminatory purposes in their decision-making, so long as there were also *other* reasons for the decision. In the words of one critic, the decision "let employers escape liability for 'overt sexism or racism . . . as long as it was not the only thing on the employer's mind.'"[163]

Wards Cove Packing v. Atonio involved a challenge to hiring practices under Title VII at an Alaskan cannery. The Court ruled employers need only offer, rather than prove, a business justification for employment practices that had a disproportionate impact on minorities, stating, "the dispositive issue is whether a challenged practice serves, in a significant way, the legitimate employment goals of the employer."[164] It also made it more difficult for employees to

---

of which have innocent, constitutionally unexceptional, explanations." Abner J. Mikva and Jeff Bleich, "When Congress Overrules the Court." California Law Review 79, no. 3 Symposium: Civil Rights Legislation in the 1990s (May 1991): 729. Nevertheless, the constitutional values and status of civil rights and equal protection were still before Congress as competing coalitions sought to evaluate how to frame and respond to the civil rights and disparate-impact-related Court decisions

[163] Reginald C. Govan, "Honorable Compromises and the Moral High Ground: The Conflict between the Rhetoric and the Content of the Civil Rights Act of 1991," Rutgers Law Review 46, no. 1 (fall 1993): 18, citing, Statement of Judith Litchman, President, Women's Legal Defense Fund, Hearings Before the House Committee on Education and Labor and the Judiciary Subcommittee on Civil and Constitutional Rights, Hearings on H.R. 4000, The Civil Rights Act of 1990, hearing, 101st Cong., 2nd sess., 20 and 27 Feb. 1990 (Washington, D.C.: GPO, 1990), 243.

[164] 490 U.S. 642, 659 (1989). As Fisher and Adler state, the Court "shifted the burden to employees to prove that racial disparities in the work force result from employment practices and are not justified by business needs. This new test conflicted with the *Griggs* ruling in 1971, which appeared to require an employee to demonstrate disparate results, not intent. Since this decision was a statutory interpretation of Title VII, Congress could rewrite the statute and

prove that an employer's personnel practices had an unlawful disparate impact on them by requiring that they identify the specific policy or requirement that allegedly produced inequalities in the workplace and demonstrate it alone had this effect. Writing for the majority, Justice Byron White stated, "[t]he ultimate burden of proving that discrimination against a protected group has been caused by a specific employment practice remains with the plaintiff at all times."[165] White continued

> [w]e acknowledge that some of our earlier decisions can be read as shifting the burden to employers to prove a business necessity for challenged practices. But from now on . . . it is up to a plaintiff to prove that he was denied employment opportunities because of unlawful discrimination. . . . The proper comparison is between the racial composition of the at-issue jobs and the racial composition of the qualified population in the relevant labor market.[166]

---

overturn the Court." Louis Fisher and David Gray Adler, American Constitutional Law, Vol. 2 Constitutional Rights: Civil Rights and Civil Liberties, 810.

[165] Justice White is quoting verbatim from Justice O'Connor's plurality opinion in *Watson v. Forth Worth Bank & Trust Co.* (1988).

[166] Joan Biskupic, "Congress May Seek to Reverse Narrow Civil Rights Ruling," *CQ Weekly Online* (June 10, 1989): 1404-1406. library.cqpress.com/cqweekly/WR101406485 (accessed April 30, 2009). In dissent, Justice Stevens replied that he could not "'join this latest sojourn into judicial activism.' The majority was 'turning a blind eye to the meaning and purpose of Title VII.' 'This casual – almost summary – rejection of the statutory construction that developed in the wake of *Griggs* is most disturbing.' 'I have always believed that the *Griggs* opinion correctly reflected the intent of the Congress that enacted Title VII. Even if I were not so persuaded, I could not join a rejection of a consistent interpretation of a federal statute. Congress frequently revisits this statutory scheme and can readily correct our mistakes if we misread its meaning.'" Supreme Court Rulings on Civil Rights Laws." CQ Electronic Library, CQ Historic Documents Series Online Edition, library.cqpress.com/historicdocuments/ hsdc89-0001181410. Originally published in Historic Documents of 1989

Martin v. Wilks dealt with "impermissible collateral attack" and allowed white firefighters in the Birmingham, Alabama Fire Department who had not been party to litigation establishing a consent decree governing the hiring and promotion of a group of African-American firefighters to bring suit challenging the decree. The majority interpreted the Federal Rules of Civil Procedure to "give white men new authority to challenge consent decrees that embody court-approved affirmative action plans. To avoid future challenges, consent decrees had to reach out to all groups that might be affected."[167]

(Washington: CQ Press, 1990); available at library.cqpress.com /historicdocuments/hsdc89-0001181410 (accessed October 23, 2007). In a separate dissent joined by Justices Brennan and Marshall, Justice Harry Blackmun wrote, "[o]ne wonders whether the majority still believes that race discrimination – or more accurately, race discrimination against non-whites – is a problem in our society, or even remembers that it ever was." "Supreme Court Rulings on Civil Rights Laws." CQ Electronic Library, CQ Historic Documents Series Online Edition, hsdc89-0001181410. Originally published in Historic Documents of 1989 (Washington: CQ Press, 1990); available at library.cqpress.com/historicdocuments/hsdc89-0001181410 (accessed October 23, 2007).

[167] 490 U.S. 755 (1989). See Louis Fisher and David Gray Adler, American Constitutional Law, Vol. 2 Constitutional Rights: Civil Rights and Civil Liberties, 810. The trial court "had barred the suit, holding that the 'impermissible collateral attack' doctrine immunizes parties to a consent decree from discrimination charges by nonparties to the decree for actions taken pursuant to it. [The] . . . Court . . . held that white firefighters could not be barred from challenging the deal struck at their expense between the local governments and the black firefighters. 'This . . . is part of our 'deep-rooted historic tradition that everyone should have his own day in court.'" Roger Clegg, "Introduction: A Brief Legislative History of the Civil Rights Act of 1991," Louisiana Law Review 54, no. 6 The Civil Rights Act of 1991: A Symposium (1993-1994): 1461, citing *Martin v. Wilks*, 490 U.S. 762, 109 S. Ct. at 2185 (quoting 18 Charles Alan Wright et al., Federal Practice and Procedure § 4449, at 417 (1981)).

Lorance v. AT&T Technologies, Inc. restricted the Title VII statute of limitations involving seniority systems.[168] It "held that the statute of limitations period for challenging an alleged[] discriminatory and unfavorable change in an employee's contractual seniority rights – which were not discriminatory on their face or as currently applied – began when the new system was adopted, rather than when the employee was actually demoted pursuant to the seniority system."[169]

Patterson v. McClean Credit Union overturned a 1976 ruling which had held that an 1866 statute could be used by individuals to challenge a private school's racially discriminatory admissions process and as the basis for lawsuits seeking monetary damages.[170] The 1866 statute gave "all persons within the jurisdiction of the United States" the same rights as "white citizens" to make and enforce contracts and allowed courts to award monetary damages to those who prevail in discrimination suits.[171] In response to the African-American plaintiff, Brenda Patterson, who claimed she had been harassed, denied promotion, and fired because of her race, the Court ruled that § 1981 "is limited to prohibiting discriminatory actions *before* someone is hired, not after, and advised Patterson that she should have acted under Title VII."[172] Justice Kennedy argued that "the right to make contracts

---

[168] Louis Fisher and David Gray Adler, American Constitutional Law, Vol. 2 Constitutional Rights: Civil Rights and Civil Liberties, 810.

[169] Roger Clegg, "Introduction: A Brief Legislative History of the Civil Rights Act of 1991." Louisiana Law Review 54, no. 6 The Civil Rights Act of 1991: A Symposium (1993-1994): 1461.

[170] *Runyon v. McCrary*, 427 U.S. 160 (1976).

[171] S. 1981 of Title 42 read "All persons within the jurisdiction of the United States shall have the same right in every State and Territory to make and enforce contracts, to sue, be parties, give evidence, and to the full and equal benefit of all laws for the security of persons and property as is enjoyed by white citizens, and shall be subject to like punishment, pains penalties, taxes, licenses, and exactions of every kind, and to no other." Roger Clegg, "Introduction: A Brief Legislative History of the Civil Rights Act of 1991," Louisiana Law Review 54, no. 6 The Civil Rights Act of 1991: A Symposium (1993-1994): 1461.

[172] Louis Fisher and David Gray Adler, American Constitutional Law, Vol. 2 Constitutional Rights: Civil Rights and Civil Liberties, 810.

does not extend to conduct by the employer after the contract relation has been established, including breach of the terms of the contract or imposition of discriminatory working conditions.'"[173]

Finally, in *Independent Federation of Flight Attendants v. Zipes*, the Court "held losing intervenors (i.e., a collective-bargaining agent for a whole group, in this case all Trans World Airlines' flight attendants, as opposed to the specific class, in this case a group of female flight attendants, seeking damages) could be required to pay the prevailing party's attorney fees only if their position had been frivolous, unreasonable, or without foundation, since they 'have not been found to have violated anyone's civil rights.'"[174]

---

[173] In dissent, Justice Brennan denounced the Court's "pinched reading" of the 1866 statute: "[w]hen it comes to deciding whether a civil-rights statute should be construed to further our nation's commitment to the eradication of racial discrimination, the Court adopts a formalistic method of interpretation antithetical to Congress' vision of a society in which contractual opportunities are equal." "Supreme Court Rulings on Civil Rights Laws," CQ Electronic Library, CQ Historic Documents Series Online Edition, hsdc89-0001181410. Originally published in Historic Documents of 1989 (Washington: CQ Press, 1990); available at library.cqpress.com/historicdocuments/hsdc89-0001181410 (accessed October 23, 2007). See also Joan Biskupic, "Rights Bill Is Almost Ready After Long Delay, Debate," CQ Weekly Online (November 11, 1989): 3055, available at library.cqpress.com/cqweekly/WR101407818 (accessed October 23, 2007).

[174] Roger Clegg, "Introduction: A Brief Legislative History of the Civil Rights Act of 1991," Louisiana Law Review 54, no. 6 The Civil Rights Act of 1991: A Symposium (1993-1994): 1462-63. Stated another way, "the Court held that prevailing plaintiffs who successfully defend the relief they received from challenge in subsequent proceedings cannot recover attorney's fees from the intervenor/challenger unless the 'intervenor's action was frivolous, unreasonable, or without foundation.'" Reginald C. Govan, "Honorable Compromises and the Moral High Ground: The Conflict between the Rhetoric and the Content of the Civil Rights Act of 1991," Rutgers Law Review 46, no. 1 (fall 1993): 19. 491 U.S. 754, 760-61 (1989). This case was not addressed in the final legislation but nevertheless contributed to the climate that existed in conjunction with the other controversial cases.

This was the landscape during the summer of 1989. To some, the Court had "provoke[ed] . . . Congress"[175] and by early the next year, an "enormously ambitious" bill was introduced in Congress to send "the Court a resounding message that it was out of touch with Congress's views on employment discrimination."[176] Debate between the branches

---

[175] Jack M. Beermann, "The Supreme Court's Narrow View on Civil Rights," The Supreme Court Review 1993 (1993): 201, n.10.

[176] Roger Clegg, "Introduction: A Brief Legislative History of the Civil Rights Act of 1991," Louisiana Law Review 54, no. 6 The Civil Rights Act of 1991: A Symposium (1993-1994): 1463. Clegg argues, "[t]his decision – to ask for essentially *every* civil rights reform on their wish list – was the most important strategic call made by the civil rights groups during the whole debate, and it turned out to be the correct one." Roger Clegg, "Introduction: A Brief Legislative History of the Civil Rights Act of 1991," Louisiana Law Review 54, no. 6 The Civil Rights Act of 1991: A Symposium (1993-1994): 1463, emphasis in original. Jack M. Beermann, "The Supreme Court's Narrow View on Civil Rights," The Supreme Court Review 1993 (1993): 243. See also Reginald C. Govan, "Honorable Compromises and the Moral High Ground: The Conflict between the Rhetoric and the Content of the Civil Rights Act of 1991," Rutgers Law Review 46, no. 1 (fall 1993): 24-25. The Senate Report on the 1990 bill stated: The impact of each of the Supreme Court decisions addressed by the legislation is described below. In many respects, however, the overall effect of the Courts decisions is more devastating than the sum of the parts. For more than thirty-five years, since *Brown v. Board of Education*, the Supreme Court has played a critical role in the nation's efforts to wipe out discrimination. This role was demonstrated through conscientious application of the Constitution's guarantee to all persons of the 'equal protection of the laws,' and through generous interpretation of federal civil rights statutes in a manner consistent with their remedial purpose. . . . In its recent decisions construing these civil rights laws, however, the Court has adopted crabbed, narrow interpretations, signalling [sic] an apparent retreat from the Court's historic vigilance for the rights of those who have been victims of prejudice." Senate Committee on Labor and Human Resources Report 101-315, 101st Congress, "Civil Rights Act of 1990," 8 June 1990, 13.

would encompass the next two years.[177] The original bill was introduced in both chambers on February 7, 1990.[178] In October it was

[177] "From April 3, 1990, less than two months after the legislation was first introduced, to October 23, 1991, two days before the announcement of a compromise agreement, the Bush administration steadfastly claimed that it would veto this behemoth package of civil rights reforms. During this period, the President . . . on at least two dozen occasions publicly discussed this matter." Neal Devins, "Reagan Redux: Civil Rights Under Bush," Notre Dame Law Review 68, no. 5 Symposium: The Civil Rights Act of 1991: Theory and Practice (1993): 983. See Nadine Cohodas, "Despite Setback, Push Still On for Civil Rights Bill," *CQ Weekly Online* (6 Feb. 1988): 254-255. library.cqpress.com/cqweekly/WR100402606 (accessed April 30, 2009); Nadine Cohodas, "Congressional Intent Disputed: Court Hears Arguments on Key Civil Rights Case," *CQ Weekly Online* (15 October 1988): 2980; available at library.cqpress.com/cqweekly/WR100404771 (accessed April 30, 2009); "Major Civil Rights Laws," CQ Weekly Online (13 May 1989): 1122. library.cqpress.com/cqweekly/WR101406216 (accessed April 30, 2009); Joan Biskupic, "Congress May Seek to Reverse Narrow Civil Rights Ruling." CQ Weekly Online (10 June 1989): 1404-1406. library.cqpress.com/cqweekly/WR101406485 (accessed April 30, 2009); Joan Biskupic and Christine C. Lawrence, "Civil Rights Bill Advancing Despite GOP Objections," CQ Weekly Online (5 May 1990): 1352-1353. library.cqpress.com/cqweekly/WR101409192 (accessed April 30, 2009); .Joan Biskupic, "Senate Ready To Begin Debate On Omnibus Civil Rights Bill," CQ Weekly Online (30 June 1990): 2070-2070. library.cqpress.com/ cqweekly/WR101409753 (accessed April 30, 2009); Joan Biskupic, "Deal on Civil Rights Measure Stymied by 'Quota' Issue," CQ Weekly Online (14 July 1990): 2225-2226. library.cqpress.com/ cqweekly/WR101409867 (accessed April 30, 2009); Joan Biskupic, "Partisan Rancor Marks Vote On Civil Rights Measure," CQ Weekly Online (21 July 1990): 2312-2316. library.cqpress.com/cqweekly/WR101409913 (accessed April 30, 2009); Joan Biskupic, "New Struggle Over Civil Rights Brings Shift in Strategy," CQ Weekly Online (9 February 1991): 366-373. library.cqpress.com/cqweekly/WR102402503 (accessed May 1, 2009); "Job Discrimination Legislation Roils Business Community," CQ Weekly Online (20 April 1991): 989-991. library.cq press.com/cqweekly/WR102402966 (accessed May 1, 2009); Joan Biskupic, "Son of 'Quotas'," CQ Weekly

vetoed by President Bush and fell one vote shy of being overridden by the Senate.[179] It was reintroduced the beginning of the next Congress, on January 3, 1991.[180] After a year of wrangling, the Act passed the Senate on October 30, 1991 by a vote of 93-5[181] and the House of

---

Online (18 May 1991): 1287. library.cq press.com/cqweekly/WR102403173 (accessed May 1, 2009); Joan Biskupic, "Behind the Fight Over Quotas Lie Divisive Racial Issues," CQ Weekly Online (1 June 1991): 1442-1445. Library.cqpress.com/cqweekly/WR1024034 82 (accessed May 1, 2009); Joan Biskupic, "CIVIL RIGHTS: Danforth Revises Legislation In Quest for a Compromise," CQ Weekly Online (22 June 1991): 1669. library.cqpress.com/cqweekly/WR102403666 (accessed May 1, 2009); Joan Biskupic, "Civil Rights: No Deal," CQ Weekly Online (3 August 1991): 2170. library.cq press.com/cqweekly/WR102404050 (accessed May 1, 2009); Joan Biskupic, "LAW/JUDICIARY: Conferees Attempt To Rescue Imperiled Civil Rights Bill," CQ Weekly Online (13 October 1990): 3428-3428. Library.cq press.com/cqweekly/WR101401673 (accessed May 1, 2009); Joan Biskupic, "PROV ISIONS: Civil Rights Act of 1991," CQ Weekly Online (7 December 1991): 3620-3622. library.cqpress.com/ cqweekly/WR102405603 (accessed May 1, 2009).

[178] S. 2104/H.R. 4000. Initial reaction to these decisions was "predictable and typified the later debate: shrill condemnation by the civil rights groups, followed with a tentative defense by the Bush administration. After a few weeks, however, the public debate for the most part lapsed into a silence lasting over half a year. During this time, the groups drafted the bill they would introduce and lined up a long list of sponsors for it. The administration began preparing its response to that bill, based on the rumors of what it would entail." Roger Clegg, "Introduction: A Brief Legislative History of the Civil Rights Act of 1991," Louisiana Law Review 54, no. 6 The Civil Rights Act of 1991: A Symposium (1993-1994): 1463.

[179] 11 Republicans joined 55 Democrats to fall one vote short on of a presidential override of S. 2104/H.R. 4000.

[180] H.R. 1. Also see Neal Devins, "Reagan Redux: Civil Rights Under Bush," Notre Dame Law Review 68, no. 5 Symposium: The Civil Rights Act of 1991: Theory and Practice (1993): 955-1001.

[181] Democrats voted 55-0. Republicans voted 38-5.

Representatives on November 7, 1991 by a vote of 381-38.[182] It was signed into law by President George H. W. Bush on November 21, 1991.[183] Standing in the Rose Garden, he made clear "[i]t d[id] not resort to quotas"[184] and that "[t]his administration is committed to action that is truly affirmative, positive action. Nothing in this bill overturns the government's affirmative action programs."[185]

---

[182] Democrats voted 252-5. Republicans voted 128-33.

[183] Pub. L. No. 102-166, 105 Stat. 1071 (1991).

[184] "'After extraordinary debate and negotiation, we have reached an agreement with Senate Republican and Democratic leaders on a civil rights bill that will be a source of pride for all Americans. It does not resort to quotas, and it strengthens the cause of equality in the workplace. Both the administration and the Congress can present this legislation to the people of America as a new standard against discrimination and for equal opportunity. This agreement was reached last night in marathon negotiations, shepherded by Sen. John Danforth, (R-Mo.), nurtured by Sen. (Bob) Dole (R-Kan.) and other leaders of both parties. It was a proud accomplishment for the Congress and the administration. And now we can go forward together in progress on civil rights in this country. I remember standing out there in the Rose Garden with Attorney General (Dick) Thornburgh more than a year and a half ago to make an unshakable commitment to the nation's civil rights leaders that I wanted a non-quota civil rights bill that I could sign. And assuming there are no changes in the bill as agreed to last night, we now have such a bill. And my promise will be kept, and I will enthusiastically sign this bill.' President Bush used the word 'quota' at least six times in his brief statement and answers to reporters." "PRESIDENTIAL NEWS CONFERENCE: Bush Hails Civil Rights Accord, Sees 'Joyous Day' for Nation," CQ Weekly Online (October 26, 1991): 3149-3150, available at library.cqpress.com/cqweekly/WR 102405149 (accessed October 23, 2007).

[185] Joan Biskupic, "PROVISIONS: Civil Rights Act of 1991," CQ Weekly Online (7 Dec. 1991): 3620-3622. library.cqpress.com/cqweekly/ WR102405603 (accessed October 19, 2007); "Bush on Job Rights Bill," CQ Electronic Library, CQ Historic Documents Series Online Edition, library.cqpress.com/historicdocuments/hsdc91-0000911038. Originally published in Historic Documents of 1991 (Washington: CQ Press, 1992).

The Act "[s]tate[d] that Congress finds that additional remedies are needed to deter unlawful harassment and intentional discrimination in the workplace" and "[s]ingles out the Supreme Court's 1989 decision in *Wards Cove Packing Co. v. Atonio*, saying it weakened the scope and effectiveness of federal civil rights protections."[186] Technically, the bill "reverse[d] or modif[ied] [the] six Supreme Court decisions from the 1988-89 term and four other high court decisions since 1985 involving awards and attorneys' fees for plaintiff-employees" by amending Title VII of the 1964 Civil Rights Act. Specifically, in addition to *Wards Cove* it reversed *Patterson v. McLean* by explicitly broadened the language of the 1866 statute concerning contracts. It also reversed *Martin v. Wilks* by narrowing the opportunities to challenge affirmative action policies in court. It allowed plaintiffs to ask for a jury trial and for victims of harassment and other intentional discrimination based on sex, religion or disability to sue for both compensatory and punitive damages up to a limit of $300,000, as opposed to the status quo ante which was that only lost pay and lawyer's fees were recoverable under Title VII of the 1964 Civil Rights Act.[187]

---

library.cqpress.com/historicdocuments/ hsdc91-0000911038 (accessed October 23, 2007).

[186] Joan Biskupic, "PROVISIONS: Civil Rights Act of 1991," CQ Weekly Online (December 7, 1991): 3620-3622, available at library.cqpress.com/cqweekly/WR102405603 (accessed October 19, 2007).

[187] Joan Biskupic, "Civil Rights Act Poised To Clear, But Bush Veto Looks *Certain,"* CQ Weekly Online (September 29, 1990): 3128-3129. http://library.cqpress.com/cqweekly/WR101401448 (accessed May 1, 2009). Other related cases were *Library of Congress v. Shaw*, 478 U.S. 310 (1985) which stated that Title VII's allowance of reasonable attorney's fees to prevailing party does not provide for recovery of interest from government; *Crawford Fitting Co. v. J.T. Gibbons, Inc.*, 482 U.S. 437 (1987) which limited reimbursement by losing party of prevailing party's expert witness fees; and *Evans v. Jeff D.*, 475 U.S. 717 (1986) which ruled that Civil Rights Attorney's Fees Awards Act of 1976 does not prohibit waiver of attorney's fees in exchange for settlement of case on the merits. Biskupic described the legislation's purpose as seeking "to provide appropriate remedies for discrimination, to codify the concepts of 'business necessity' and 'job related' offered by the Supreme Court in *Griggs v. Duke Power Co.* in 1971,

However, Congress, using "vague, open-ended language to settle the most controversial questions. . . . [which were] left to federal courts

---

and in related Supreme Court decisions before *Wards Cove Packing Co. v. Atonio*, to provide statutory guidelines for disparate-impact lawsuits under Title VII of the Civil Rights Act of 1964, to respond to recent court decisions by expanding the scope of relevant civil rights statutes to provide adequate protection to victims of discrimination." Joan Biskupic, "PROVISIONS: Civil Rights Act of 1991," CQ Weekly Online (December 7, 1991): 3620-3622. library.cqpress.com/cqweekly/WR102405603 (accessed October 19, 2007). The Equal Employment Opportunity Commission describes the bill as: "The 1991 Act amended several of the statutes enforced by EEOC, both substantively and procedurally. Previously, jury trials were possible only in cases brought under the EPA (Equal Pay Act of 1963) or the ADEA (Age Discrimination in Employment of 1967). Under the provisions of the 1991 Act, parties could now obtain jury trials, and recover compensatory and punitive damages in Title VII and ADA lawsuits involving intentional discrimination. The Act placed statutory caps on the amount of damages that could be awarded for future pecuniary losses, pain and suffering, and punitive damages, based on employer size. The maximum award of compensatory and punitive damages combined was set at $300,000 for the largest employers (more than 500 employees). . . . In addition, the 1991 Act added a new subsection to Title VII, codifying the disparate impact theory of discrimination, essentially putting the law back as it had been prior to *Wards Cove*. And in response to *Price-Waterhouse*, the Act provided that where the plaintiff shows that discrimination was a motivating factor for an employment decision, the employer is liable for injunctive relief, attorney's fees, and costs (but not individual monetary or affirmative relief) even though it proves it would have made the same decision in the absence of a discriminatory motive. The Act also provided employment discrimination protection to employees of Congress and some high-level political appointees. Lastly, Title VII and ADA coverage was extended to include American and American-controlled employers operating abroad." http://www.eeoc.gov /abouteeoc/35th/1990s/civilrights.html. See also Douglas S. McDowell, ed. The Civil Rights Act of 1991: A Legislative History, Volume I (Employment Policy Foundation, 1992), i-ii.

interpreting the law,"[188] passed a bill called by some a "classic, convoluted legislative deal"[189] and "little more than a truce designed to get some sort of deal passed."[190] It "did not fully define standards for justifying work practices, such as achievement tests, that appear fair but have a disproportionately adverse effect on women, blacks or other minorities."[191] The bill also did not decide the issue of retroactivity,[192] it excluded the two thousand Asian-American workers of Wards Cove, and the Act failed to define "business necessity," already an inexact term.[193]

---

[188] Joan Biskupic, "PROVISIONS: Civil Rights Act of 1991," CQ Weekly Online (December 7, 1991): 3620-3622, available at library.cqpress.com/cqweekly/WR102405603 (accessed October 19, 2007).

[189] Stuart Taylor, "The Civil Rights Bill: Punt to the Courts," Legal Times (4 Nov. 1991): 25.

[190] Douglas S. McDowell, ed. The Civil Rights Act of 1991: A Legislative History, Volume I (Employment Policy Foundation, 1992), ii.

[191] Joan Biskupic, "PROVISIONS: Civil Rights Act of 1991," CQ Weekly Online (December 7, 1991): 3620-3622, available at library.cqpress.com/ cqweekly/WR102405603 (accessed October 19, 2007).

[192] Ronald D. Rotunda, "The Civil Rights Act of 1991: A Brief Introductory Analysis of the Congressional Response to Judicial Interpretation," Notre Dame Law Review 68, no. 5 Symposium: The Civil Rights Act of 1991: Theory and Practice (1993): 951.

[193] *Griggs* "used seven different formulations to describe the concept of 'business necessity.' In six of these, the Court described 'business necessity' as requiring an employer to show that its practices related, in some way, to 'job performance' or 'job capability.' In the seventh, the Court stated that the practice must 'have a manifest relationship to the employment in question.'" *Griggs v. Duke Power Company*, 401 U.S. at 426, 431-33, 436, 432 (1971). See Peter M. Leibold, Stephen A. Sola, and Reginald E. Jones, "Civil Rights Act of 1991: Race to the Finish – Civil Rights, Quotas, and Disparate Impact in 1991," Rutgers Law Review 45 (1992-93): 1046-47 (n.23). In the original Kennedy bill, the term was defined as "required by business necessity" and "essential to effective job performance." S. 2104, Section 3. In a 1975 case, the Court defined "business necessity" as "job related." *Albermarle Paper Co. v. Moody*, 422 U.S. 405, 425 (1975). In a 1977 case, the Court defined it

How such an agreement was reached was "itself an unresolved mystery."[194] Some believed the final bill was the result of a "backroom deal" with little input from most members of the Senate.[195] There were also other external political issues possibly affecting the political environment. The Americans with Disabilities Act of 1990 was signed

---

as "essential to effective job performance." *Dothard v. Rawlinson*, 433 U.S. 301, 331 (1977). In 1979, it was defined as "legitimate employment goals are significantly served by, even if they do not require," the challenged practice. *New York City Transit Authority v. Beazer*, 440 U.S. 568, 587 (n.31) (1979). In 1988, the term was defined as "based on legitimate business reasons." *Watson v. Fort Worth Bank & Trust*, 487 U.S. 977, 998 (1988). In *Wards Cove* the Court had said a disputed practice must "serve in a significant way the legitimate employment goals on the employer." In the final language of the 1991 Civil Rights Act, a challenged practice must be "job-related and consistent with business necessity." See Peter M. Leibold, Stephen A. Sola, and Reginald E. Jones, "Civil Rights Act of 1991: Race to the Finish – Civil Rights, Quotas, and Disparate Impact in 1991," Rutgers Law Review 45 (1992-93): 1073-1074.

194 Roger Clegg, "Introduction: A Brief Legislative History of the Civil Rights Act of 1991," Louisiana Law Review 54, no. 6 The Civil Rights Act of 1991: A Symposium (1993-1994): 1469.

195 According to William McGurn, "[i]n the case of the civil-rights bill, Dole made good on his promise to accommodate Mitchell. The package was hatched in one of those backroom deals in Dole's office with almost no other Republicans knowing what he was up to. The next day, staffer Sheila Burke kept Republicans from even *looking* at the bill until after the Democrats had had a chance to consider it at their morning conference. Republicans didn't get to discuss the compromise until the afternoon, by which time Teddy Kennedy had already put his spin on it (the bill would negate several Supreme Court decisions, Kennedy welcomed the President's change of heart, etc.). No wonder some call Dole the 'Assistant Majority Leader' behind his back." William McGurn, "The Two Bobs: Meet Bobs Michel and Dole, establishmentarians extraordinaire. As long as they're the Minority Leaders, they don't seem to mind that their troops are more of a minority with every election," National Review (2 December 1991): 35.

into law July 26, 1990.[196] The 1990 North Carolina Senate race between incumbent Jesse Helms and Harvey Gantt, an African-American from Charlotte, featured the infamous "hands" campaign commercial, and there were upcoming presidential and congressional elections, including an election involving David Duke for governor of Louisiana.[197] There had been a "public normative alarm" about the undermining of a "bedrock statute."[198] Judge Clarence Thomas was nominated for the Supreme Court on July 1, 1991 with the hearings involving the testimony of Anita Hill occurring in October. Thomas was confirmed October 15th and some believe compromise on the Act was reached in their "wake."[199]

---

[196] Pub. L. 101-366, 104 Stat. 327 (1990), codified at 42 U.S.C. § 12101.

[197] Mary H. Cooper, "Racial Quotas," CQ Researcher Online 1 (May 17, 1991): 277-300, available at library.cqpress.com/cqresearcher/cqresrre1991051700 (accessed August 22, 2008).

[198] Eskridge and Ferejohn argue that, "[f]or the particular justices on that Court, there was nothing greatly remarkable about their narrow construction in those cases. . . . The Court's methodology was emblematic of ordinary statutory construction: hew closely to statutory plain meaning without undue intrusion into common law rights and obligations. What the majority justices did not sufficiently appreciate was that the political process did not regard these as ordinary cases. The decisions triggered a public normative alarm that a bedrock statute was being undermined, and large majorities in Congress approved the Civil Rights Act of 1991, which reaffirmed *Griggs* (explicitly) and *Weber* (implicitly). This normative feedback had some effect on the Rehnquist Court, even though its membership became more conservative. The continuing and indeed strengthened popular support for a strong anti-discrimination – and pro-integration – principle has swept the field." William N. Eskridge Jr. and John Ferejohn, "Quasi-Constitutional Law: The Rise of Super-Statutes," in Congress and the Constitution, eds. Devins and Whittington (Durham: Duke University Press, 2005), 206.

[199] Joan Biskupic, "PROVISIONS: Civil Rights Act of 1991," CQ Weekly Online (December 7, 1991): 3620-3622, available at library.cqpress.com/cqweekly/WR102405603 (accessed October 19, 2007). See also Pamela Fessler, Joan Biskupic, and Phil Kuntz, "Rights Bill Rises From the Ashes Of Senate's Thomas Fight," CQ Weekly Online (October 26, 1991): 3124-3126, available at library.cqpress.com /cqweekly/

DELIBERATION

VALUES, FIGURES, & FRAMERS

Members on both sides of the issues often appealed to generic values like fairness, equality, and justice. Some said that "[f]reedom and justice are not achieved by statistical balance of employees,"[200] while others stated that "[t]he real issues at stake here are issues of integrity, issues of justice, issues of fairness."[201] Sen. Jeffords believed that "[t]here is no higher moral principle in a democracy than ensuring equal rights. That is the very principle that we seek to strengthen today"[202] while several Senate Republicans believed "[t]here is unanimous support in Congress for the basic principle of equal employment opportunity for all Americans without regard to race, ethnicity, religion, or gender, as required by Title VII of the Civil Rights Act of 1964. The promise of S. 2104, however, is equal

---

WR102405172 (accessed May 1, 2009); Joan Biskupic, "CIVIL RIGHTS: Bush Signs Anti-Job Bias Bill Amid Furor Over Preferences," CQ Weekly Online (November 23, 1991): 3463, available at library.cqpress.com/cqweekly/WR102405422 (accessed May 1, 2009); Roger Clegg, "Introduction: A Brief Legislative History of the Civil Rights Act of 1991," Louisiana Law Review 54, no. 6 The Civil Rights Act of 1991: A Symposium (1993-1994): 1469; Louis Fisher and David Gray Adler, American Constitutional Law, Vol. 2 Constitutional Rights: Civil Rights and Civil Liberties, 7th edition (Carolina Academic Press: Durham, North Carolina, 2007): 811; Joan Biskupic, "Senate passes sweeping measure to overturn court rulings," CQ Weekly (2 Nov. 1991): 3200.

200 Rep. Susan Molinari (R-NY), Congressional Record, 101st Cong., 2nd sess., 1990, H6751 (3 Aug. 1990).

201 Sen. Howard Metzenbaum (D-OH), Congressional Record, 101st Cong., 2nd sess., 1990, S15334 (16 Oct. 1990).

202 Sen. James Jeffords (R-VT), Congressional Record, 101st Cong., 2nd sess., 1990, S15337 (16 Oct. 1990)

outcomes for groups, not equal opportunity for individuals."[203] Rep. Panetta stated:

> Mr. Chairman, during this debate all of us have said that we adhere to the fundamental principle this Nation was founded upon, that we are all created equal. But there is also a fundamental reality in this Nation that we do not always do what we say. Indeed the history of civil rights is really the history of that double standard. Our forefathers declared in this founding of this Nation that we were all equal under God, but accepted slavery. This Nation bled in a civil rights way, the Civil War, to basically free the slaves, but yet a few years later reinstituted slavery under the guise of 'separate but equal' in the *Plessy versus Ferguson* decision. And when the Supreme Court in the *Brown* decision declared that 'separate' is inherently unequal, it took almost 25 years to end the dual school system in this country.[204]

While Rep. Owens stated that:

> [A]s a layman I have found the discussion, this very technical discussion, back and forth among the lawyers quite interesting. I am going to take a different approach. I do think what I have to say is germane, however, because I think that the quest for justice and the quest for a higher morality is very important here. Sometimes, as I listened, I wondered, about that statement that law often has nothing to do with justice, is not concerned with morality. . . . I think that the Supreme

---

[203] Senate Committee on Labor and Human Resources Report, The Civil Rights Act of 1990, Minority Views of Senators Hatch, Thurmond, and Coats, 101st Cong., 2nd sess., 8 June 1990, appearing in Douglas S. McDowell, ed. The Civil Rights Act of 1991: A Legislative History, Volume I (Employment Policy Foundation, 1992), 120. For another reference to this debate, see Sen. Orrin Hatch (R-UT), Congressional Record, 101st Cong., 2nd sess. 136 S457 (29 Jan. 1990, Legislative day of 23 January 1990).

[204] Rep. Leon Panetta (D-CA), Congressional Record, 102nd Cong., 1st sess., 1991, H3901 (4 June 1991).

> Court certainly has provided some bad leadership in making certain recent decisions without taking into consideration history and background, and the fact that, we are talking basically about a condition that was created by an institution called slavery, then after slavery, Jim Crow and discrimination for many years. Two hundred and some years of slavery and after that about a hundred years of intense oppressive second-class citizenship. People were not even allowed until very recently, relatively recently, to apply for jobs on the fire department or the police department in Birmingham or other southern cities. . . . Blacks were not allowed to get licenses to be plumbers or to be carpenters or be electricians. The fallout of that still exists. On and on we go.[205]

In addition, during the congressional deliberation invocations to authoritative figures and references were also common. Appeals were made to Martin Luther King, Jr.,[206] King's "Letter from a Birmingham Jail,"[207] "human rights,"[208] racism on college campuses,[209] South

---

[205] Rep. Major R. Owens (D-NY), Congress, House of Representatives, Joint Hearings before the Committee on Education and Labor and the Subcommittee on Civil and Constitutional Rights of the Committee on the Judiciary, Hearings on HR 4000, The Civil Rights Act of 1990 – Volume 2, 101st Cong., 2nd sess., 13 and 20 March 1990 (Washington, D.C.: GPO, 1990), 386-388.

[206] Sen. Jesse Helms (R-NC), Congressional Record, 101st Cong., 2nd sess., 1990, 136, no. 86 S9339 (Tuesday 10 July 1990).

[207] Rep. Glen Poshard (D-IL), Congressional Record, 102nd Cong., 1st sess., 1991, H3904 (4 June 1991).

[208] Rep. Matthew G. Martinez (D-CA), Congress, House of Representatives, Committee on Education and Labor, Hearings on H.R. 4000, The Civil Rights Act of 1990 – Volume 3, 101st Cong., 2nd sess., 25 April 1990 (Washington, D.C.: GPO, 1990), 59.

[209] Rep. Jose E. Serrano (D-NY), Congress, House of Representatives, Committee on Education and Labor, hearing, Hearings on H.R. 1, The Civil Rights Act of 1991, 102nd Cong., 1st sess., 27 February and 5 March 1991 (Washington, D.C.: GPO, 1991), 29.

Africa,[210] Eastern Europe,[211] and the Gettysburg Address.[212] Figures appealed to included Willie Horton,[213] Sen. Hubert Humphrey,[214] Sen. Sam Ervin,[215] Frederick Douglass,[216] Justice William O. Douglas,[217] Alexander Bickel,[218] F. W. de Klerk and Nelson Mandela,[219] the biblical figure Job,[220] David Duke,[221] and Andrew Johnson.[222]

---

[210] Rep. Jose E. Serrano (D-NY), Congress, House of Representatives, Committee on Education and Labor, hearing, Hearings on H.R. 1, The Civil Rights Act of 1991, 102nd Cong., 1st sess., 27 February and 5 March 1991 (Washington, D.C.: GPO, 1991), 29.

[211] Sen. Paul Simon (D-IL), Congress, Senate, Committee on Labor and Human Resources, hearing, Civil Rights Act of 1990, 101st Cong., 1st sess., 23 and 27 February and 1 and 7 March 1990 (Washington, D.C.: GPO, 1990), 57.

[212] Rep. Edolphus Towns (D-NY), Congressional Record, 102nd Cong., 1st sess., 1991, H3894 (4 June 1991).

[213] Rep. Douglas Owens (D-UT), Congressional Record, 102nd Cong., 1st sess., 1991, H3906 (4 June 1991); Rep. Theodore Weiss (D-NY), Congressional Record, 102nd Cong., 1st sess., 1991, H3956 (5 June 1991).

[214] Sen. Jesse Helms (R-NC), Congressional Record, 102nd Cong., 1st sess., 1991, S8560 (25 June 1991). For other appeals to Sen. Humphrey see Paul Wellstone (D-MN), Congressional Record, 102nd Cong., 1st sess., 1991, S8683-8684 (26 June 1991); Sen. Steven Symms (R-ID), Congressional Record, 102nd Cong., 1st sess., 1991, S 12777 (11 Sept. 1991); Sen. McCain (R-AZ), Congressional Record, 101st Cong., 2nd sess., S9894 (18 July 1990); Rep. Stephen Neal (D-NC), Congressional Record, 101st Cong., 2nd sess., 1990, H6806 (2 Aug. 1990); Sen. Jesse Helms (R-NC), Congressional Record, 101st Cong., 2nd sess., 1990, 136, no. 86 S9339 (Tuesday 10 July 1990).

[215] Sen. Jesse Helms (R-NC), Congressional Record, 102nd Cong., 1st sess., 1991, S8560 (25 June 1991).

[216] Sen. Jesse Helms (R-NC), Congressional Record, 102nd Cong., 1st sess., 1991, S8562 (25 June 1991). See also, Sen. Jesse Helms (R-NC), Congressional Record, 101st Cong., 2nd sess., 1990, 136, no. 86 S9339 (Tuesday 10 July 1990).

[217] Sen. Jesse Helms (R-NC), Congressional Record, 102nd Cong., 1st sess., 1991, S8562 (25 June 1991).

[218] Sen. Jesse Helms (R-NC), Congressional Record, 101st Cong., 2nd sess., 1990, 136, no. 86 S9339 (10 July 1990). See also, Congressional Record,

Members also made explicit appeals to the founding era and our founding documents, most frequently the Declaration of Independence.[223] Rep. Hyde argued "[l]et us vote no on H.R. 1 and, thus, reaffirm our Constitution and the Civil Rights Act of 1964,"[224] while Rep. Fish stated that "[i]n addressing redress for discriminatory employment practices, we implement the 'equal protection of the law' clause of our Constitution. Surely discriminating employment practices without redress is a denial of equal protection."[225] Rep. AuCoin asked his colleagues:

> what is our fundamental purpose here in Congress? Is it not to preserve and protect the rights guaranteed to Americans by our Constitution and legislate accordingly? So how can we allow the strength of the Civil Rights Act of 1964 to be slowly eroded away by an indifferent Supreme Court? Today it is our moral imperative to restore by statute the full spirit of civil rights and equality to our laws. We have been through this debate before. In 1964, we provided stronger protection for

---

101st Cong., 2nd sess., 1990, 136, no. 86, S16584 (24 October 1990); Congressional Record, 102nd Cong., 1st sess., 1991, S8562 (25 June 1991).

219 Sen. Edward Kennedy (D-MA), Congressional Record, 101st Cong., 2nd sess., 136 S9320 (10 July 1990).

220 Sen. Jesse Helms (R-NC), Congressional Record, 101st Cong., 2nd sess., 1990, 136, no. 86 S9339 (Tuesday 10 July 1990).

221 Sen. Howard Metzenbaum (D-OH), Congressional Record, 101st Cong., 2nd sess., 1990, S15334 (16 Oct. 1990).

222 Rep. Don Edwards (D-CA), Congressional Record, 101st Cong., 2nd sess., 1990, H9977 (17 Oct. 1990).

223 Rep. William Lacy Clay (D-MO), Congressional Record, 102nd Cong., 1st sess., 1991, H3895 (4 June 1991). See also Rep. Marilyn Lloyd (D-TN), Congressional Record, 101st Cong., 2nd sess., 1990, H6332 (2 Aug. 1990).

224 Rep. Henry Hyde (R-IL), Congressional Record, 102nd Cong., 1st sess., 1991, H3929 (5 June 1991).

225 Rep. Hamilton Fish (R-NY), Congressional Record, 102nd Cong., 1st sess., 1991, H3946 (5 June 1991).

> rights guaranteed by the Constitution, protections against race discrimination.[226]

Rep. Washington stated, "Mr. Chairman, my problem is I believed in the Constitution. My problem is I believed in the Declaration of Independence"[227] while Sen. Bradley believed that "[t]his bill sets our Nation forth once again on the path of continuous progress toward the open and free society envisioned in the Declaration of Independence."[228] Rep. Washington stated:

> You see, my problem is that even though I am 49 years old, I am still impatient. I think that when I read the Constitution that I love so much and I look at the Declaration of Independence and all of those things that those great people wrote down years ago, I believe them. My problem is I believe that those words were promises that were made to all of us, not black or white or brown or rich or poor or old or young, but those words were great because this is a great country. . . . We need to show the entire world that looks to us for direction and guidance that although we have many cultures, many religions, various kinds of people, we can live together in this country as one people, and that what we wrote down in our Declaration of Independence and what we wrote down in our Constitution means something to all of us.[229]

Rep. de la Garza argued:

> That is what we are about today, justice and equality. . . . We hear so often the words that our Founding Fathers left with us,

---

[226] Rep. Les AuCoin (D-OR), Congressional Record, 102nd Cong., 1st sess., 1991, H3952 (5 June 1991).

[227] Rep. Craig Washington (D-TX), Congressional Record, 101st Cong., 2nd sess., 1990, H6758 (3 Aug. 1990).

[228] Sen. Bill Bradley (D-NJ), Congressional Record, 101st Cong., 2nd sess., 1990, S15381 (16 Oct. 1990).

[229] Rep. Craig Washington (D-TX), Congressional Record, 101st Cong., 2nd sess., 1990, H9978 (17 Oct. 1990).

> that there are certain unalienable rights bestowed upon us by the Creator of the human beings. This is but another step in the never-ending process of trying to achieve the ultimate in that vow, and that promise and that challenge of the Founding Fathers. . . . I would say, and I have heard all of the arguments, that there is not that much difference. But should there be difference, justice demands that the doubt be given in the favor of those who suffered.[230]

Rep. Hoyer addressed the Court by stating:

> And so we speak to five Supreme Court cases, and we speak in a way that says we meant what we said in 1964 and we expect people in America to honor the civil rights commitment that this Nation really made in 1776 and in 1787 and in the 1860's in the adoption of significant amendments to our Constitution, but which we know and which was said so eloquently in 1963, that we have still not lived out the promises of those documents, and that is true today.[231]

INTENT, EFFECTS, & QUOTAS

Many members engaged in deliberation over the intention of the 1964 Civil Rights Act, *Griggs v. Duke Power Company*, *Wards Cove Packing v. Atonio*, and the use of "quotas." The Act "represented a significant step forward in our pursuit of equal justice for all."[232] Sen. Symms believed "there is a wide disparity between nondiscriminatory purposes of the Civil Rights Act of 1964 as it was originally enacted

---

[230] Rep. Kika de la Garza (D-TX), Congressional Record, 101st Cong., 2nd sess., 1990, H6754 (3 Aug. 1990).

[231] Rep. Steny Hoyer (D-MD), Congressional Record, 101st Cong., 2nd sess., 1990, H6793 (2 Aug. 1990).

[232] Sen. Alan Cranston (D-CA), Congressional Record, 101st Cong., 2nd sess., 1990, S9942 (18 July 1990).

and the color-conscious perversion which some judges derived from it."[233] The 1964 Act was thus "colorblind."[234] As Sen. Helms argued:

> Mr. President, the Civil Rights Act of 1964 -- which the current legislation would irreparably alter -- did not purport to establish racial classifications. It outlawed discrimination on all fronts. In matters of employment, title VII of the act declared that no employer shall be permitted to "fail or refuse to hire or discharge any individual, or otherwise discriminate against any individual . . . because of such individual's race, color, religion, sex, or national origin."[235]

After President Bush's veto, Sen. Hatch exclaimed, "Title VII of the 1964 Civil Rights Act promised colorblind treatment of all Americans in the workplace, where every citizen should be treated on the basis of his or her talents and merit."[236] "What we need is a color-blind society with equal opportunity for all Americans, and not a color-conscious society with equal results for all."[237]

On the other hand, "[w]hat we want to accomplish today is to restore the degree of civil rights protection provided by the . . . 1964 act[].[238] Therefore, "[p]assage of the Civil Rights Act of 1990 is vital if we are to reaffirm the original intent of civil rights laws, and protect the

---

[233] Sen. Steven Symms (R-ID), Congressional Record, 102nd Cong., 1st sess., 1991, S12777 (11 Sept. 1991).

[234] Sen. Malcolm Wallop (R-WY), Congressional Record, 102nd Cong., 1st sess., S15363 (29 October 1991).

[235] Sen. Jesse Helms (R-NC), Congressional Record, 101st Cong., 2nd sess., 1990, 136, no. 86 S9339 (10 July 1990).

[236] Sen. Orrin Hatch (R-UT), Congressional Record, 101st Cong., 2nd sess., 1990, S16565 (24 Oct. 1990).

[237] Rep. Barbara Vucanovich (R-NV), Congressional Record, 102nd Cong., 1st sess., 1991, H3860 (4 June 1991).

[238] Rep. Marilyn Lloyd (D-TN), Congressional Record, 101st Cong., 2nd sess., 1990, H6332 (2 Aug. 1990).

future from the forces that would divide us, not unite us."[239] The bill was "a reaffirmation of the Civil Rights Act of 1964."[240] Rep. Gephardt stated the "Civil Rights Act that we meet on today, passed in 1964, changed America. . . . I say to my colleagues . . . Stand up for the values of this country and our Constitution, and, if you will, will reaffirm the acts of courage of 1964."[241]

The threat and purported non-existence of quotas were heatedly verbalized. Rep. Hyde argued:

> I would advise all employers to abandon the outdated claim, 'An Equal Opportunity Employer,' for the more accurate claim, 'A Statistically Proportional Employer' and I would recommend all help wanted signs revert to the old 'Irish need not apply' signs in 19th century Boston, and perhaps advertisements can specify: 'Help Wanted, four women, two African-American males, and one Hispanic required. . . . My old-fashioned reading of the Constitution is that the promise of the 5th and 14th Amendments is equal protection, not proportional protection of the law.[242]

Likewise, Sen. Wallop stated:

> On July 2 1964 - the day the 1964 Act became law - Sen. Humphrey inserted into the record 'A concise explanation of the Civil Rights Act of 1964.' – 'to provide Americans with a short and understandable explanation of the civil rights bill. . . . that the American people may find useful.' – [Title VII] does not provide that any preferential treatment shall be given to

---

[239] Rep. Norman Mineta (D-CA), Congressional Record, 101st Cong., 2nd sess., 1990, H6794 (2 Aug. 1990).

[240] Rep. Augustus Hawkins (D-CA), Congressional Record, 101st Cong., 2nd sess., 1990, H6799 (2 Aug. 1990).

[241] Rep. Richard Gephardt (D-MO), Congressional Record, 101st Cong., 2nd sess., 1990, H6766 (3 Aug. 1990).

[242] Rep. Henry Hyde (R-IL), Congressional Record, 102nd Cong., 1st sess., 1991, H3839 (4 June 1991).

> Negroes or to any other persons or groups. It does not provide that any quota systems may be established to maintain racial balance in employment. In fact, the title prohibits preferential treatment for any particular group.'[243]

Rep. Fawell denied the 1964 Act was ever meant to encompass statistical disparities: "we have to remember that we're talking about something the legislature never in its wisdom created – unintentional discrimination."[244] Sen. Wallop "believe[d] it [was] high time we as a Nation return to the notion of civil rights as being the province of individuals, as the Constitution requires, not as a booty for specific groups."[245] Sen. Helms asserted "we have [a] quota bill before us – quota bill, not civil rights bill. It is a quota bill."[246] Sen. Gordon agreed:

> This bill is designed to and will result in the establishment of quotas, the abandonment of merit as the principal reason for hiring and for promotions, and the abandonment of a system in

---

243 Sen. Malcolm Wallop (R-WY), Congressional Record, 102nd Cong., 1st sess., 1991, S15363 (29 October 1991).

244 Rep. Harris W. Fawell (R-IL), Congress, House of Representatives, Committee on Education and Labor, hearing, Hearings on H.R. 1, The Civil Rights Act of 1991, 102nd Cong., 1st sess., 27 February and 5 March 1991 (Washington, D.C.: GPO, 1991), 490.

245 Sen. Malcolm Wallop (R-WY), Congressional Record, 102nd Cong., 1st sess., 1991, S15363 (29 October 1991).

246 Sen. Jesse Helms (R-NC), Congressional Record, 101st Cong., 2nd sess., 1990, 136, no. 86 S9339 (10 July 1990). See also Sen. John McCain (R-AZ), Congressional Record, 101st Cong., 2nd sess., 1990, 136 S9894 (18 July 1990). "But there is a major point of disagreement in this bill as it stands that is of utmost concern to many civil rights advocates – from Hubert Humphrey on – and that is the imposition of racial quotas." Exchange between Rep. Steve Gunderson (R-WI) and witness William Burns, Pacific Gas & Electric, Congress, House of Representatives, Committee on Education and Labor and the Subcommittee on Civil and Constitutional Rights of the House Judiciary Committee, Hearings on H.R. 4000, The Civil Rights Act of 1990 – Volume 2, 101st Cong., 2nd sess., 1990, 13 and 20 March (Washington, D.C.: GPO, 1990), 182.

> America in which hard work and qualifications are the primary ground for getting ahead.[247]

Sen. Hatch stated:

> Mr. President, the decision before us is not about restoring prior antidiscrimination law. It is about whether the Senate wishes to lead this country down a short road to quota hiring and promotion. It is about whether the Senate wants to slam the courthouse door on some Americans who wish to assert claims of a denial of their civil rights, and it is about whether we will turn title VII into a litigation bonanza for lawyers.[248]

Others disputed the charge. Sen. Kennedy stated that "[t]wo decades of experience are clear: The *Griggs* rule does not lead to quotas, and never has. It is a mockery of civil rights and the fundamental principle of equal justice under law for opponents of this legislation to raise the false hue and cry of quotas."[249] Rep. Ford stated:

> We all abhor quotas. The legislation we are considering explicitly rejects quotas. Hiring pay and promotion decisions must be based on individual qualifications. I have lived my life sharing with most Americans a commitment to the basic principle that the opportunity to get ahead should be based on individual effort and merit. I will not yield in that commitment The fruits of our labor on H.R. 1 must sustain that fundamental common sense view.[250]

---

[247] Sen. Slade Gorton (R-WA), Congressional Record, 101st Cong., 2nd sess., 1990, S15398 (16 Oct. 1990).

[248] Sen. Orrin Hatch (R-UT), Congressional Record, 101st Cong., 2nd sess., 1990, S15401 (16 Oct. 1990).

[249] Sen. Edward Kennedy (D-MA), Congress, Senate, Committee on Labor and Human Resources, hearing, Civil Rights Act of 1990, 101st Cong., 1st sess., 23 and 27 February and 1 and 7 March 1990 (Washington, D.C.: GPO, 1990), 1-2.

[250] Rep. William D. Ford (D-MI), Congress, House of Representatives, Committee on Education and Labor, hearing, Hearings on H.R. 1, The Civil

Rep. Edwards agreed:

> Mr. Chairman, ironically, the quota argument was raised in 1964 when title VII was being debated. As a result, Section 703(j) was added to title VII saying, "[title VII] does not require preferential treatment . . . on account of imbalance." between an employer's work force and the general population. This means an employer is not required to grant preferential treatment to correct any perceived racial gender or ethnic imbalance in his/her work force.[251]

Sen. Simon defended the use of employment proportionality: "[y]ou cannot use statistics, for all practical purposes, as a result of the *Wards Cove* case. That really ultimately is going to have a devastating effect on seeing to it that justice and opportunity are part of our society."[252]

Committee witnesses did try and draw members into a deeper discussion involving many of the historical issues and case law previously touched upon but their statements went singularly into the record. Former Secretary Coleman stated that "the great steps taken by

---

Rights Act of 1991, 102nd Cong., 1st sess., 27 February and 5 March 1991 (Washington, D.C.: GPO, 1991), 23.

[251] Rep. Don Edwards (D-CA), Congressional Record, 101st Cong., 2nd sess., 1990, H6809 (2 Aug. 1990). Law Professor Douglas W. Kmiec points to Section 703(j), 42 U.S.C. § 2000e-2(j). "Senator Humphrey said the bill 'does not provide that any quota systems may be established to maintain racial balance in employment. In fact, the title [Title VII] . . . prohibit[s] preferential treatment for any particular group, and any person, whether or not a member of any minority group." (Congressional Record, 88th Cong., 2nd sess., 1964, 110, S11848 (1964). To further emphasize the point, it was explicitly provided in Title VII that nothing in the legislation should be interpreted to require preferential treatment because of race." Douglas W. Kmiec, "Foreword: The 1991 Civil Rights Act: A Constitutional, Statutory, and Philosophical Enigma," Notre Dame Law Review 68, no. 5 Symposium: The Civil Rights Act of 1991: Theory and Practice (1993): 915.

[252] Sen. Paul Simon (D-IL), Congress, Senate, Committee on Labor and Human Resources, hearing, Civil Rights Act of 1990, 101st Cong., 1st sess., 23 and 27 February and 1 and 7 March 1990 (Washington, D.C.: GPO, 1990), 9.

this Congress after the Civil War were subsequently nullified by the U.S. Supreme Court, which misconstrued the 13th Amendment, the 14th Amendment and the 15th Amendment, and the 19th century civil rights laws."[253] Another witness said

> I would remind this panel – and if we would want to read, I'd be happy to send you the Civil rights Act of 1875, that dealt with public accommodations. A Post-Reconstruction Supreme Court struck that down. It was not until 1964 that we passed again what we had done in 1875. If I could recount the agony, the injustice, the suffering, the shame, the indignity, the inhumanity, of years and years of this country having to live under 'separate but equal' because the Supreme Court refused to obey the mandates of Congress and Congress would not set the Supreme Court straight. . . . We have suffered so much in this country because we tried after the Civil War to do some of the very same things that we did in the 1950s and 1960s.[254]

The Fourteenth Amendment was mentioned but not specifically correlated to a justification for criticizing the Court's decisions.[255] Rep.

---

[253] Hon. William T. Coleman, senior partner O'Melveny and Myers, Washington, D.C., former clerk of Justice Frankfurter, Secretary of Transportation in the Ford administration, Congress, Senate, Committee on Labor and Human Resources, hearing, Civil Rights Act of 1990, 101st Cong., 1st sess., 23 and 27 February and 1 and 7 March 1990 (Washington, D.C.: GPO, 1990), 13.

[254] Benjamin L. Hooks, CEO/Executive Director, National Association for the Advancement of Colored People, Congress, House of Representatives, Joint Hearings before the Committee on Education and Labor and the Subcommittee on Civil and Constitutional Rights of the Committee on the Judiciary, Hearings on H.R. 4000, the Civil Rights Act of 1990, Vol. 1, hearing, 101st Cong., 2nd sess., 20 and 27 Feb. 1990 (Washington, D.C.: GPO, 1990), 30.

[255] "Every American citizen who has bothered to spend any time examining the Constitution of the United States, if not familiar with those words [the 14th Amendment] exactly, understands that, if they have lived any life at all here,

Hyde mentioned it in mocking the legislative tilt toward upholding disparate analysis.[256] One representative went so far as to accuse the previous administration of attacking the Bill of Rights and not enforcing the 13th Amendment banning slavery.[257] One member did point out important amendment language:

> The framers of the 14th amendment understood the difference between merely granting a right and providing a legal remedy. That's why they specifically included a section that simply reads: 'The Congress shall have power to enforce, by appropriate legislation, the provisions of this article.' They understood that it would take real laws establishing legal

---

that fundamental principle is something we all share, live by, and under. . . . In fact, anyone who might try to detract from that fundamental statement of principle would be considered, I think, by most to be in fundamental violation of our values and principles embraced in our Constitution. To be protected and not to be denied the equal protection of the laws of this country is as fundamental as anything. . . . The decisions, these five decisions, represent, in my view, an unprecedented retreat on the part of the Court from the enforcement of the antidiscrimination laws in our Nation." Sen. Christopher Dodd (D-CT), Congressional Record, 101st Cong., 2nd sess., 1990, S9914 (18 July 1990).

[256] "Now, the 5th amendment, and I need not tell you scholars that, and the 14th amendment, I need not tell you that, guarantees to every person equal protection of the laws. Now, I know everyone is equal, some are just more equal than others. And this bill moves in that direction. . . . But I would just like to recall to your mind the ideal as set forth in our Constitution: equal protection of the law." Rep. Henry Hyde (R-IL), Congressional Record, 101st Cong., 2nd sess., 1990, H6749 (3 Aug. 1990).

[257] "Mr. Chairman, in the last 11 years we have witnessed 3 significant points in civil rights. The first was the wholesale political program by the Reagan administration to attack the Bill of Rights and the judicial and legislative advancements that we have made in this country in enforcing the 13th, 14th, and 15th amendments to the Constitution over the last 30 years." Rep. John Conyers (D-MI), Congressional Record, 102nd Cong., 1st sess., 1991, H3851 (4 June 1991).

remedies to make the rights granted in the 14th Amendment real rights.[258]

DIALOGUES

INTER-BRANCH DESCRIPTIONS

As already alluded to and demonstrated, the Court was frequently criticized throughout deliberations regarding the Civil Rights Act of 1991.[259] Congress needed to "rectify several Supreme Court decisions,"[260] "halt the erosion of Title VII,"[261] and "reverse" the

---

[258] Rep. Cardiss Collins (D-IL), Congressional Record, 102nd Cong., 1st sess., 1991, H3859 (4 June 1991).

[259] One majority report stated "Congress finds that (1) in a series of recent decisions addressing employment discrimination claims under Federal law, the Supreme Court cut back dramatically on the scope and effectiveness of civil rights protections. . . . (b) Purposes – The purposes of this Act are to – (1) respond to the Supreme Court's recent decisions by restoring the civil rights protections that were dramatically limited by those decisions. . . . and to overrule the treatment of business necessity as a defense in *Wards Cove Packing Co., Inc. v. Atonio* (109 S. Ct. 2115 (1989)." Congress, House of Representatives, Committee on Education and Labor, hearing, Hearings on H.R. 1, The Civil Rights Act of 1991, 102nd Cong., 1st sess., 27 February and 5 March 1991 (Washington, D.C.: GPO, 1991), 5.

[260] Rep. Craig A. Washington (D-TX), Congress, House of Representatives, Committee on Education and Labor, hearing, Hearings on H.R. 1, The Civil Rights Act of 1991, 102nd Cong., 1st sess., 27 February and 5 March 1991 (Washington, D.C.: GPO, 1991), 29.

[261] Rep. John F. Reed (D-RI), Congress, House of Representatives, Committee on Education and Labor, hearing, Hearings on H.R. 1, The Civil Rights Act of 1991, 102nd Cong., 1st sess., 27 February and 5 March 1991 (Washington, D.C.: GPO, 1991), 32. "The Civil Rights Act of 1991 seeks to halt the erosion of Title VII of past civil rights legislation and address recent interpretations of such laws."

Court.[262] Rep. Hayes stated that "[w]hat we are proposing here is to try to restore the damage that was done in some of the recent decisions of the Supreme Court."[263] Opponents argued that the Court "destroyed [a] balanced system"[264] and did not recognize the history of slavery and discrimination.[265] The Court had "served as a retreat in the enforcement

---

[262] Rep. William J. Jefferson (D-LA), Congress, House of Representatives, Committee on Education and Labor, hearing, Hearings on H.R. 1, The Civil Rights Act of 1991, 102nd Cong., 1st sess., 27 February and 5 March 1991 (Washington, D.C.: GPO, 1991), 378-79.

[263] Rep. Charles A. Hayes (D-IL), Congress, House of Representatives, Hearings before the Committee on Education and Labor, Hearing on H.R. 4000, The Civil Rights Act of 1990 – Volume 3, 101st Cong., 2nd sess., 25 April 21 May 1990 (Washington, D.C.: GPO, 1990), 168.

[264] William C. Burns, Pacific Gas & Electric, Congress, House of Representatives, Joint Hearings before the Committee on Education and Labor and the Subcommittee on Civil and Constitutional Rights of the Committee on the Judiciary, Hearings on HR 4000, The Civil Rights Act of 1990 – Volume 2, 101st Cong., 2nd sess., 13 and 20 March 1990 (Washington, D.C.: GPO, 1990), 79.

[265] Rep. Major R. Owens (D-NY), Congress, House of Representatives, Joint Hearings before the Committee on Education and Labor and the Subcommittee on Civil and Constitutional Rights of the Committee on the Judiciary, Hearings on HR 4000, The Civil Rights Act of 1990 – Volume 2, 101st Cong., 2nd sess., 13 and 20 March 1990 (Washington, D.C.: GPO, 1990), 387. Sometimes, as I listened, I wondered, about that statement that law often has nothing to do with justice, is not concerned with morality. . . . I think that the Supreme Court certainly has provided some bad leadership in making certain recent decisions without taking into consideration history and background, and the fact, we are talking basically about a condition that was created by an institution called slavery, then after slavery, Jim Crowe and discrimination for many years. Two hundred and some years of slavery and after that about a hundred years of intense oppressive second-class citizenship. People were not even allowed until very recently, relatively recently, to apply for jobs on the fire department or the police department in Birmingham or other southern cities. . . . Blacks were not allowed to get licenses to be plumbers or to be carpenters or be electricians. The fallout of that still exists. On and on we go."

of anti-discrimination laws."[266] The Court lost sight of "the full meaning of the United States Constitution" and Congress should be focused on "the restoration of the rights that we all have come to understand and believe were within the full meaning of the Constitution."[267] The Court "destroyed the credibility of the effectiveness of Title VII as a[n] antidiscrimination law that is able to be enforceable generally."[268] Sen. Metzenbaum argued:

> In 1971, Chief Justice Burger, for the unanimous U.S. Supreme Court in *Griggs*, recognized that title VII requires the removal of artificial, arbitrary, and unnecessary barriers to employment when the barriers operate invidiously to discriminate on the basis of racial or other impermissible classification. . . . Some 18 years later, the new U.S. Supreme Court majority, in *Wards Cove*, held that such discriminatory barriers may remain in place. . . . Worse, the new majority, led by three Reagan appointees, sent a clear signal that new barriers may be erected with impunity. . . . The Civil Rights Act of 1990 sends a completely different signal. The bill stands for the simple proposition that all barriers to equal

---

[266] Rep. Donald M. Payne (D-TX), Congress, House of Representatives, Hearings before the Committee on Education and Labor, Hearing on H.R. 4000, The Civil Rights Act of 1990 – Volume 3, 101st Cong., 2nd sess., 25 April 21 May 1990 (Washington, D.C.: GPO, 1990), 311.

[267] Rep. Craig A. Washington (D-TX), Congress, House of Representatives, Joint Hearings before the Committee on Education and Labor and the Subcommittee on Civil and Constitutional Rights of the Committee on the Judiciary, Hearings on HR 4000, The Civil Rights Act of 1990 – Volume 2, 101st Cong., 2nd sess., 13 and 20 March 1990 (Washington, D.C.: GPO, 1990), 2.

[268] Herbert B. Newberg, Esq., Congress, House of Representatives, Joint Hearings before the Committee on Education and Labor and the Subcommittee on Civil and Constitutional Rights of the Committee on the Judiciary, Hearings on HR 4000, The Civil Rights Act of 1990 – Volume 2, 101st Cong., 2nd sess., 13 and 20 March 1990 (Washington, D.C.: GPO, 1990), 479.

> employment opportunity, whether intentional or not, must come down.[269]

The Supreme Court had "cut back dramatically on the scope and effectiveness of civil rights protections."[270] They "broke ranks with Congress and the consensus of the American people on our march toward the goal of equal justice and equal employment opportunity for all regardless of race, gender, religion, and national origin."[271] They "signal[ed] a swift retreat from the principles we hold dearly. The list is long, but the result is clear: victims are being thrown out of court without a remedy at an alarming rate."[272] The Court had "shirked" their "responsibility" "in protecting the rights of other people."[273] The Court

---

[269] Sen. Howard Metzenbaum (D-OH), Congress, Senate, Committee on Labor and Human Resources, hearing, Civil Rights Act of 1990, 101st Cong., 1st sess., 23 and 27 February and 1 and 7 March 1990 (Washington, D.C.: GPO, 1990), 237.

[270] Congress, House of Representatives, Committee on Education and Labor and the Subcommittee on Civil and Constitutional Rights of the Committee on the Judiciary, hearing, Hearings on H.R. 4000, the Civil Rights Act of 1990, Vol. 1, 101st Cong., 2nd sess., 20 and 27 February 1990 (Washington, D.C.: GPO, 1990), 3-4.

[271] Rep. Augustus F. Hawkins (D-CA), Congress, House of Representatives, Committee on Education and Labor and the Subcommittee on Civil and Constitutional Rights of the Committee on the Judiciary, hearing, Hearings on H.R. 4000, the Civil Rights Act of 1990, Vol. 1, 101st Cong., 2nd sess., 20 and 27 February 1990 (Washington, D.C.: GPO, 1990), 18.

[272] Rep. Don Edwards (D-CA), Congress, House of Representatives, Joint Hearings before the Committee on Education and Labor and the Subcommittee on Civil and Constitutional Rights of the Committee on the Judiciary, Hearings on H.R. 4000, the Civil Rights Act of 1990, Vol. 1, hearing, 101st Cong., 2nd sess., 20 and 27 Feb. 1990 (Washington, D.C.: GPO, 1990), 19.

[273] Rep. Kweisi Mfume (D-MD), Congress, House of Representatives, Joint Hearings before the Committee on Education and Labor and the Subcommittee on Civil and Constitutional Rights of the Committee on the Judiciary, Hearings on H.R. 4000, the Civil Rights Act of 1990, Vol. 1,

was not doing their "job" to "defend[] minorities."[274] The Court wanted to "turn back the clock" and "restrict racial progress."[275] The rulings were a "retreat from the Court's historic vigilance for the rights of those who have been victims of prejudice."[276] One Senate Committee Report stated that "the Act's purposes are both to respond to the Court's recent decisions by restoring the civil rights protections that were so dramatically limited."[277] This was an example of "some of the most extreme form of judicial activism . . . in reversing progress."[278] The Court had "turned against the victims of discrimination."[279] Rep. Kennedy stated that "[i]n an earlier time, the Supreme Court set the moral tone of our Nation's commitment to equality. Not it endeavors to resurrect the barriers that most folks thought were knocked down years

---

hearing, 101st Cong., 2nd sess., 20 and 27 Feb. 1990 (Washington, D.C.: GPO, 1990), 226.

[274] Sen. Paul Simon (D-IL), Congress, United States Senate, Hearing before the Committee on Governmental Affairs, To Amend the Civil Rights Act of 1964: Permitting Minority Set-Asides, hearing, 101st Cong., 2nd sess., 1990 (Washington, D.C.: GPO, 1990), 3.

[275] Henry L. Marsh III, city councilman, Richmond, VA, Congress, United States Senate, Hearing before the Committee on Governmental Affairs, To Amend the Civil Rights Act of 1964: Permitting Minority Set-Asides, hearing, 101st Cong., 2nd sess., 1990 (Washington, D.C.: GPO, 1990), 22.

[276] Senate Committee on Labor and Human Resources Report, The Civil Rights Act of 1990, 101st Cong., 2nd sess., 8 June 1990, appearing in Douglas S. McDowell, ed. The Civil Rights Act of 1991: A Legislative History, Volume I (Employment Policy Foundation, 1992), 94.

[277] Senate Committee on Labor and Human Resources Report, The Civil Rights Act of 1990, 101st Cong., 2nd sess., 8 June 1990, appearing in Douglas S. McDowell, ed. The Civil Rights Act of 1991: A Legislative History, Volume I (Employment Policy Foundation, 1992), 108.

[278] Rep. Meldon Levine (D-CA), Congressional Record, 101st Cong., 2nd sess., 1990, H6783 (2 Aug. 1990).

[279] Rep. Constance Morella (R-MD), Congressional Record, 101st Cong., 2nd sess., 1990, H6788 (2 Aug. 1990).

ago."[280] They had "erode[d] basic civil rights."[281] The Court was losing its status as a defender of minority rights.[282] Congress must be the "watchdog" for civil rights if the Court would not.[283] The Court had become "out of touch with the mainstream of American thinking"[284] and therefore "Congress must take an active role, indeed the leadership, to end . . . discrimination."[285] Sen. Akaka agreed: "[w]here we once turned towards the Court to safeguard our basic rights and freedoms, we must now turn to Congress."[286] Rep. Mineta stated that "if the

---

[280] Rep. Patrick Kennedy (D-MA), Congressional Record, 101st Cong., 2nd sess., 1990, H6756 (3 Aug. 1990).

[281] Sen. Paul Simon (D-IL), Congressional Record, 101st Cong., 2nd sess., 1990, S15339 (16 Oct. 1990).

[282] "Mr. President, we stand today at a historic juncture. For more than 35 years, the U.S. Supreme Court led the way as America struggled to free itself from the legacy of discrimination that has stained the fabric of this land. But in 1989, the Supreme Court handed down a series of decisions that significantly undermined the struggle to end prejudice in the workplace. They were ominous steps backward, away from the goal of equal opportunity and justice for all Americans." Sen. Edward Kennedy (D-MA), Congressional Record, 101st Cong., 2nd sess., 1990, 136, no. 91 S9810 (17 July 1990).

[283] "Mr. President, I close by saying that we must look upon our country not as a peerless example of democracy and equality in action, but as a country constantly perfecting its own search and journey toward true equal rights for all. With this reality in mind, Congress must be aggressive in its dedication to the perfecting of our civil rights movement. As long as discrimination in the workplace exists, there must be a watchdog. If the Supreme Court refuses to assume this role then Congress must." Sen. Alan Cranston (D-CA), Congressional Record, 101st Cong., 2nd sess., 1990, S9942 (18 July 1990).

[284] Rep. Marilyn Lloyd (D-TN), Congressional Record, 101st Cong., 2nd sess., 1990, H6332 (2 Aug. 1990).

[285] Rep. Nancy Pelosi (D-CA), Congressional Record, 101st Cong., 2nd sess., 1990, H6780 (2 Aug. 1990).

[286] Sen. Daniel Akaka (D-HI), Congressional Record, 101st Cong., 2nd sess., 1990, S15379 (16 Oct. 1990).

President and his advisers persist in their myopia, Congress must not fail to stand up for fairness and the spirit of our Constitution."[287]

The inter-branch environment is helpful in terms of understanding the context of the bill negotiations. That environment was one of mistrust toward the Administration on the part of bill supporters. These critics did not shy away from criticizing the former and current administrations for their perceived lack of support for civil rights. Sen. Metzenbaum was particularly enraged.

> Over the last 9 years we have seen a marked increase in the tolerance for racism and sexism. The Reagan administration launched a campaign against civil rights. Ronald Reagan did more to set back the clock on civil rights than any President in this century. His administration consistently turned a deaf ear to the complaints of the victims of discrimination. . . . It is no wonder, then, that the U.S. Supreme Court, with the three Reagan appointees tipping the balance, slammed the door in the face of the victims of discrimination.[288]

---

[287] Rep. Norman Mineta (D-CA), Congressional Record, 102nd Cong., 1st sess., 1991, H3862 (4 June 1991).

[288] Sen. Howard Metzenbaum (D-OH), Congress, Senate, Committee on Labor and Human Resources, hearing, Civil Rights Act of 1990, 101st Cong., 1st sess., 23 and 27 February and 1 and 7 March 1990 (Washington, D.C.: GPO, 1990), 238. In July, Sen. Metzenbaum would exclaim, "[t]oday we have civil rights laws in this country but, unfortunately, the Supreme Court has turned the clock back. The Reagan-Bush administration led an aggressive assault on civil rights that was unprecedented in this century. The culmination of the assault was the wholesale retreat of the civil rights protection by the Supreme Court in a series of decisions announced 1 year ago. . . . What has happened to America? What has happened to the Supreme Court? What kind of leadership did we get from the President and the Vice President in trying to move backward on civil rights and indeed doing just that? Make no mistake about it, the Reagan appointees to the Supreme Court lived up to their advanced billing and turned back the clock on civil rights protection. . . . With the lone exception of Justice O'Connor's support for the victim of sex discrimination in the *Price Waterhouse* case last spring, the Justices

Rep. Edwards believed the Bush Administration was "very hostile" to "civil rights legislation."[289] Sen. Kennedy said "[t]his is no time for . . . the White House . . . to retreat on civil rights."[290]

---

appointed by the Reagan-Bush administration uniformly and consistently voted against protecting the civil rights of women and minorities. We, here in the Congress, are called upon to undo that wrong. . . . We are at a crossroads in the history of civil rights in this country. We can reject the legislation and continue the policy of the Reagan-Bush years by turning our backs on women and minorities who seek equal opportunity. That policy has fueled intolerance and bigotry and frustration. That policy has led to a dramatic increase in hate crimes, like the ugly incidents in Bensonnhurst and Howard Beach. That policy has created an audience for the venom of a David Duke or a Lewis Farrakhan. . . . Unfortunately, Mr. President, we stand here today while the White House is playing Tweedledee-Tweedledum with the language. They want some specific language to take care of this 'problem' or that 'problem' because some employers are worried about its impact. . . . Let us ring the bell here on the floor of the U.S. Senate. We welcome the support of the President of the United States. Let us quit playing Tweedledee-Tweedledum with civil rights in this country. Let us stand up for civil rights as they were once in this country before the Reagan-Bush appointees on the Supreme Court turned back the clock. Let us quit twiddling with the language, and let us move forward. . . . We can stand together to send a message to restore the moral climate of this Nation by enacting this bill. We can announce that America will not retreat on civil rights, that America will reject bigotry and prejudice, and that America still stands for fair treatment and equal opportunity." Sen. Howard Metzenbaum (D-OH), Congressional Record, 101st Cong., 2nd sess., 136, no. 86, S9319 (10 July 1990).

289 Rep. Don Edwards (D-CA), Congress, House of Representatives, Joint Hearings before the Committee on Education and Labor and the Subcommittee on Civil and Constitutional Rights of the Committee on the Judiciary, Hearings on H.R. 4000, the Civil Rights Act of 1990, Vol. 1, hearing, 101st Cong., 2nd sess., 20 and 27 Feb. 1990 (Washington, D.C.: GPO, 1990), 383. Rep. Edwards' entire statement was the following: "[o]n all of the civil rights bills in the 1980s, the Administration was just generally opposed to all of them. On the 1981Voting Rights Extension, the Attorney General refused to testify. We never did get him to testify. On the Fair

JUDICIAL SUPREMACY

There were a few references to judicial supremacy, even though the Court was being so heavily criticized. Sen. Specter stated:

> Mr. President, there are many reasons why *Wards Cove* ought to be repudiated. It ought to be repudiated on the merits because it is a major step backward on civil rights. But it also ought to be repudiated because it is a flagrant example of judicial usurpation where the Supreme Court has stepped into what is a legislative prerogative on legislative intent on the statute which we have passed. . . . Let me explain why. If you have a constitutional interpretation, the Supreme Court is *the final arbiter* of the Constitution. If you have a statute which is passed and you have a question as to what is the intent of the Congress, that is up to the Congress. When the Supreme Court of the United States, by a unanimous court, in an opinion written by Chief Justice Burger, who is not known to be a flaming liberal, hands down the *Griggs* decision and Congress lets it stand for 18 years, that establishes conclusively the congressional stamp of approval that that definition of business necessity and that definition of the Civil Rights Act is what Congress intended. . . . Now, what happens in 1989? Five Supreme Court Justices, by a 5-to-4 vote, come along and say 'Never mind what Congress has approved. We know better; we are going to interpret the Civil Rights Act of 1964 differently from what is the conclusive congressional intent on the subject.' . . . It is more than judicial activism. It is the Court taking over the function of the Congress."[291]

Housing bill, we couldn't get any assistance at all. Of course, on the Civil Rights Restoration Act, the President vetoed the bill and the bill was enacted over his veto. So we have generally a very hostile Administration to civil rights legislation."

[290] Sen. Edward Kennedy (D-MA), Congressional Record, 101st Cong., 2nd sess., 136 S1019 (7 Feb. 1990).

[291] Sen. Arlen Specter (R-PA), Congressional Record, 101st Cong., 2nd sess., 1990, S15372 (16 Oct. 1990). Emphasis added.

Sen. Packwood believed that "[i]f we pass this bill and this goes to the courts and it goes to the U.S. Supreme Court and the U.S. Supreme Court says this is unconstitutional, *there is nothing we can do about that* short of amending the Constitution. There is nothing we can do about that."[292]

A few members did defend the Court as in institution, without going so far as to endorse supremacy. Rep. Goodling thought that "[p]erhaps we should spend less time looking over the shoulders of the Supreme Court and more time on these very pressing problems."[293] Rep. Fawell invoked President Roosevelt's Court-packing effort in questioning the bill and Congress' attempt to "silence" the Court.

> has there ever been – and I don't know the answer to this question – but has there ever been such a rush to silence the Supreme Court, and indeed, to do it retroactively? I don't know of any. Perhaps not since FDR tried to pack the Court many years ago, and maybe these are not perfect analogies. But how many of us have read the decisions? I have, but I must confess I have many questions in my mind. But more important, having read them, how many of us understand them within the historical context of civil rights law decisions since the passage of the 1964 Civil Rights Act. . . . Mr. Chairman, those who would eradicate in one bill the writings of these many Supreme Court decisions, which to my knowledge is new in the history of this Congress, it seems to me are . . . asking a lot of this Congress and a lot of the people of this Nation we represent.[294]

---

[292] Sen. Robert Packwood (R-OR), Congressional Record, 102nd Cong., 1st sess., S15351 (29 October 1991).

[293] Rep. William F. Goodling (R-PA), Congress, House of Representatives, Joint Hearings before the Committee on Education and Labor and the Subcommittee on Civil and Constitutional Rights of the Committee on the Judiciary, Hearings on H.R. 4000, the Civil Rights Act of 1990, Vol. 1, hearing, 101st Cong., 2nd sess., 20 and 27 Feb. 1990 (Washington, D.C.: GPO, 1990), 21.

[294] Rep. Harris W. Fawell (R-IL), Congress, House of Representatives, Joint Hearings before the Committee on Education and Labor and the

CONCLUSION

Civil rights issues obviously continued to remain in the forefront of the nation's political life throughout the 1990s. However, one of the first statistical studies of the 1991 Act concluded that fears of "quotas" had been unfounded, but that the Act negatively impacted the employment opportunities of minorities and females.[295] Employers were hesitant to hire because of the enlarged monetary awards for firing-based discrimination lawsuits contained in the Act. Other research had also discovered a trend prior to the Act's passage that focused on the shift away from hiring-based employment lawsuits toward firing-based lawsuits.[296] Nevertheless, disparate impact analysis and broad-based

---

Subcommittee on Civil and Constitutional Rights of the Committee on the Judiciary, Hearings on H.R. 4000, the Civil Rights Act of 1990, Vol. 1, hearing, 101st Cong., 2nd sess., 20 and 27 Feb. 1990 (Washington, D.C.: GPO, 1990), 24. Rep. Fawell also asked, "[d]o any of the gentlemen at the table remember a similar undertaking by Congress, where in one fell swoop we are to eradicate the writings of five or six Supreme Court decisions? Maybe it's good. Maybe that's what we should be doing. But I don't recall it ever having been done. . . . [It was a] tremendous never before undertaking of Congress." Rep. Harris W. Fawell (R-IL), Congress, House of Representatives, Joint Hearings before the Committee on Education and Labor and the Subcommittee on Civil and Constitutional Rights of the Committee on the Judiciary, Hearings on H.R. 4000, the Civil Rights Act of 1990, Vol. 1, hearing, 101st Cong., 2nd sess., 20 and 27 Feb. 1990 (Washington, D.C.: GPO, 1990), 220, 715.

[295] Paul Oyer and Scott Schaefer, "The Unintended Consequences of the '91 Civil Rights Act," Regulation 26, no. 2 (summer 2003): 42-47.

[296] John J. Donohue III and Peter Siegelman, "The Changing Nature of Employment Discrimination Litigation," Stanford Law Review 43 (1990-1991): 983-1034. For an overview of both articles in the context of the 1991 Act, see Stuart Taylor Jr., "The 1991 Civil Rights Act Has Hurt Its Intended Beneficiaries: The nondiscrimination law made employers in traditionally white-male industries less likely to hire minorities," The Atlantic Online from National Journal 9 Sept. 2003, previously available at http:///www.theatlantic.com/politics/nj/taylor2003-09-09.html.

class-action type employment issues remain controversial as administrations differed on whether to focus on individual or group-based discrimination suits.[297]

This case and its aftermath affirm the insights of political regime and political time analysis, as well as what we know about the contemporary Congress within those constructs. While President Reagan may have been, as Skowronek argues, a reconstructive president, even he did not attain all he sought in the area of civil rights, much less an affiliated president like his predecessor, the first President Bush. Affiliated presidents may have a national coalition largely instituted by the reconstructive leader before them, but coalitions are nevertheless often fragile and temporary.[298] Even though there was a fundamental "settled" norm in relation to a broad, nation-encompassing, understanding of civil rights and its enforcement by the federal government, on the secondary level of "unsettled" values and how far either a color-blind constitutional, or affirmative-action supporting, paradigm would venture was left uncertain.[299] Thus, affiliated presidents, while having power, but limited power, are often susceptible to the limited strength of their coalition and to challenges from within their own coalition.[300] They are unsure whether to embrace

---

[297] See, for example, Charlie Savage, "Justice Department to Recharge Civil Rights Enforcement," The New York Times 1 Sept. 2009, available at http://www.nytimes.com/2009/09/01/us/politics/01rights.html.

[298] "A political coalition may be delicate, even if it is dominant." Keith E. Whittington, "The Political Foundations of Judicial Supremacy," in Sotirios A. Barber and Robert P. George, eds., Constitutional Politics: Essays on Constitution Making, Maintenance, and Change (Princeton: Princeton University Press, 2001), 277.

[299] "Affiliated leaders are not weak presidents; they are simply limited. Their goals do not extend to the foundations of the regime." Keith E. Whittington, "The Political Foundations of Judicial Supremacy," in Sotirios A. Barber and Robert P. George, eds., Constitutional Politics: Essays on Constitution Making, Maintenance, and Change (Princeton: Princeton University Press, 2001), 276.

[300] Keith E. Whittington, "The Political Foundations of Judicial Supremacy," in Sotirios A. Barber and Robert P. George, eds., Constitutional Politics: Essays

or distance themselves from an aligned-Court's rulings extending or cementing, in their mind, the reconstructive leader's legacy.[301] In addition, we then see members of Congress attempting to shift public opinion by framing, often in dire and extreme terms, their opponents as outside the mainstream and unworthy of a respectable or credible deference in the realm of public policy.

---

on Constitution Making, Maintenance, and Change (Princeton: Princeton University Press, 2001), 268.

[301] The "institutional powers of the presidency are specific and limited. The president cannot, for example, govern by decree. He must usually win support for his policies from Congress and, ultimately, the Court." Keith E. Whittington, "The Political Foundations of Judicial Supremacy," in Sotirios A. Barber and Robert P. George, eds., Constitutional Politics: Essays on Constitution Making, Maintenance, and Change (Princeton: Princeton University Press, 2001), 268.

CHAPTER 3

The Partial-Birth Abortion Ban Act of 2003

No one would dispute that, for many, D&E is a procedure itself laden with the power to devalue human life.[302]

The issue of and discussions related to "partial-birth" abortion can elicit technical terminology, definitional disagreements, and emotively controversial statements. Abortion itself has been defined as "the termination of a pregnancy after, accompanied by, resulting in, or closely followed by the death of the embryo or fetus [through the] spontaneous expulsion of a human fetus during the first 12 weeks of gestation [or the] induced expulsion of a human fetus."[303] According to the American Pregnancy Association "medical" and "surgical" are the two types of abortion procedures used during particular trimesters.[304]

---

[302] *Gonzales v. Carhart*, 550 U.S. ___, 28 (2007) (Justice Kennedy, majority opinion).

[303] Merriam-Webster Online Dictionary, s.v. "abortion," available at http://www.merriam-webster.com/dictionary.

[304] During the first trimester, the following procedures are available: Methotrexate & Misoprostol (MTX) (medical), Mifepristone and Misoprostol (i.e. RU-486) (medical), and Suction Aspiration (surgical). During the second trimester, the following procedures are available: Dilation & Curettage (D&C) (surgical), Dilation & Evacuation (D&E) (surgical), and Induction Abortion (surgical). D&E is "the most common form of legal abortions performed in the second trimester of pregnancy. . . . [It] accounts for 95 percent of second-trimester abortions [and] the fetus is terminated inside the womb." Jeffrey Rosen, "Partial Solution: John Roberts, centrist?,"

Specifically in relation to this case study, Dilation and Extraction, "also known as D&X, Intact D&X, Intrauterine Cranial Decompression and Partial Birth Abortion," is a "surgical abortion procedure used to terminate a pregnancy after 21 weeks of gestation."[305]

LEGISLATIVE HISTORY

Abortion-related legislation and jurisprudence has an over forty year long history.[306] Initially, the focus was on the state of Connecticut.

The New Republic, 11 Dec. 2006, 8. During the third trimester, the following procedures are available: Induction Abortion (surgical), Dilation and Extraction (surgical). See the American Pregnancy Association, found at www.american pregnancy.org. The Association is "a national health organization committed to promoting reproductive and pregnancy wellness through education, research, advocacy, and community awareness." Also see Sarah Glazer, "*Roe v. Wade* At 25: Will the landmark abortion ruling stand?," CQ Researcher 7, no. 44 (28 Nov. 1997): 1033-1056, available at http://library.cqpress.com/cqresearcher/cqresrre1997112800 (accessed April 22, 2009) and Karen J. Lewis and Jon O. Shimabukuro, Legislative Attorneys, American Law Division, "Abortion Law Development: A Brief Overview," CRS Report for Congress, Prepared for Members and Committees of Congress, Updated January 2, 2001, available at http://www.law.umaryland.edu/marshall/crsreports/crsdocuments/95-724_A.pdf.

[305] Further description is given by the American Pregnancy Association: "[t]wo days before the procedure, laminaria is inserted . . . to dilate the cervix. [After a woman's] water . . . break[s] on the third day [she] return[s] to the clinic. The fetus is rotated and forceps are used to grasp and pull the legs, shoulders and arms through the birth canal. A small incision is made at the base of the skull to allow a suction catheter inside. The catheter removes the cerebral material until the skull collapses. Then the fetus is completely removed." See http://www.americanpregnancy.org, "Pregnancy Options," "Surgical Abortions." According to the Centers for Disease Control and Prevention, for the last year in which it has data (2005), 820,151 "legal induced abortions" were reported. Of these, 88% were performed within the first twelve weeks of pregnancy. See http://www.cdc.gov/reproductivehealth/ Data_Stats/Abortion.htm.

[306] See Sarah Glazer, "Roe v. Wade At 25: Will the landmark abortion ruling stand?," CQ Researcher 7, no. 44 (28 Nov. 1997): 1033-1056, available at

There, in the 1960s, due to an 1879 statute which "made it a crime for any person to use any drug or article to prevent conception," the Executive and Medical Directors of the Planned Parenthood League were "convicted for giving married persons information on how to prevent conception" and "for giving medical advice on conception and for prescribing a contraceptive device for a married woman."[307]

Resulting litigation eventually led to the Supreme Court where on June 7th, 1965 the Supreme Court issued *Griswold v. Connecticut* in which Justice William O. Douglas recognized a "zone of privacy" and said "specific guarantees in the Bill of Rights have penumbras, formed by emanations from those guarantees that help given them life and substance."[308] Seven years later in *Eisenstadt v. Baird*, the Court

---

http://library.cqpress.com/cqresearcher/ cqresrre1997112800 (accessed April 22, 2009) and Lewis and Shimabukuro, "Abortion Law Development: A Brief Overview."

307 Estelle Griswold and C. Lee Buxton, respectively. Louis Fisher and David Gray Adler, American Constitutional Law, Vol. 2 Constitutional Rights: Civil Rights and Civil Liberties, 900.

308 381 U.S. 479, 484 (1965). Douglas highlighted the 1st, 3rd, 4th, 5th, and 9th Amendments. In dissent, Justice Hugo Black wrote, "[t]he Court talks about a constitutional 'right to privacy' as though there is some constitutional provision or provisions forbidding any law ever to be passed which might abridge the 'privacy' of individuals. But there is not. There are, of course, guarantees in certain specific constitutional provisions which are designed in part to protect privacy at certain times and places with respect to certain activities. . . . I like my privacy as well as the next one, but I am nevertheless compelled to admit that government has a right to invade it unless prohibited by some specific constitutional provision." 381 U.S. 479, 508, 510 (1965). The initial challenge to the Connecticut statute was *Poe v. Ullman*. In it, Justice John M. Harlan, foreshadowing the language of *Griswold*, dissented by writing, "[T]his . . . legislation . . . violates the Fourteenth Amendment. I believe that a statute making it a criminal offense for married couples to use contraceptives is an intolerable and unjustifiable invasion of privacy in the conduct of the most intimate concerns of an individual's personal life." 367 U.S. 497, 539 (1961). For a brief synopsis of the history of *Griswold v. Connecticut*, see Laura Kalman, "The Promise and Peril of Privacy," Review

extended *Griswold*'s holding to include the right of unmarried people to obtain birth control. In the words of Justice Brennan, "[i]f the right to privacy means anything, it is the right of the individual, married or single, to be free from unwanted governmental intrusions into matters so fundamentally affecting a person as the decision whether to bear or beget a child."[309]

Ten months after *Eisenstadt*, the twin cases that would define a subsequent era were issued. In *Doe v. Bolton*, a case regarding the Model Penal Code law recently adopted in the state of Georgia, "the Court held . . . a state may not unduly burden a woman's fundamental right to abortion by prohibiting or substantially limiting accesses to the means of effectuating her decision. . . . the Fourteenth Amendment['s] right of personal privacy encompassed a woman's decision whether to carry a pregnancy to term."[310] In *Roe v. Wade*, a case challenging a Texas life-of-the-mother statute, the Court "determined that the Constitution protects a woman's decision whether or not to terminate her pregnancy."[311] Justice Harry Blackmun, writing for the same 7-2 majority as in *Doe*, said they need "not resolve the difficult question of when life begins" in order to adjudicate the issue.

> The right of privacy, whether it be founded in the Fourteenth Amendment's concept of personal liberty and restrictions upon state action as we feel it is or as the District Court

---

of Liberty and Sexuality: The Right to Privacy and the Making of *Roe v. Wade*, by David Garrow Reviews in American History 22, no. 4 (Dec. 1994): 725-731.

[309] *Eisenstadt v. Baird*, 405 U.S. 438, 453 (1972). Justice Brennan added, "If under *Griswold* the distribution of contraceptives to married persons cannot be prohibited, a ban on distribution to unmarried persons would be equally impermissible. It is true that in *Griswold* the right of privacy in question inhered in the marital relationship. Yet the marital couple is not an independent entity with a mind and heart of its own, but an association of two individuals each with a separate intellectual and emotional makeup." 453.

[310] 410 U.S. 179 (1973). Lewis and Shimabukuro, "CRS Report for Congress. Abortion Law Development: A Brief Overview."

[311] 410 U.S. 113 (1973). Lewis and Shimabukuro, "CRS Report for Congress. Abortion Law Development: A Brief Overview."

> determined in the Ninth Amendment's reservation of rights to the people is broad enough to encompass a woman's decision whether or not to terminate her pregnancy. We therefore conclude that the right of personal privacy includes the abortion decision.[312]

This right, however, was ostensibly not absolute. Within the newly created trimester framework of pregnancy, where the state could show a compelling state interest in limiting abortion the Court would approve such limitations. Thus, in the first trimester, "the abortion decision . . . must be left to the medical judgment of the pregnant woman's attending physician." In the second, the state could "regulate the abortion procedure in ways . . . reasonably related to maternal health."[313] Finally, "subsequent to viability" abortion could be "proscribed" "except where it is necessary, in appropriate medical judgment, for the preservation of the life or health of the mother."[314]

Since these important precedents, abortion has been central in our political debates within all levels of state and federal governments. One reason for this significance being that much was still unclear. The Court

> did not address a number of important abortion-related issues which [were] raised subsequently by state actions seeking to restrict the scope of the Court's rulings. These include[d] the issues of informed consent, spousal consent, parental consent,

---

[312] 410 U.S. 113, 153 (1973). For a history of *Griswold*, see Laura Kalman, "The Promise and Peril of Privacy," Review of Liberty and Sexuality: The Right to Privacy and the Making of *Roe v. Wade*, by David Garrow Reviews in American History 22, no. 4 (Dec. 1994): 725-731.

[313] 410 U.S. 113, 164 (1973).

[314] 410 U.S. 113, 164-65 (1973). In *Roe*, Blackmun said the two opinions were to be read together. Thus, as Blackmun explained in *Doe*, "medical judgment may be exercised in the light of all factors – physical, emotional, psychological, familial, and the woman's age – relevant to the wellbeing of the patient. All these factors may relate to health." 410 U.S. 179, 192, 197 (1973).

> and reporting requirements [as well as] what, if any, type of abortion procedures may be required or prohibited by statute.[315]

Thus, Congress passed the Hyde Amendment barring the federal funding of abortion in 1976 which was upheld by the Court in 1980.[316] Human Life Amendment hearings were held in Congress in 1981[317] and two years later Justice Sandra Day O'Connor would famously cast doubt upon the trimester framework of *Roe* and foreshadow its abandonment nine years later.

> [N]either sound constitutional theory nor our need to decide cases based on the application of neutral principles can accommodate an analytical framework that varies according to the 'stages' of pregnancy, where those stages, and their concomitant standards of review, differ according to the level of medical technology available when a particular challenge to state regulation occurs.

She added:

> The *Roe* framework . . . is clearly on a collision course with itself. As the medical risks of various abortion procedures decrease, the point at which the state may regulate for reasons of maternal health is moved further forward to actual childbirth. As medical science becomes better able to provide

---

[315] Lewis and Shimabukuro, "CRS Report for Congress. Abortion Law Development: A Brief Overview," Summary.

[316] *Harris v. McRae*, 448 U.S. 297 (1980).

[317] For further treatment of this time period, see Susan R. Burgess, Contest for Constitutional Authority: The Abortion and War Powers Debates (Lawrence, KS: University Press of Kansas, 1992), 28-64. Burgess covers *Roe v. Wade*, as well as the proposed Human Life Bill of 1981, (*City of*) *Akron v. Akron Center for Reproductive Health*, 462 U.S. 416 (1983), debates over the Hyde Amendment, and *Thornburgh v. American College of Obstetricians and Gynecologists*, 476 U.S. 747 (1986).

> for the separate existence of the fetus, the point of viability is moved further back toward conception.[318]

Three years after *Thornburgh*, the Court "indicated . . . it was willing to apply a less stringent standard of review to state restrictions respecting a woman's right to an abortion" and invited states to revisit the issue of abortion restrictions.[319] In doing so, the Court said that "[w]hen the constitutional invalidity of a State's abortion statute actually turns upon the constitutional validity of *Roe*, there will be time enough to reexamine *Roe*. And to do so carefully."[320]

---

[318] *(City of) Akron* v. *Akron Center for Reproductive Health*, 462 U.S. 416, 457-458 (1983). Three years later, Justice Byron White would offer the same assessment. He stated "there is no nonarbitary line separating a fetus from a child or, indeed, an adult human being." *Thornburgh v. American College of Obstetricians & Gynecologists*, 476 U.S. 747, 792 (1986). Also in *Thornburgh*, O'Connor would write, "[t]his Court's abortion decisions have already worked a major distortion in the Court's constitutional jurisprudence. Today's decision goes further, and makes it painfully clear that no legal rule or doctrine is safe from ad hoc nullification by this Court when an occasion for its application arises in a case involving state regulation of abortion. The permissible scope of abortion regulation is not the only constitutional issue on which this Court is divided, but - except when it comes to abortion - the Court has generally refused to let such disagreements, however longstanding or deeply felt, prevent it from evenhandedly applying uncontroversial legal doctrines to cases that come before it. That the Court's unworkable scheme for constitutionalizing the regulation of abortion has had this institutionally debilitating effect should not be surprising, however, since the Court is not suited to the expansive role it has claimed for itself in the series of cases that began with *Roe* v. *Wade*." 476 U.S. 747, 816 (1986) (Citations omitted).

[319] Lewis and Shimabukuro, "CRS Report for Congress. Abortion Law Development: A Brief Overview," Summary.

[320] *Webster v. Reproductive Services*, 492 U.S. 490 (1989). As W. John Moore explains more fully, "[m]any thought this would be done soon enough and that *Roe* was on the path to being overruled. During the 1970s and early 1980s, it appeared that courts were sympathetic to the arguments of those who were pro-choice on the issue of abortion. Consequently, the pro-choice

That time would come in the summer of 1992. In *Planned Parenthood v. Casey* a 5-4 majority upheld "all of Pennsylvania's contested restrictions but one (a requirement for spousal notification) and affirm[ed] the right of states to restrict abortions." More importantly, however, the Court, appealing to a "common mandate rooted in the Constitution" and the value of *and* correlation between *stare decisis* and regime stability, upheld "*Roe*'s essential holding," which was "a recognition of the right of the woman to choose to have an abortion before viability and to obtain it without undue interference from the State."[321] Finally, the majority also jettisoned the *Roe*-created strict scrutiny standard and ruled post-viability restrictions should be

---

community concentrated on litigation while the pro-life group appealed to the legislatures, the President, and governors. By the end of the 1980s, as a result of appointments by Presidents Nixon, Ford, Reagan, and Bush, the Supreme Court indicated that it would give less protection to the interests sought by the pro-choice organizations. Consequently, they now turned to Congress for support. [I]n June . . . 1991 . . . NARAL, which had relied on the courts in the past, now stated: 'Clearly Congress is our Court of Last Resort. All hopes of protecting our constitutional right to choose depends upon our elected representatives in Congress responding to the will of the American people.' The American Civil Liberties Union, which had also depended heavily on litigation, sounded a similar theme: 'Congress is increasingly asked to look at these issues because there is nobody else. It is now the court of last resort.'" W. John Moore, "In Whose Court?," National Journal, 5 Oct. 1991, 2400, quoted in Fisher and Gray, American Constitutional Law, Vol. 1 Constitutional Structures: Separated Powers and Federalism, 24-25.

321 505 U.S. 833 (1992). Peter J. Boyer, "The Right to Choose: Why the Democrats are moving toward compromise," The New Yorker (14 Nov. 2005). More specifically, the "[f]ive provisions of the Pennsylvania Abortion Control Act required that a woman give her informed consent, receive certain information at least 24 hours before the abortion, required a minor to receive the informed consent of one parent (subject to a judicial bypass procedure), required women to first notify their husband (with some exceptions), and imposed certain reporting requirements on facilities providing abortion services." Fisher and Adler, American Constitutional Law, Vol. 2 Constitutional Rights: Civil Rights and Civil Liberties, 922.

upheld unless they placed "undue interference" on the woman seeking an abortion "which endanger[ed] [her] life or health."[322]

Abortion did not cease to be an issue after *Casey*. In the halls of Congress, "partial-birth abortion" took center stage. In fact, throughout the 1990s, Congress "tried four times to enact a law banning the procedure." In the 104th Congress, H.R. 1833 passed the House 288-139, November 1st, 1995. On December 7th, an amended version passed the Senate 54-44. The House passed the Senate's version 286-129 the following March. President Clinton vetoed the bill April 10th, 1996. On September 19th, the House voted 285-137 to override the veto. Six days later the Senate fell nine votes. In the 105th Congress, H.R. 1122 passed the House 295-136 on March 20th, 1997. On May 20th, an amended version passed the Senate 64-36. The House passed the Senate's version 296-132 on October 8th and President Clinton vetoed the bill

---

[322] 505 U.S. 833, 867, 846 (1992). "Undue burden" had a long history in the jurisprudential thought of Justice O'Connor. As Stern explains, "[i]t was an idea she had advanced almost as long as she had been on the court. In a 1983 case, she first laid out her undue burden test as a high bar that would strike down regulations only 'in situations involving absolute obstacles or severe limitations on the abortion decision.' She offered it in dissent after dissent throughout the 1980s without winning any converts among fellow justices. But the undue standard really found its power in . . . *Webster v. Reproductive Health Services*, in which a divided Supreme Court abandoned *Roe*'s 'trimester formula' governing abortion regulations in considering whether abortion regulations in the state of Missouri were constitutional. In *Webster*, the court splintered; some justices wanted to uphold *Roe* and others wanted to uphold the regulations. But among the nine, the only justice who wanted to uphold both the regulations and the precedent of *Roe* was O'Connor. She was thus pivotal in the case, and so was her opinion. The Missouri law, she said, did not constitute an 'undue burden on women' seeking an abortion." Seth Stern, "The Legacy of 'Undue Burden,'" <u>CQ Weekly Online</u> (7 Nov. 2005): 2960-2961, available at http://library. cqpress.com/cqweekly/ weeklyreport109-000001950657 (accessed October 19, 2007). See also Boyer, "The Right to Choose: Why the Democrats are moving toward compromise" and Lewis and Shimabukuro, "CRS Report for Congress. Abortion Law Development: A Brief Overview," Summary.

two days later. The House overrode the veto 296-132 on July 23rd, 1998 but two months later the Senate fell three votes short. In the 106th Congress, the Senate passed S. 1692 63-34 on October 21st, 1999. The House passed H.R. 3660 287-141 on April 5th, 2000. In the 107th Congress, the House passed H.R. 4965 274-151 on July 24th, 2002 but the Senate did not vote on a bill.[323]

The 2003 version[324] was written in response to the Supreme Court decision three years prior, *Stenberg v. Carhart.*[325] That decision struck down a Nebraska state ban on the late-term abortion procedure. The 5-4 majority ruled the statute was overly vague, given, it was argued, it could encompass more abortion procedures than the dilation and extraction procedure, and was an "undue burden" on women seeking abortions because it lacked a health exception.[326] Rebuked, supporters

---

[323] See "'Partial Birth' Abortion: A Long Legislative History," CQ Weekly Online (25 Oct. 2003): 2635, available at http://library.cqpress.com/ cqweekly/ weeklyreport108-000000878454 (accessed October 19, 2007).

[324] The "Partial-Birth Abortion Ban Act." 18 U.S.C. § 1531, Public Law 108-105.

[325] 530 U.S. 914 (2000). An analysis of deliberation post-*Stenberg* is a constructive demarcation given the rebuttal from the Supreme Court. A new effort and new legislative language and tactics had to be forged, if, given the political and inter-branch understandings and dynamics of the time, actual passage was to be sought and judicial overrule was not to be feared. Pre-*Stenberg* and post-*Stenberg* were basically two separate endeavors by proponents of the ban (Staff Interview, 2008).

[326] 530 U.S. 914, 11 (2000). Fisher and Gray elaborate: "Dr. Leroy Carhart, a physician, brought this lawsuit against Attorney General Don Stenberg of Nebraska, charging that Nebraska's law banning 'partial birth abortion' violated the Federal Constitution. The District Court held the statute unconstitutional, the Eighth Circuit affirmed, and the Supreme Court granted cert to decide whether the statute . . . constituted an 'undue burden' on a woman's right to choose to have an abortion. Much of the opinion by Justice Breyer turns on the legislative intent of the Nebraska statute." Louis Fisher and David Gray Adler, American Constitutional Law, Vol. 2 Constitutional Rights: Civil Rights and Civil Liberties, 7th edition (Carolina Academic Press: Durham, North Carolina, 2007), 925.

of a ban tried to again legislatively act by introducing this Act, the Partial-Birth Abortion Ban Act of 2003.

S. 3, "A bill to prohibit the procedure commonly known as partial-birth abortion,"[327] was sponsored by Sen. Rick Santorum (R-PA) and had forty-five Senate co-sponsors. H.R. 760 was sponsored by Rep. Steve Chabot (R-OH) and had one-hundred sixty-one House co-sponsors. On February 13th, 2003 introductory remarks were made and the bill was referred to the House Judiciary Committee, where the Constitution Subcommittee and full committee both held hearings and mark-ups. In the Senate, the bill was introduced and read February 14th, 2003. On February 24th it was read a second time and placed on the Senate Legislative Calendar. March 10th the measure was laid before the Senate by unanimous consent. On March 11th and 12th it was considered by the Senate and on the latter a motion by Senator Boxer (D-CA) to commit it to the Senate Judiciary Committee with instructions was rejected 42-56. On the 13th it was again considered by the Senate, passed with an amendment (affirming *Roe*), 64-33, and held at the desk in House. The House debated and passed the bill June 4th by a vote of 282-139. Four months later, on October 2nd, 2003, the House passed conference report 281-142 and on October 21st the Senate agreed to the conference report 64-34.

DELIBERATION

VALUES . . .

During debate, there was an intense battle to define the terms of the debate. Throughout the course of the deliberation, opponents of the ban referred to the "so-called partial-birth abortion"[328] and "the language of propaganda rather than the language of medical science."[329] It was "simply . . . a procedure that doctors were using to save the lives of

---

327 Located at THOMAS (Library of Congress), available at http://thomas.loc.gov. "S.3." "All congressional action."

328 Rep. John Conyers (D-MI), Congressional Record, 107th Cong., 1st sess., 2001, vol. 147, no. 158, E2101 (15 Nov. 2001).

329 Rep. Jerrold Nadler (D-NY), Congressional Record, 107th Cong., 2nd sess., 2002, vol. 148, no. 102, H5357 (24 Jul. 2002).

mothers who wanted to have children"[330] and the ban was ridiculed as "extreme . . . vicious, mean-spirited, antiwoman, and . . . unconstitutional."[331]

Conversely, supporters of the ban used many terms to indicate their disapproval of the procedure. It was a "devious and evil practice,"[332] a "deplorable. . . . violent and crude procedure,"[333] "one of the most barbaric acts known to mankind,"[334] "infanticide,"[335] "barbarous, to say the least,"[336] "[a] a horrific procedure that is tantamount to murder,"[337] "a most horrible procedure,"[338] "a death sentence. . . . [and a] repulsive procedure,"[339] "a fringe procedure,"[340]

---

[330] Rep. Sheila Jackson-Lee (D-TX), Congressional Record, 107th Cong., 1st sess., 2001, vol. 147, no. 54, H1632 (26 Apr. 2001).

[331] Rep. Carolyn Maloney (D-NY), Congressional Record, 108th Cong., 1st sess., 2003, vol. 149, no. 81, H4930 (4 Jun. 2003).

[332] Rep. Mike Pence (R-IN), Congressional Record, 107th Cong., 2nd sess., 2002, vol. 148, no. 82, H3674 (19 Jun. 2002).

[333] Rep. Robert Aderholt (R-AL), Congressional Record, 107th Cong., 2nd sess., 2002, vol. 148, no. 86, H3866-67 (25 Jun. 2002).

[334] Rep. Joseph Pitts (R-PA), Congressional Record, 107th Cong., 2nd sess., 2002, vol. 148, no. 87, H3933 (26 Jun. 2002).

[335] Rep. Jim Ryun (R-KS), Congressional Record, 107th Cong., 2nd sess., 2002, vol. 148, no. 87, H3932 (26 Jun. 2002).

[336] Rep. Mike Pence (R-IN), Congressional Record, 107th Cong., 2nd sess., 2002, vol. 148, no. 97, H4860 (17 Jul. 2002).

[337] Rep. Melissa Hart (R-PA), Congressional Record, 107th Cong., 2nd sess., 2002, vol. 148, no. 102, H5358 (24 Jul. 2002).

[338] Sen. Jeff Sessions (R-AL), Congressional Record, 107th Cong., 2nd sess., 2002, vol. 148, no. 151, S11669-70 (20 Nov. 2002).

[339] Rep. Barbara Cubin (R-WO), Congressional Record, 108th Cong., 1st sess., 2003, vol. 149, no. 27, E249 (13 Feb. 2003).

[340] Sen. Bill Frist (R-TN), Congressional Record, 108th Cong., 1st sess., 2003, vol. 149, no. 174, S16078 (25 Nov. 2003).

and "cruel and unusual punishment."[341] The House sponsor of the ban labeled the practice

> the termination of the life of a living baby just seconds before it takes its first breath outside the womb. The procedure is violent. It is gruesome. It is infanticide. . . . A moral, medical, and ethical consensus exists that the practice of performing a partial-birth abortion is a gruesome and inhumane procedure that is never medically necessary and should be prohibited. . . . [It is a] national tragedy.[342]

. . . & MORE VALUES

Members on both sides of the issue also appealed to other values and authoritative sources. For example, there were discussions about "American values,"[343] women's health,[344] the medical issues involved,[345] the interconnectedness of international and domestic human rights,[346] the societal impact of partial-birth abortion,[347] and

---

341 Rep. Roscoe Bartlett (R-MD), Congressional Record, 108th Cong., 1st sess., 2003, vol. 149, no. 138, H9138 (2 Oct. 2003).

342 Rep. Steve Chabot (R-OH), Congressional Record, 107th Cong., 2nd sess., 2002, vol. 148, no. 82, E1096-97 (19 Jun. 2002).

343 Rep. Nita Lowey (D-NY), Congressional Record, 108th Cong., 1st sess., 2003, vol. 149, no. 81, H4927 (4 Jun. 2003).

344 Sen. Jon Corzine (D-NJ), Congressional Record, 108th Cong., 1st sess., 2003, vol. 149, no. 41, S3655 (13 Mar. 2003).

345 See Sen. Bill Frist (R-TN), Congressional Record, 108th Cong., 1st sess., 2003, vol. 149, no. 39, S3457-59 (11 Mar. 2003).

346 Rep. Joe Pitts (R-PA), Congressional Record, 108th Cong., 1st sess., 2003, vol. 149, no. 41, H1815 (13 Mar. 2003).

347 Sen. Jesse Helms (R-NC), Congressional Record, 107th Cong., 1st sess., 2001, vol. 147, no. 7, S332-333 (22 Jan. 2001); Sen. Rick Santorum (R-PA), Congressional Record, 108th Cong., 1st sess., 2003, vol. 149, no. 40, S3591 (12 Mar. 2003).

about respect and civility.[348] There were also references to engaging the larger abortion debate,[349] personhood and conception,[350] the virtue of autonomy,[351] and about women's rights.[352] The United Nations Declaration of Human Rights was invoked.[353] The fundamental tension between the competing values of "the liberty of a woman" and "the life of a baby" was mentioned but not elaborated upon.[354] Also mentioned were Prohibition, the wartime internment of Japanese-Americans, and the system of Jim Crow,[355] the three-fifths clause[356] and the Declaration of Independence.[357] The Senate sponsor of the ban was particularly

---

[348] Sen. Russ Feingold (D-WI), Congressional Record, 108th Cong., 1st sess., 2003, vol. 149, no. 40, S3611-12 (12 Mar. 2003).

[349] Sen. Bill Frist (R-TN), Congressional Record, 107th Cong., 1st sess., 2001, vol. 147, no. 100, S7849 (18 Jul. 2001).

[350] Sen. Richard Durbin (D-IL), Congressional Record, 108th Cong., 1st sess., 2003, vol. 149, no. 40, S3572 (12 Mar. 2003).

[351] Sen. Russ Feingold (D-WI), Congressional Record, 108th Cong., 1st sess., 2003, vol. 149, no. 40, S3611-12 (12 Mar. 2003).

[352] Sen. Olympia Snowe (R-ME), Congressional Record, 108th Cong., 1st sess., 2003, vol. 149, no. 40, S3577 (12 Mar. 2003); Sen. Hillary Clinton (D-NY), Congressional Record, 108th Cong., 1st sess., 2003, vol. 149, no. 40, S3587 (12 Mar. 2003).

[353] Rep. Ileana Ros-Lehtinen (R-FL), Congressional Record, 108th Cong., 1st sess., 2003, vol. 149, no. 137, H9036 (1 Oct. 2003).

[354] Sen. Lamar Alexander (R-TN), Congressional Record, 108th Cong., 1st sess., 2003, vol. 149, no. 45 S4159 (20 Mar. 2003).

[355] Sen. Christopher Dodd (D-CT), Congressional Record, 108th Cong., 1st sess., 2003, vol. 149, no. 128, S11602 (17 Sept. 2003).

[356] Sen. Sam Brownback (R-KS), Congressional Record, 108th Cong., 1st sess., 2003, vol. 149, no. 40, S3597-98 (12 Mar. 2003).

[357] Sen. Mike Enzi (R-WY), Congressional Record, 108th Cong., 1st sess., 2003, vol. 149, no. 39, S3482-83 (11 Mar. 2003). See also, Rep. Todd Akin (R-MO), Congressional Record, 108th Cong., 1st sess., 2003, vol. 149, no. 137, H9113 (1 Oct. 2003); Rep. Roscoe Bartlett (R-MD), Congressional Record, 108th Cong., 1st sess., 2003, vol. 149, no. 138, H9138 (2 Oct. 2003); Rep.

active in recurrently referencing and discussing *Dred Scott v. Sanford*, the difference between liberty "rights" and life "rights," as well as the nature of slavery, the teaching of the Declaration of Independence, and the meaning of "ordered liberty."[358]

A PASSING GLANCE

Sometimes members appealed to the Constitution as an obvious source of authority without elaborating on the content or consequences of such an appeal. Other times they made constitutional comparisons without drawing out the specific constitutional implications for this particular bill.

For example, Sen. Santorum said he believed "it is important to define when a child is protected by the Constitution"[359] and that previous justices had "found a right that was not written in this Constitution. I don't think anyone will make the comment that the right to an abortion is written in the black letters of the Constitution. It is not."[360] Sen. Boxer stated that she did not "see it in the Constitution that I should outlaw a medical procedure that doctors are saying to me is necessary to save the life and health of a woman."[361] Rep. Schakowsky simply said "[a]bortion is a constitutionally protected

---

Barbara Cubin (R-WY), Congressional Record, 108th Cong., 1st sess., 2003, vol. 149, no. 138, H9151 (2 Oct. 2003).

[358] See Sen. Rick Santorum (R-PA), Congressional Record, 108th Cong., 1st sess., 2003, vol. 149, no. 40, S3591 (12 Mar. 2003). See also, Congressional Record, 108th Cong., 1st sess., 2003, vol. 149, no. 40, S3608 (12 Mar. 2003). Congressional Record, 108th Cong., 1st sess., 2003, vol. 149, no. 40, S3644-45 (12 Mar. 2003); Congressional Record, 108th Cong., 1st sess., 2003, vol. 149, no. 127, S11551-52 (16 Sept. 2003).

[359] Sen. Rick Santorum (R-PA), Congressional Record, 107th Cong., 1st sess., 2001, vol. 147, no. 83, S6329 (14 Jun. 2001).

[360] Sen. Rick Santorum (R-PA), Congressional Record, 108th Cong., 1st sess., 2003, vol. 149, no. 40, S3644-45 (12 Mar. 2003).

[361] Sen. Barbara Boxer (D-CA), Congressional Record, 108th Cong., 1st sess., 2003, vol. 149, no. 38, S3398 (10 Mar. 2003).

medical procedure in this country"[362] and that "[f]or us to be true to the Constitution, to be true to the sentiments of equality and freedom, women must have control over their bodies. Instead, proponents of this bill, including the Bush administration, are using this bill as part of a broader agenda to take away a woman's constitutionally guaranteed right to choose."[363] Sen. Feingold said he would "oppose S. 3 . . . and instead w[ould] support a constitutionally sound alternative."[364] Rep. Nadler hoped "the Constitution still serves as a bulwark against such efforts [to restrict abortion]."[365] Sen. Durbin said the ban "violates a woman's constitutional right to have her health protected."[366]

Sen. Mikulski believed a particular amendment "offers the Senate a sensible alternative, one that would prohibit post-viability abortions while respecting the Constitution and protecting women's lives."[367] Sen. Murray argued the bill "shows that nothing[,] not war, not the stagnant economy[,] will stop hardliners in Congress from trying to appease their political base by pushing an unconstitutional, deceptive, extreme agenda on American women."[368] Rep. Lee described at length that:

> Pregnancy and childbirth are among the most intimate and the most personal experiences of a woman's life. . . . Our freedom to choose is every woman's fundamental right. This should be

---

[362] Rep. Jan Schakowsky (D-IL), Congressional Record, 107th Cong., 2nd sess., 2002, vol. 148, no. 102, H5365 (24 Jul. 2002).

[363] Rep. Schakowsky (D-IL), Congressional Record, 108th Cong., 1st sess., 2003, vol. 149, no. 81, H4928 (4 Jun. 2003).

[364] Sen. Russ Feingold (D-WI), Congressional Record, 108th Cong., 1st sess., 2003, vol. 149, no. 40, S3611-12 (12 Mar. 2003).

[365] Rep. Jerrold Nadler (D-NY), Congressional Record, 108th Cong., 1st sess., 2003, vol. 149, no. 138, H9144 (2 Oct. 2003).

[366] Sen. Richard Durbin (D-IL), Congressional Record, 108th Cong., 1st sess., 2003, vol. 149, no. 39, S3480-81 (11 Mar. 2003).

[367] Sen. Barbara Mikulski (D-MD), Congressional Record, 108th Cong., 1st sess., 2003, vol. 149, no. 77, S6973 (22 May 2003).

[368] Sen. Patty Murray (D-WA), Congressional Record, 108th Cong., 1st sess., 2003, vol. 149, no. 38, S3388 (10 Mar. 2003).

> a medical decision made between a woman, her family, and her doctor and her clergy. Government has no right to interfere. This bill is outrageous.[369]

Similarly, Rep. Johnson, while appropriately raising the issue of "conflicting rights," did not explain the constitutional foundations of nor solutions to this dilemma.

> This is a very important issue because it involves the balancing of conflicting rights, the right of the fetus and the right of the mother; and it is because balancing rights is the very hardest thing a democracy has to do that this is a constitutional issue. It ought to matter to the proponents that every single State law has been found wanting and been overturned because it does not balance these rights fairly. It does not allow the mother, the woman, to consider her health; but the system can only consider her life and every court has overturned every single State law for this constitutional deficiency.[370]

THE TEXT

Occasionally and to varying degrees, members did invoke the constitutional text specifically, usually in relation to the 14th Amendment. For example, Rep. Hyde asked, "at what point does that tiny member of the human family get protected by the Equal Protection Clause and due process of our Constitution? No person shall be deprived of life, liberty and the pursuit of happiness, nor shall any person be deprived of equal protection of the law."[371] Sen. Feinstein stated "[t]he Senator has talked about the liberty clause. And *Roe v.*

---

[369] Rep. Barbara Lee (D-CA), Congressional Record, 108th Cong., 1st sess., 2003, vol. 149, no. 138, H9149 (2 Oct. 2003).

[370] Rep. Nancy Johnson (R-CT), Congressional Record, 108th Cong., 1st sess., 2003, vol. 149, no. 81, H4942 (4 Jun. 2003).

[371] Rep. Henry Hyde (R-IL), Congressional Record, 107th Cong., 2nd sess., 2002, vol. 148, no. 102, H5361 (24 Jul. 2002).

Wade . . . did come from the liberty clause of the due process clause of the 14th amendment and other parts of the Constitution."[372] Rep. Jackson-Lee said that "[i]n *Roe v. Wade*, the court held that women had a privacy interest in electing to have an abortion, based on the 5th and 14th Amendments' concept of personal liberty."[373]

Likewise, Sen. Santorum, acknowledged, "[s]o where did this right spring from? Where did this right emerge from? It emerged from the liberty clause of the 14th amendment."[374] Rep. Kucinich invoked the equal protection clause to make his case: "[t]his bill likely will not prevent a single abortion, but it does defeat the rights of women. I believe that equal protection under the law and the right to privacy should be freedoms enjoyed by women as well as men, but women will not be equal to men if this constitutionally protected right is denied. This bill infringes on those rights for women."[375] Finally, in this perplexing example, Sen. Landrieu offered numerous and seemingly conflicting perspectives on the 14th Amendment:

> Let me read, for the pro-life community, from this decision [*Roe v. Wade*], which was delicately crafted to address a very complex constitutional provision that was framed initially in the Bill of Rights, supported by the Constitution, and those principles are the principles of life, liberty, and happiness, not just for the fetus, for the unborn, for young children, but life, liberty, and happiness for people of all ages and all conditions in life, male and female, slave and free. . . . For the pro-life community, let me read what the Justices said: A State criminal abortion statute of the current Texas type, that excepts from criminality only a lifesaving procedure on behalf

---

[372] Sen. Dianne Feinstein (D-CA), Congressional Record, 108th Cong., 1st sess., 2003, vol. 149, no. 40, S3608 (12 Mar. 2003).

[373] Rep. Sheila Jackson-Lee (D-TX), Congressional Record, 108th Cong., 1st sess., 2003, vol. 149, no. 81, H4936 (4 Jun. 2003).

[374] Sen. Rick Santorum (R-PA), Congressional Record, 108th Cong., 1st sess., 2003, vol. 149, no. 40, S3644-45 (12 Mar. 2003). Also see Congressional Record, 108th Cong., 1st sess., 2003, vol. 149, no. 40, S3591 (12 Mar. 2003).

[375] Rep. Dennis Kucinich (D-OH), Congressional Record, 108th Cong., 1st sess., 2003, vol. 149, no. 81, H4928 (4 Jun. 2003).

> of the mother, without regard to pregnancy stage and without recognition of the other interests involved . . . is violative of the Due Process Clause of the Fourteenth Amendment. . . . I suggest unless there are a majority of Senators willing to change the Constitution and remove the 14th amendment, this debate is going nowhere. The fact is that the Constitution supports a framework in which life and liberty for everyone, including the unborn, have to be taken into consideration.[376]

ROE, ROE, & ROE

Members often invoked prior cases or the words of former justices to buttress or stand in the place of their own original arguments. Such examples included *Dred Scott v. Sandford,*[377] *Landmark Communications, Inc. v. Virginia,*[378] *Doe v. Bolton,*[379] *Planned Parenthood v. Casey,*[380] and *Stenberg v. Carhart.*[381]

---

[376] Sen. Mary Landrieu (D-LA), Congressional Record, 108th Cong., 1st sess., 2003, vol. 149, no. 40, S3575 (12 Mar. 2003). This is confusing. The first part of the statement seems to be arguing from aspirational principle or a mistaken textual belief that the equality language from the Declaration is actually in the Bill of Rights and the possibly elsewhere in the Constitution. The latter part of the statement seems to be arguing that embedded in the Constitution is a contradiction: the 14th Amendment allows for an abortion license but the Constitution "supports a framework" in which the life of the unborn "have to be taken into consideration." Whatever the truth of this statement, no further explication was given.

[377] 60 U.S. 393 (1857). Rep. Mike Pence (R-IN), Congressional Record, 108th Cong., 1st sess., 2003, vol. 149, no. 141, H9366 (8 Oct. 2003).

[378] Sen. Dianne Feinstein (D-CA), Congressional Record, 108th Cong., 1st sess., 2003, vol. 149, no. 148, S12937-38 (21 Oct. 2003).

[379] Sen. Mike DeWine (R-OH), Congressional Record, 108th Cong., 1st sess., 2003, vol. 149, no. 40, S3604-05 (12 Mar. 2003); Also, Sen. Rick Santorum (R-PA), Congressional Record, 108th Cong., 1st sess., 2003, vol. 149, no. 40, S3606 (12 Mar. 2003).

[380] The Pennsylvania statute which precipitated the ruling, the Pennsylvania Abortion Control Act, was discussed as was the case's most famous

More importantly and as one would expect, both supporters and opponents of the Partial-Birth Abortion Ban Act of 2003 discussed *Roe v. Wade* at great length. *Roe* was described as a "moderate decision, a moderate mainstream decision,"[382] "the most difficult and contentious social issue of our day. . . . one of those elephants in the living room,"[383] and "a decision that recognized [that] the fundamental right to privacy extends to a woman's decision whether or not to have an abortion with freedom from government intrusion. *Roe* transformed women's experiences in many ways: saved their lives, protected their health, fostered equality and paved the way for greater partnership with men in all aspects of our nation's life."[384] The bill "undermine[d the] basic tenets of *Roe v. Wade*"[385] and was an attempt "to get somebody

---

"mystery of life" passage. See Sen. Rick Santorum (R-PA), Congressional Record, 108th Cong., 1st sess., 2003, vol. 149, no. 40, S3644-45 (12 Mar. 2003); Sen. Lindsey Graham (R-SC) and Sen. Rick Santorum (R-PA), Congressional Record, 108th Cong., 1st sess., 2003, vol. 149, no. 40, S3583 (12 Mar. 2003). *Casey* was mentioned in name only by Sen. Tom Daschle (D-SC), Congressional Record, 108th Cong., 1st sess., 2003, vol. 149, no. 41, S3660-61 (13 Mar. 2003).

381 Del. Eleanor Holmes Norton (D-D.C.), Congressional Record, 108th Cong., 1st sess., 2003, vol. 149, no. 138, H9139 (2 Oct. 2003); Sen. Rick Santorum (R-PA), Congressional Record, 108th Cong., 1st sess., 2003, vol. 149, no. 40, S3577-78 (12 Mar. 2003); Rep. Chet Edwards (D-TX), Congressional Record, 107th Cong., 2nd sess., 2002, vol. 148, no. 102, 5350 (24 Jul. 2002); Sen. Susan Collins (R-ME), Congressional Record, 108th Cong., 1st sess., 2003, vol. 149, no. 39, S3483 (11 Mar. 2003).

382 Sen. Barbara Boxer (D-CA), Congressional Record, 108th Cong., 1st sess., 2003, vol. 149, no. 40, S3597 (12 Mar. 2003).

383 Sen. Sam Brownback (R-KS), Congressional Record, 108th Cong., 1st sess., 2003, vol. 149, no. 40, S3597-98 (12 Mar. 2003).

384 Rep. Pete Stark (D-CA), Congressional Record, 108th Cong., 2nd sess., 2004, vol. 150, no. 4, E43 (23 Jan. 2004).

385 Sen. Olympia Snowe (R-ME), Congressional Record, 108th Cong., 1st sess., 2003, vol. 149, no. 40, S3577 (12 Mar. 2003).

new on the Supreme Court and to turn the clock back completely, to overrule *Roe v. Wade*."[386]

Roe was considered equivalent with the Constitution or at least precedentially sacrosanct. Sen. Boxer stated to a colleague, "[y]ou thought [*Stenberg*] met the *Roe v. Wade* requirements as well. You were wrong and you were faulty. . . . it is really about meeting the constitutional requirements of *Roe*,[387] and that "[i]n [*Roe*] the Court found that a woman's reproductive decisions are a privacy right guaranteed by the Constitution."[388] Rep. Davis said, "[t]his ban is also unconstitutional because it is in blatant violation of *Roe v. Wade*."[389] Sen. Jeffords commented that "[e]nactment of this legislation, if upheld, would erode the *Roe* decision by banning an abortion procedure that is used previability of the fetus. Thus, this legislation can be clearly seen as an attempt to undermine the legal underpinnings of the *Roe* decision."[390] Sen. Cantwell said *Roe* "was carefully crafted to be balanced and responsible while holding the rights of women in America paramount in reproductive decisions."[391]

---

[386] Sen. Hillary Clinton (D-NY), Congressional Record, 108th Cong., 1st sess., 2003, vol. 149, no. 40, S3588 (12 Mar. 2003).

[387] Sen. Barbara Boxer (D-CA) to Sen. George Voinovich (R-OH), Congressional Record, 108th Cong., 1st sess., 2003, vol. 149, no. 38, S3397 (10 Mar. 2003).

[388] Sen. Barbara Boxer (D-CA), Congressional Record, 108th Cong., 1st sess., 2003, vol. 149, no. 126, S11454 (15 Sept. 2003).

[389] Rep. Davis adds in an intriguing note, "Might I remind the House, this landmark decision leaves the regulation of post vitality or late term abortions to the States, not the Federal Government." Rep. Davis seems to be asserting that the bill is wrong *because* Congress is proposing a *federal* ban and that instead, states are the ones with that power. Rep. Danny Davis (D-IL), Congressional Record, 108th Cong., 1st sess., 2003, vol. 149, no. 84, E1185 (10 Jun. 2003).

[390] Sen. Jim Jeffords (I-VT), Congressional Record, 108th Cong., 1st sess., 2003, vol. 149, no. 40, S3611-12 (12 Mar. 2003). Emphasis added.

[391] Sen. Maria Cantwell (D-WA), Congressional Record, 108th Cong., 1st sess., 2003, vol. 149, no. 40, S3598 (12 Mar. 2003).

Some members disagreed as to whether *Roe* allowed a complete abortion license or allowed significant limitations in the second and third trimesters,[392] or if *Roe* was even an issue, given the focus on this one particular method.[393] Others emphasized *Roe*'s distinction between pre-viability and post-viability abortions.[394] In the Senate, members also voted on a resolution offered by Sen. Harkin affirming the rightness of *Roe v. Wade*: "I want to make sure with all of this going on that we send a strong signal to the women of this country that *Roe v. Wade* is appropriate, it was a good decision, and it is not going to be overturned.[395]

---

[392] Sen. Rick Santorum (R-PA), Congressional Record, 108th Cong., 1st sess., 2003, vol. 149, no. 39, S3456 (11 Mar. 2003). For opposite view, see, for example, Sen. Christopher Dodd (D-CT), Congressional Record, 108th Cong., 1st sess., 2003, vol. 149, no. 41, S3661 (13 Mar. 2003) or Sen. Barbara Boxer (D-CA), Congressional Record, 108th Cong., 1st sess., 2003, vol. 149, no. 40, S3578 (12 Mar. 2003).

[393] "But the D&X procedure is not an ordinary abortion. It is not contemplated by the *Roe v. Wade* decision. Even the *Stenberg* court confirmed, and I quote, 'By no means must physicians [be granted] 'unfettered discretion' in their selection of abortion methods.' So this is not about overturning *Roe v. Wade*[,] that is a red herring." Sen. Orrin Hatch (R-UT), Congressional Record, 108th Cong., 1st sess., 2003, vol. 149, no. 39, S3467 (11 Mar. 2003).

[394] Sen. Jon Corzine (D-NJ), Congressional Record, 108th Cong., 1st sess., 2003, vol. 149, no. 41, S3655 (13 Mar. 2003); Sen. Richard Durbin (D-IL), Congressional Record, 108th Cong., 1st sess., 2003, vol. 149, no. 39, S3479 (11 Mar. 2003). Also see pages S3480-81. For other member discussions along this vein, see Sen. Patty Murray (D-WA), Congressional Record, 108th Cong., 1st sess., 2003, vol. 149, no. 39, S3423 (11 Mar. 2003); Sen. Richard Durbin (D-IL), Congressional Record, 108th Cong., 1st sess., 2003, vol. 149, no. 40, S3572 (12 Mar. 2003); Sen. Pete Domenici (R-NM), Congressional Record, 108th Cong., 1st sess., 2003, vol. 149, no. 40, S3603 (12 Mar. 2003); and Sen. Barbara Mikulski (D-MD), Congressional Record, 108th Cong., 1st sess., 2003, vol. 149, no. 40, S3576 (12 Mar. 2003).

[395] Sen. Tom Harkin (D-IA), Congressional Record, 108th Cong., 1st sess., 2003, vol. 149, no. 40, S3581-82 (12 Mar. 2003). The amendment passed 52-46. Although it was observed that "you did not have a whole lot of people coming down here to engage in that debate." Sen. Rick Santorum (R-PA),

Finally, *Roe* was discussed as an issue involving representation, legislatures, and judicial power,[396] as a reminder the abortion license was not absolute,[397] as relating to philosophical beliefs about the "the legal status of a young human,"[398] and about the proper understanding of "settled law."[399]

PRECEDENT

While it obviously overlaps with previous discussions, it is worth pointing out that Supreme Court precedent was also frequently discussed. This could be seen as entirely predictable given that any discussion of an issue that has been debated within the three branches of government, especially in the Courts, for the last thirty years is bound to include discussions of precedent, if for no other reason than to understand the terms of the debate and the issue. Nevertheless, it is worth considering the nature of this behavior and the implications.

The health exception mentioned in *Doe v. Bolton* and emphasized in *Stenberg v. Carhart* was frequently cited, although usually in terms of merely mentioning its necessity for perceived constitutionality rather than discussing its normative context.[400] Rep. Edwards said, "if there is

---

Congressional Record, 108th Cong., 1st sess., 2003, vol. 149, no. 40, S3644-45 (12 Mar. 2003).

396 Sen. Sam Brownback (R-KS), Congressional Record, 108th Cong., 1st sess., 2003, vol. 149, no. 40, S3597-98 (12 Mar. 2003). Sen. Rick Santorum (R-PA), Congressional Record, 108th Cong., 1st sess., 2003, vol. 149, no. 40, S3644-45 (12 Mar. 2003).

397 Sen. Mary Landrieu (D-LA), Congressional Record, 108th Cong., 1st sess., 2003, vol. 149, no. 40, S3575 (12 Mar. 2003).

398 Sen. Sam Brownback (R-KS), Congressional Record, 108th Cong., 1st sess., 2003, vol. 149, no. 40, S3597-98 (12 Mar. 2003).

399 Sen. Rick Santorum (R-PA), Congressional Record, 108th Cong., 1st sess., 2003, vol. 149, no. 40, S3609 (12 Mar. 2003).

400 "Undue burden" was also mentioned, but not as frequently. Here, Sen. Boxer discusses it: "[w]e had a Supreme Court that argues that the *Stenberg* case, the legally identical bill to this, is unconstitutional on its face. . . Unconstitutional because it put an undue burden on women because the

one frivolous late-term abortion in America, in my book that is one too many. But this bill is a false promise. . . . it is clearly unconstitutional, since it has no health exception."[401] Sen. Durbin and Sen. Boxer exchanged comments over *Stenberg* and a health exception, in which Sen. Durbin asked: "why are we now considering S. 3, this bill, which defies the Supreme Court and says to them, we know better, we are going to change your mind, we are going to send you something that doesn't meet the test [a health exception] in light of the Nebraska statute?"[402]

Sen. Cantwell agreed, arguing that "[d]espite the Supreme Court's very clear mandate, the legislation before us today does not provide an exception for the health of the mother. For this reason, this legislation, like the one struck down in *Stenberg*, is unconstitutional."[403] Defending his amendment to the bill, Sen. Durbin argued it had "a health exception not contained in S. 3 . . . [and therefore] more likely to withstand the constitutional challenge and scrutiny across the street at the Supreme Court."[404] Sens. DeWine and Santorum disagreed with

---

definition is vague. Undue burden[,] very important words. You cannot put an undue burden on a woman because abortion under *Roe* is legal and in the late stages it is not legal if the State says it isn't, except for life and health. But it puts an undue burden because we don't know at what stage the woman is going to get this abortion and whether this procedure applies to it or not." Sen. Barbara Boxer (D-CA), Congressional Record, 108th Cong., 1st sess., 2003, vol. 149, no. 38, S3395 (10 Mar. 2003).

401 Rep. Edwards (D-TX), Congressional Record, 108th Cong., 1st sess., 2003, 149, no. 81, H4929 (4 Jun. 2003).

402 Sen. Richard Durbin (D-IL), Congressional Record, 108th Cong., 1st sess., 2003, vol. 149, no. 126, S11458 (15 Sept. 2003). See also, Sen. Richard Durbin (D-IL) and Sen. Barbara Boxer (D-CA), Congressional Record, 108th Cong., 1st sess., 2003, vol. 149, no. 126, S11456 (15 Sept. 2003); and Rep. (Tom) Udall (D-NM), Congressional Record, 108th Cong., 1st sess., 2003, vol. 149, no. 141, E2011 (8 Oct. 2003).

403 Sen. Maria Cantwell (D-WA), Congressional Record, 108th Cong., 1st sess., 2003, vol. 149, no. 40, S3598 (12 Mar. 2003).

404 Sen. Richard Durbin (D-IL), Congressional Record, 108th Cong., 1st sess., 2003, vol. 149, no. 39, S3481 (11 Mar. 2003). See also, for example, Sen. Susan Collins (R-ME), Congressional Record, 108th Cong., 1st sess., 2003,

this emphasis, arguing that medical judgment is a "loophole[] so big that abortion providers would be able to continue to perform virtually all the partial-birth abortions they perform today"[405] and that

> 'medical judgment' has, of course, a great deal of built-in flexibility. Specifically, under the precedent set by the U.S. Supreme Court, in 1973, in the *Doe v. Bolton* case: Medical judgment may be exercised in the light of all factors_physical, emotional, psychological, familial, and the woman's age_relevant to the well being of the patient. All these factors may relate to health. . . .That is from *Doe v. Bolton.*[406]

DIALOGUES

COOPERATION & COMMUNICATION

As has been shown, sometimes members simply made comments merely acknowledging the existence of the other branches of government (in this case primarily the Court), or stating the basic belief that branches of government have worked together or should work together in some particular fashion.

One way this occurred during deliberation over this bill was through debate over congressional fact finding. This was extremely important because supporters of the ban inserted findings of fact they claimed demonstrated the lack of need for a health exception, thus making the bill constitutionally adequate given current Court

---

vol. 149, no. 39, S3483 (11 Mar. 2003); Sen. Jim Jeffords (I-VT), Congressional Record, 108th Cong., 1st sess., 2003, vol. 149, no. 40, S3611-12 (12 Mar. 2003). Emphasis added.

405 Sen. Mike DeWine (R-OH), Congressional Record, 108th Cong., 1st sess., 2003, vol. 149, no. 40, S3574-75 (12 Mar. 2003).

406 Sen. Mike DeWine (R-OH), Congressional Record, 108th Cong., 1st sess., 2003, vol. 149, no. 40, S3574-75 (12 Mar. 2003).

precedents.[407] Others argued the findings were evidentially insufficient.[408] Sen. Feinstein stated:

> The Framers of the Constitution did not intend that Congress be able to evade Supreme Court precedent and effectively amend the Constitution just by holding a hearing and generating questionable testimony from handpicked witnesses. In fact, the Supreme Court has made crystal clear that Congress cannot simply ignore a constitutional ruling they dislike by adopting a contrary legislative finding and telling the Court that they have to defer to it. That is just what is being done here. . . . So make no mistake about it. You can say anything you want in the findings, and it isn't going to be dispositive as to whether the statute meets the test of the Constitution of the United States.[409]

Sen. Jeffords agreed:

> The proponents of this legislation will point to the pages of findings contained in the legislation as to why it is unnecessary to have an exception for the health of the mother. There are two problems with this rationale, first the Supreme Court has shown an unwillingness to consider Congressional findings of fact in recent decisions, such as *Morrison*, *VAWA*, and *Kimmel*, *ADEA*. Second, during the debate on the *Carhart* decision, the Supreme Court had knowledge of these findings, yet still ruled that because the Nebraska statute did not have an explicit health exception the law was unconstitutional.[410]

---

[407] Sen. Santorum (R-PA), stated, "[c]learly, we believe we have addressed the issue of health." Sen. Rick Santorum (R-PA), Congressional Record, 108th Cong., 1st sess., 2003, vol. 149, no. 39 S3429 (11 Mar. 2003).

[408] Rep. John Conyers (D-MI), Congressional Record, 108th Cong., 1st sess., 2003, vol. 149, no. 81, H4925 (4 Jun. 2003).

[409] Sen. Dianne Feinstein (D-CA), Congressional Record, 108th Cong., 1st sess., 2003, vol. 149, no. 148, S12937-38 (21 Oct. 2003).

[410] Sen. Jim Jeffords (I-VT), Congressional Record, 108th Cong., 1st sess., 2003, vol. 149, no. 40, S3611-12 (12 Mar. 2003).

Supporters of the ban offered arguments why congressional fact finding was appropriate. Rep. Pence said, "[w]e have changed the bill, adding findings of fact to overcome constitutional barriers, and I am confident that it will survive judicial review."[411] Rep. Sensenbrenner cited numerous quotations from previous Court decisions supporting the efficacy of congressional fact finding.[412] Citing one such case, *Turner Broadcasting System*, Rep. Chabot stated:

> the United States Congress is entitled to reach its own factual findings, findings that the Supreme Court consistently relies upon and accords great deference, and to enact legislation based upon these findings so long as it seeks to pursue a legitimate interest that is within the scope of the Constitution and draws reasonable inferences based upon substantial evidence.[413]

In the Senate, Sen. Santorum agreed:

> Congress has, on repeated occasions, made findings of fact in preparation for review by the courts, and in a vast number of these cases, the courts have been very deferential to Congress, as a body, that gets into much more detail through the process

---

[411] Rep. Mike Pence (R-IN), Congressional Record, 107th Cong., 2nd sess., 2002, vol. 148, no. 97, H4860 (17 Jul. 2002).

[412] Rep. James Sensenbrenner (R-WI), Congressional Record, 108th Cong., 1st sess., 2003, vol. 149, no. 81, H4932 (4 Jun. 2003). See also, Sen. Orrin Hatch (R-UT), Congressional Record, 108th Cong., 1st sess., 2003, vol. 149, no. 39, S3467 (11 Mar. 2003); Sen. Rick Santorum (R-PA), Congressional Record, 108th Cong., 1st sess., 2003, vol. 149, no. 39, S3422 (11 Mar. 2003); Sen. Rick Santorum (R-PA), Congressional Record, 108th Cong., 1st sess., 2003, vol. 149, no. 39, S3429 (11 Mar. 2003).

[413] Rep. Steve Chabot (R-OH), Congressional Record, 108th Cong., 1st sess., 2003, vol. 149, no. 81, H4925 (4 Jun. 2003). See also, Rep. Steve Chabot (R-OH), Congressional Record, 107th Cong., 2nd sess., 2002, vol. 148, no. 82, E1097 (19 Jun. 2002).

> of hearings. We have had numerous hearings about this procedure in both the Senate and the House.[414]

CHECKS & BALANCES

Other statements reflected the belief by members that they were participating in a system of checks and balances, particularly with the Court. Sometimes members recognized that rather than acting completely independently, they were responding to the Court, or even giving implicit or explicit deferential acknowledgment to it. This makes rational sense if, rather than seeking merely symbolic votes or gestures, legislation which would not instantly be ruled unconstitutional by the perceived preference of a majority of the Court was the desired outcome.

For example, Sen. Mikulski said, "[t]he Supreme Court's acknowledgment of the fundamental 'right to privacy' in our Constitution gave every woman the right to decide what to do with her own body."[415] Sen. Murray stated, "this ban is unconstitutional. The U.S. Supreme Court has already ruled that this very type of restriction violates the Constitution."[416] Rep. Brown commented that "[t]he Supreme Court agrees that medical decisions should be made by the patient and her doctor and not by a bunch of politicians in Washington and their special interests."[417] In support of the bill, Rep. Ryun said, "[a]lthough language banning this procedure has been struck down in the past by the Supreme Court, this new legislation has been tailored to address the Court's concerns."[418] Others backers of the ban echoed this belief that the bill rectified the health and definitional deficiencies in

---

[414] Sen. Rick Santorum (R-PA), Congressional Record, 108th Cong., 1st sess., 2003, vol. 149, no. 39 S3429 (11 Mar. 2003).

[415] Sen. Barbara Mikulski (D-MD), Congressional Record, 108th Cong., 1st sess., 2003, vol. 149, no. 128, S11603 (17 Sept. 2003).

[416] Sen. Patty Murray (D-WA), Congressional Record, 108th Cong., 1st sess., 2003, vol. 149, no. 39, S3424 (11 Mar. 2003).

[417] Rep. Corrine Brown (D-FL), Congressional Record, 108th Cong., 1st sess., 2003, vol. 149, no. 81, H4916 (4 Jun. 2003).

[418] Rep. Jim Ryun (R-KS), Congressional Record, 107th Cong., 2nd sess., 2002, vol. 148, no. 87, H3932 (26 Jun. 2002).

the Nebraska statute.[419] Sen. Santorum argued for his bill by explaining:

> The Senator from California said: We meant to cover more than one procedure with this language. . . . Why would we want to do that? The Supreme Court said: The reason we are striking down your language is that we believe it covers more than one procedure. So we are going to craft language so the Supreme Court can come back and say, well, it covers more than one procedure? . . . Maybe my colleagues think we are not serious about banning this procedure. Let me assure them, I am serious as a heart attack about banning this procedure, and we have crafted language to do just that, and only that. . . . The language is different. It is not identical to the Nebraska statute.[420]
>
> I am simply trying, to the best of my ability, to adequately and sufficiently describe a procedure to include that procedure and exclude all others. Because that is what the Court asked us to do[,] to define this procedure so specifically as to exclude others. . . . The Court went through great detail, talking about other procedures where a child could still be alive and portions of that child could be outside the mother. They could be doing another form of abortion and an arm or a leg or some portion of the body could go outside of the mother in the process of

---

[419] Sen. Jon Kyl (R-AZ), Congressional Record, 108th Cong., 1st sess., 2003, vol. 149, no. 38, S3399 (10 Mar. 2003). See also, Sen. Charles Grassley (R-IA), Congressional Record, 108th Cong., 1st sess., 2003, vol. 149, no. 41, S3655 (13 Mar. 2003); Sen. George Voinovich (R-OH), Congressional Record, 108th Cong., 1st sess., 2003, vol. 149, no. 38, S3397 (10 Mar. 2003); Sen. George Voinovich (R-OH), Congressional Record, 108th Cong., 1st sess., 2003, vol. 149, no. 39, S3461-63 (11 Mar. 2003). See also, Sen. Rick Santorum (R-PA), Congressional Record, 108th Cong., 1st sess., 2003, vol. 149, no. 38, S3384 (10 Mar. 2003).

[420] Sen. Rick Santorum (R-PA), Congressional Record, 108th Cong., 1st sess., 2003, vol. 149, no. 40, S3568 (12 Mar. 2003).

killing the child in the womb. So they said the original definition was not clear enough.[421]

On the other hand, numerous members justified their opposition by highlighting the unconstitutionality of the bill, usually through the paradigm of judicial primacy. Many members expressed their perspective that because there was no health exception in the bill, and because the Court had ruled in *Stenberg* the need for one in the Nebraska statute, this ban would be found unconstitutional.[422] Sen. Mikulski asserted that "[t]he Santorum bill before us [.] . . . is unconstitutional. . . . The Santorum bill is unconstitutional. . . . The Santorum bill violates the key principles of *Roe v. Wade* and other Court decisions."[423] Sen. Feinstein agreed, saying, "The bill violates *Roe* and other Supreme Court opinions because it doesn't protect the health of the woman. . . . My amendment follows the Constitution. It is constitutional."[424] Rep. Tauscher asked, "are we just wasting everybody's time and beating our chests just to pass something that we know will be overturned by the Supreme Court?"[425] Rep. Kirk stated

[421] Sen. Rick Santorum (R-PA), Congressional Record, 108th Cong., 1st sess., 2003, vol. 149, no. 40, S3610 (12 Mar. 2003). See also, Sen. Mike DeWine (R-OH), Congressional Record, 108th Cong., 1st sess., 2003, vol. 149, no. 38, S3391 (10 Mar. 2003).

[422] See Rep. Diana DeGette (D-CO), Congressional Record, 107th Cong., 2nd sess., 2002, vol. 148, no. 102, H5361 (24 Jul. 2002); Rep. Richard Gephardt (D-MO), Congressional Record, 107th Cong., 2nd sess., 2002, vol. 148, no. 102, H5368-69 (24 Jul. 2002); Rep. Chet Edwards (D-TX), Congressional Record, 107th Cong., 2nd sess., 2002, vol. 148, no. 102, 5350 (24 Jul. 2002); Rep. Bobby Scott (D-VA), Congressional Record, 107th Cong., 2nd sess., 2002, vol. 148, no. 102 H5350 (24 Jul. 2002).

[423] Sen. Barbara Mikulski (D-MD), Congressional Record, 108th Cong., 1st sess., 2003, vol. 149, no. 77, S6973 (22 May 2003); See also Rep. Sheila Jackson-Lee (D-TX), Congressional Record, 108th Cong., 1st sess., 2003, vol. 149, no. 81, H4953 (4 Jun. 2003).

[424] Sen. Dianne Feinstein (D-CA), Congressional Record, 108th Cong., 1st sess., 2003, vol. 149, no. 40, S3609 (12 Mar. 2003).

[425] Rep. Ellen Tauscher (D-CA), Congressional Record, 108th Cong., 1st sess., 2003, vol. 149, no. 81, H4944 (4 Jun. 2003).

that "[u]nlike H.R. 760, the Greenwood substitute bans late-term abortions in a way the Supreme Court will sustain. Passage of the Greenwood substitute would mean a quick end to litigation and a rapid change in U.S. law. . . . Failure to pass the substitute means continuing litigation and defeat at the hands of the Supreme Court."[426] Rep. Lee thought that "[m]eddling in these intensely personal private affairs violates our Constitution. . . . This bill is . . . reckless and it is unconstitutional. . . . Otherwise, the Supreme Court will rule it unconstitutional. *Roe v. Wade* must be upheld.[427]

Rep. DeGette asked, "[i]f this bill were passed into law, the Supreme Court would find it unconstitutional. Why on Earth would we pass a bill we know for a fact is unconstitutional?"[428] Rep. Holmes Norton stated:

> The bill tries to simply hop over *Roe versus Wade* with 15 pages of congressional findings. But congressional findings cannot overrule a Supreme Court decision. Congressional findings cannot nullify a woman's constitutional right. Congressional findings cannot defeat a woman's right to have an abortion if her health is in danger. . . . It is plainly unconstitutional.[429]

Two months later, she added:

> I want to speak to the constitutional issues. . . . because each and every time this and similar bills have been overturned. Worse, there is no health exception. It is as if Roe versus Wade never said that in order to be constitutional there always had to be a health exception. . . . It was unconstitutional 3

---

[426] Rep. Mark Kirk (R-IL), Congressional Record, 108th Cong., 1st sess., 2003, vol. 149, no. 81, H4941 (4 Jun. 2003).

[427] Rep. Barbara Lee (D-CA), Congressional Record, 108th Cong., 1st sess., 2003, vol. 149, no. 138, H9149 (2 Oct. 2003).

[428] Rep. Diana DeGette (D-CO), Congressional Record, 107th Cong., 2nd sess., 2002, vol. 148, no. 102, H5361 (24 Jul. 2002).

[429] Rep. Eleanor Holmes Norton (D-DC), Congressional Record, 107th Cong., 2nd sess., 2002, vol. 148, no. 102, H5365 (24 Jul. 2002).

> years ago, my friends. It is unconstitutional today, even if we enact it.[430]

Sen. Daschle exclaimed:

> The Supreme Court has struck down what many experts claim is a 'legally identical' bill, the Nebraska law banning this procedure. In previous Congresses, I have expressed my concern that this legislation may not withstand an inevitable constitutional challenge. . . . Now that the Court has ruled in the Nebraska case, that concern is even greater. But the sponsors of this bill have chosen to take that gamble, claiming their '20 word changes' have resolved the constitutional concerns. Those 20 words, by the way, are allegedly powerful enough to change the outcome in the Supreme Court, but not significant enough to merit a hearing in the Judiciary Committee. . . . At this point, it is my hope that this Senate bill will go quickly to the President so that the Supreme Court can rule on it. If the Court strikes it down, then I hope people on both sides of this issue will be willing to work together to stop all post-viability abortions except those that are absolutely necessary to protect a woman's life and health.[431]

Rep. Conyers declared, "[e]ven if it passes the House and the Senate, the Supreme Court still will tell us the same thing; that we must have an exception for the life and health and safety of the mother, or this provision is not valid. . . . there is no chance of this ever becoming law."[432] Sen. Murray agreed, stating, "[o]ne of the reasons I oppose S. 3, the so-called Partial Birth Abortion Act, was because I know this legislation is unconstitutional. It simply does not meet the constitutional test that requires providing some consideration for the

---

[430] Rep. Eleanor Holmes Norton (D-DC), Congressional Record, 108th Cong., 1st sess., 2003, vol. 149, no. 138, H9139 (2 Oct. 2003).

[431] Sen. Tom Daschle (D-SC), Congressional Record, 108th Cong., 1st sess., 2003, vol. 149, no. 41, S3660-61 (13 Mar. 2003).

[432] Rep. John Conyers (D-MI), Congressional Record, 107th Cong., 2nd sess., 2002, vol. 148, no. 102, H5356 (24 Jul. 2002).

health of the woman. . . . The Court has been extremely clear on this point."[433] Other members equated Court precedent with the Constitution's apparently clear meaning. Rep. Hoyer said, "[w]e ought to protect those lives. But we have to balance it. That is what the Court says, that is what the Constitution of the United States says."[434] Sen. Rockefeller felt the same:

> The comprehensive ban I supported[,] offered as an amendment by Senator Durbin[,] would have put an end to all late-term post-viability abortions . . . . [and would have] included a very narrow exception for the rare case when a woman's life or health is threatened by a troubled pregnancy, as required by the United States Supreme Court *and the Constitution*. . . . I want to emphasize that if we are serious about ending the practice of late-term abortions then we must pass a law that will be upheld by our courts. The U.S. Supreme Court has been quite clear that to be deemed constitutional, any law banning late-term abortions must be narrowly focused and must include an exception for the health of the mother. Several previous bans ignored these tests and were struck down, and consequently there has been no end to this troubling practice. Senator Santorum's bill does not adequately meet the Court's requirements for constitutionality and will almost surely meet the same fate. . . . The Durbin amendment, on the other hand, was a clear and comprehensive ban that does comply with the constitutionality tests set forth by the U.S. Supreme Court. . . . I continue to hope that in the end we will find a way to enact a comprehensive ban on late-term abortions that meets the demands of the U.S. Supreme

---

[433] Sen. Patty Murray (D-WA), Congressional Record, 108th Cong., 1st sess., 2003, vol. 149, no. 128, S11601 (17 Sept. 2003).

[434] Rep. Steny Hoyer (D-MD), Congressional Record, 108th Cong., 1st sess., 2003, vol. 149, no. 81, H4946 (4 Jun. 2003).

> Court *and Constitution* by protecting the life and physical health of the mother in extreme situations.[435]

THE FINAL ARBITER

In combination with using Court precedent to justify their opposition to the bill, many members also expressed outright beliefs in judicial supremacy during this deliberation. For example, Rep. Maloney said, ""[t]he writers of this bill are trying to be both the Supreme Court and every woman's doctor. They are making a mockery of the separation of powers and are stealing decisions from women and their doctors."[436] Rep. Van Hollen stated, "[m]oreover, we cannot exert a power we do not have. The Supreme Court, in *Roe v. Wade*, has determined that a woman has a constitutional right to choose a safe and legal abortion during the pre-viability period."[437] Sen. Feingold argued, "I feel very strongly that Congress should seek to regulate abortions *only within the constitutional parameters set forth by the U.S. Supreme Court*. That is why I supported the inclusion of language in S. 3 reaffirming the Senate's commitment to *Roe* and its belief that *Roe* should not be overturned."[438] According to Sen. Murray, this was an issue that "was decided by the U.S. Supreme Court years ago."[439] Sen. Durbin wondered, "[i]f the Supreme Court has reached the conclusion that this language fails to meet the test of *Roe v. Wade*, why in the world are we going through this exercise again? . . . The Santorum approach, S. 3, violates a woman's constitutional right to choose under *Roe v. Wade*.

---

[435] Sen. Jay Rockefeller (D-WV), Congressional Record, 108th Cong., 1st sess., 2003, vol. 149, no. 41, S3662 (13 Mar. 2003). Emphasis added.

[436] Rep. Carolyn Maloney (D-NY), Congressional Record, 107th Cong., 2nd sess., 2002, vol. 148, no. 102, H5360 (24 Jul. 2002).

[437] Rep. Chris Van Hollen (D-MD), Congressional Record, 108th Cong., 1st sess., 2003, vol. 149, no. 81, H4932 (4 Jun. 2003).

[438] Sen. Russ Feingold (D-WI), Congressional Record, 108th Cong., 1st sess., 2003, vol. 149, no. 128, S11602 (17 Sept. 2003). Also see statement and exchange with Sen. Jeffords (I-VT), Congressional Record, 108th Cong., 1st sess., 2003, vol. 149, no. 40, S3611-12 (12 Mar. 2003).

[439] Sen. Patty Murray (D-WA), Congressional Record, 108th Cong., 1st sess., 2003, vol. 149, no. 39, S3424 (11 Mar. 2003).

Don't take my word, take the word of the Supreme Court."[440] Rep. Jackson-Lee said, "[t]he drafters of H.R. 760 are clearly wrong in asserting that they can overrule *Carhart* through legislation. Prior attempts by Congress to undo disfavored Supreme Court rulings . . . have been soundly rejected by the Supreme Court."[441] Rep. Slaughter told her colleagues that:

> S. 3 brazenly seeks to sidestep the Constitution. . . . But the Court has squarely said that '*the power to interpret the Constitution* in a case of controversy remains in the judiciary.' And the Court has said that simply because Congress makes a conclusion does not necessarily make it so. Just because the findings in the bill assert that there is no medical reason for a health exception does not make that true, and it does not change the demands of the Constitution.[442]

Other members utilized other arguments. Rep. Kind even equated his oath of office to Supreme Court precedent:

> As a Member of the U.S. Congress, I took an oath to uphold the Constitution of the United States. I will not betray that oath. Now that the Supreme Court has determined the constitutional parameters for a partial-birth abortion ban in the Stenberg case, I must adhere to that decision and cannot vote for a bill that is blatantly unconstitutional. H.R. 760 does not comply with the Court's decision.[443]

---

[440] Sen. Richard Durbin (D-IL), Congressional Record, 108th Cong., 1st sess., 2003, vol. 149, no. 39, S3480-81 (11 Mar. 2003).

[441] Rep. Sheila Jackson-Lee (D-TX), Congressional Record, 108th Cong., 1st sess., 2003, vol. 149, no. 81, H4937 (4 Jun. 2003).

[442] Rep. Louise Slaughter (D-NY), Congressional Record, 108th Cong., 1st sess., 2003, vol. 149, no. 138, H9136 (2 Oct. 2003). Emphasis added. See also Congressional Record, 108th Cong., 1st sess., 2003, vol. 149, no. 81, H4911-12 (4 Jun. 2003).

[443] Rep. Ron Kind (D-WI), Congressional Record, 108th Cong., 1st sess., 2003, vol. 149, no. 81, H4947 (4 Jun. 2003).

Sen. Kennedy did likewise:

> The Republican leadership has chosen to make as its top priority a flatly unconstitutional piece of legislation. . . . From the time of the 1973 decision in *Roe v. Wade* through the *Stenberg v. Carhart* decision in 2000, the Supreme Court of the United States has made clear that the Constitution allows states to restrict post-viability abortions as long as [there is a health exception]. . . . *The role of the United States Senate is to protect and defend the Constitution of the United States. Each of us in this body has taken that oath of office. And that oath of office and the Constitution require me to oppose this legislation.* . . . This bill unconstitutionally seeks to restrict abortions in cases before viability and it does not provide an exception to protect the mother's health after viability.[444]

Warning against congressional interpretive assertions against the Court, Rep. Nadler stated:

> Members should know better than to believe that this activist conservative Supreme Court that we now have, we should know that they do not feel any particular need to defer to Congress. Members should know what comes of Congress ignoring the will of the Supreme Court. Whatever power Congress had under section 5 of the 14th amendment to effectuate the purposes of 14th amendment as a result of *Katzenbach v. Morgan*, which was cited by the proponents of the bill, and is cited copiously in the bill's findings, I think the more recent *Boerne* decision of the Supreme Court vastly undercuts those powers. And even if *Katzenbach* was still fully good law, as I personally wish it were for other reasons, that case empowered Congress only to expand rights under the 14th amendment, not to curtail rights under the 14th amendment. . . . The Supreme Court has held that the right to choose to have an abortion is a woman's right under the 14th amendment, with some limits that the Supreme Court has

---

[444] Sen. Edward Kennedy (D-MA), Congressional Record, 108th Cong., 1st sess., 2003, vol. 149, no. 40, S3612-13 (12 Mar. 2003). Emphasis added.

> recognized; and the *Katzenbach* decision says those rights can be expanded, but not curtail them. This bill aims to curtail those rights.[445]

Several members invoked *Marbury v. Madison*, claiming that it was the foundation for *Roe v. Wade* and for judicial supremacy. Rep. Lowey proclaimed that:

> The supporters of H.R. 760 disagree with the Court's reflection of our society and reject the principles embodied in its decisions. Holding their opinion is their right. Disregarding the Constitution is wrong. . . . The Supreme Court's decisions in *Roe v. Wade* and *Stenberg v. Carhart* rested on precedent, including *Marbury v. Madison*, decided 200 years ago this year. *Marbury* was critically important to the development of our democracy because it established the Supreme Court as the final and ultimate authority on what the Constitution means. . . . In 1803, the Supreme Court became in fact, not just on paper, an equal partner in government, co-equal with the executive and the legislature. But in 2003, this Congress has decided to ignore the Court.[446]

Rep. Nadler declared:

> Mr. Speaker, we are told that the Supreme Court must defer to congressional fact-finding even if Congress' so-called facts conflict with the preponderance of evidence in litigation before the Court. But the drafters of this bill are wrong. First, it is one of the fundamental tenets of our constitutional structure which establishes three separate branches of the

---

[445] Rep. Jerrold Nadler (D-NY), Congressional Record, 107th Cong., 2nd sess., 2002, vol. 148, no. 102, H357 (24 Jul. 2002). See also, Rep. Jerrold Nadler (D-NY), Congressional Record, 108th Cong., 1st sess., 2003, vol. 149, no. 81, H4926 (4 Jun. 2003).

[446] Rep. Nita Lowey (D-NY), Congressional Record, 108th Cong., 1st sess., 2003, vol. 149, no. 81, H4927 (4 Jun. 2003).

> Federal Government that Congress can enact laws, but it cannot decide whether those laws are constitutional. *That is exclusively the Supreme Court's role*. . . . I realize that one of the members of the Committee on the Judiciary said that the Supreme Court wrongly decided *v. Madison*, but for 200 years that has been the law of the land.[447]

Rep. Jackson-Lee agreed:

> That is the basis of this Nation, three distinct branches of government; the *Marbury* decision suggesting that the Supreme Court is the supreme law of the land. . . . Justice Breyer says that this court, in the course of a generation, has determined and then redetermined that the Constitution offers basic protection to the woman's right to choose, and we shall not revisit those legal principles. We shall not revisit these legal principles. Rather, we apply them to the circumstances of this case.[448]

DEPARTMENTALISM

There were statements of varying emphasis made by members reflecting an inter-branch view of departmentalism, wherein each branch posses the power and duty to articulate and explicate their own interpretation of the Constitution. For example, Rep. Jackson-Lee acknowledged that "Congress has in its past overridden the United States Supreme Court; but at the same time, the Supreme Court can come back and say it is unconstitutional. It is the highest law of the land, and so we can keep going back and forth and back and forth."[449] Rep. Miller commented that "[i]n response to the Supreme Court's split

---

[447] Rep. Jerrold Nadler (D-NY), Congressional Record, 107th Cong., 2nd sess., 2002, vol. 148, no. 102, H5357-58 (24 Jul. 2002). Emphasis added.

[448] Rep. Sheila Jackson-Lee (D-TX), Congressional Record, 107th Cong., 2nd sess., 2002, vol. 148, no. 102, H5359 (24 Jul. 2002).

[449] Rep. Sheila Jackson-Lee (D-TX), Congressional Record, 107th Cong., 2nd sess., 2002, vol. 148, no. 102, H5349 (24 Jul. 2002).

decision in the *Stenberg-Carhart* ruling, this will help give clear guidelines to what is considered constitutional and prohibited."[450]

Others were more direct. Rep. Davis said, "[b]ut even if it were certain that this legislation as soon as it was passed would be struck down by an imperial judiciary, we must, as Members of Congress, discharge our duties to at least attempt to protect the civil rights of the most vulnerable, those least able to protect themselves."[451] Rep. Hyde asked, "[a]s far as the Supreme Court, we can keep trying to have them get it right, can we not? You would not be satisfied with *Dred Scott*, would you?"[452] Rep. Toomey stated, "[t]he Constitution does not guarantee a right to have abortions. A few Supreme Court Justices on the other hand, decided that they would rather be legislators than Justices and so they invented this right. They wrote it in a decision. . . . It is a terrible misreading of the Constitution."[453] Rep. Linder asserted Congress' prerogative by declaiming: "Although I certainly respect the Supreme Court exercising its article III duties, I believe the Congress has its own duty to create and pass laws that protect the people of this country."[454] Sen. Santorum agreed: "The reason we are back is not just to say the Court was wrong or that we disagree with the Court's

---

[450] Rep. Jeff Miller (R-FL), Congressional Record, 107th Cong., 2nd sess., 2002, vol. 148, no. 102, H5366 (24 Jul. 2002).

[451] Rep. Jo Ann Davis (R-VA), Congressional Record, 107th Cong., 2nd sess., 2002, vol. 148, no. 102, H5360 (24 Jul. 2002).

[452] Rep. Henry Hyde (R-IL), Congressional Record, 107th Cong., 2nd sess., 2002, vol. 148, no. 102, H5363 (24 Jul. 2002).

[453] Rep. Patrick Toomey (R-PA), Congressional Record, 108th Cong., 1st sess., 2003, vol. 149, no. 138, H9140 (2 Oct. 2003).

[454] Rep. John Linder (R-GA), Congressional Record, 107th Cong., 2nd sess., 2002, vol. 148, no. 102 H5349 (24 Jul. 2002). Prior to this statement, the speaker added, "I find that argument [judicial supremacy] ironic, considering 413 Members of this body voted to pass a child pornography bill last month after the Supreme Court told us in *Ashcroft v. Free Speech Coalition* that we could not."

judgment on constitutionality, although I do."[455] The next day he added, "I guess I am saying something . . . about the decision of *Roe v. Wade* because I think it gets it wrong. The Supreme Court got it wrong."[456] At length he argued:

> They have proscribed in elected representatives the right to have any impact on that. . . . The courts have completely trumped the legislature. They have decided to take an entire body of law away from us and the State legislatures. I believe the Senator was in the State legislature at one point. That is my recollection. They have taken it away from the State legislatures, taken it away from the Congress, taken it away from people in our democracy, in our Republic, and decided to hold it up across the street where nine, at the time men, decided to take the law into their own hands by creating a right that did not exist. It just did not exist.[457]

Rep. Delay asserted:

> I did not come to the House to make a decision for the courts. I came to the House to pass very strong, important legislation and then to fight in the courts for my position. I do not let the courts decide what direction I go. I do not make those decisions in this Chamber. If Members want to make decisions for the courts, then go down to the White House and get a nomination from the President.[458]

Rep. Paul stated that "[p]artial-birth abortion . . . clearly demonstrates how close we are to legalizing infanticide. This problem should be

---

[455] Sen. Rick Santorum (R-PA), Congressional Record, 108th Cong., 1st sess., 2003, vol. 149, no. 39, S3456 (11 Mar. 2003).

[456] Sen. Rick Santorum (R-PA), Congressional Record, 108th Cong., 1st sess., 2003, vol. 149, no. 40, S3609 (12 Mar. 2003).

[457] Sen. Rick Santorum (R-PA), Congressional Record, 108th Cong., 1st sess., 2003, vol. 149, no. 40, S3608 (12 Mar. 2003).

[458] Rep. Tom DeLay (R-TX), Congressional Record, 108th Cong., 1st sess., 2003, vol. 149, no. 81, H4946 (4 Jun. 2003).

dealt with by the States and without the Federal courts or the U.S. Congress ['] involvement."[459] Two months later, he argued:

> while it is the independent duty of each branch of the Federal Government to act Constitutionally, Congress will likely continue to ignore . . . its Constitutional limits. . . . by expanding the class of victims to which unconstitutional (but already-existing) Federal murder and assault statutes apply, the Federal Government moves yet another step closer to a national police state. . . . Of course, it is much easier to ride the current wave of federalizing every human misdeed in the name of saving the world from some evil than to uphold a Constitutional oath which prescribes a procedural structure by which the nation is protected from what is perhaps the worst evil, totalitarianism. Who, after all, wants to be amongst those members of Congress who are portrayed as soft on violent crimes initiated against the unborn? . . . Protection of life (born or unborn) against initiations of violence is of vital importance. So vitally important, in fact, it must be left to the States' criminal justice systems. We have seen what a legal, constitutional, and philosophical mess results from attempts to federalize such an issue. Numerous States have adequately protected the unborn against assault and murder and done so prior to the Federal Government's unconstitutional sanctioning of violence in the *Roe v. Wade* decision. Unfortunately, H.R. 503 ignores the danger of further federalizing that which is properly reserved to State governments and, in so doing, throws legal philosophy, the Constitution, the Bill of Rights, . . . out with the baby and the bathwater.[460]

---

[459] Rep. Ron Paul (R-TX), Congressional Record, 107th Cong., 1st sess., 2001, vol. 147, no. 18, H234 (8 Feb. 2001).

[460] Rep. Ron Paul (R-TX), Congressional Record, 107th Cong., 1st.sess., 2001, vol. 147, no. 54, H1636-37 (26 Apr. 2001).

Later, he would discuss the commerce clause, the general welfare clause, and the proper authorial dimension in which criminal law should normatively be dealt under a proper understanding of the Constitution.[461]

> The legal problems of protecting life stem from the ill-advised *Roe v. Wade* ruling, a ruling that constitutionally should never have occurred. . . . The best solution, of course, is not now available to us. That would be a Supreme Court that recognizes that for all criminal laws, the several states retain jurisdiction. Something that Congress can do is remove the issue from the jurisdiction of the lower federal courts, so that states can deal with the problems surrounding abortion, thus helping to reverse some of the impact of *Roe v. Wade*. . . . Another problem with this bill is its citation of the interstate commerce clause as a justification for a federal law banning partial-birth abortion. This greatly stretches the definition of interstate commerce. The abuse of both the interstate commerce clause and the general welfare clause is precisely the reason our Federal Government no longer conforms to constitutional dictates but, instead, balloons out of control in its growth and scope. H.R. 760 inadvertently justifies federal government intervention into every medical procedure through the gross distortion of the interstate commerce clause.[462]

---

461 "The best solution, of course, is not now available to us. That would be a Supreme Court that recognizes that for all criminal laws, the several states retain jurisdiction. Something that Congress can do is remove the issue from the jurisdiction of the lower federal courts, so that states can deal with the problems surrounding abortion, thus helping to reverse some of the impact of *Roe v. Wade*." Rep. Ron Paul (R-TX), Congressional Record, 107th Cong., 2nd sess., 2002, vol. 148, no. 102, H5367 (24 Jul. 2002).

462 Rep. Ron Paul (R-TX), Congressional Record, 108th Cong., 1st sess., 2003, vol. 149, no. 81, H4934-35 (4 Jun. 2003). Two months prior, Rep. Ryan introduced his own bill, the Life-Protecting Judicial Limitation Act of 2003. According to Rep. Ryan, "provides that the inferior courts of the United States do not have jurisdiction to hear abortion-related cases. Congress must use the authority granted to it in Article 3, Section 1 of the Constitution. The

CONCLUSION

On November 5th, 2003, President George W. Bush signed the Partial-Birth Abortion Ban Act into public law.[463] Several lower courts, in response to three legal challenges filed immediately after the Ban was passed, all quickly ruled that it was unconstitutional. Attorney General Alberto Gonzales appealed a ruling of the Eighth Circuit Court of Appeals in favor of LeRoy Carhart.[464] The Supreme Court upheld the Ban on April 18th, 2007 in *Gonzales v. Carhart.*[465] In it, Justice Kennedy discussed the state's interest in the promotion of life as well as the ambiguous medical testimony surrounding the issue. Drawing on his own language from fifteen years prior, wrote that the ban did not impose an

> undue burden on a woman's right to abortion based on its overbreadth or lack of a health exception. . . . It is self-evident that a mother who comes to regret her choice to abort must struggle with grief more anguished and sorrow more profound when she learns, only after the event, what she once did not know: that she allowed a doctor to pierce the skull and

---

district courts of the United States, as well as the United States Court of Federal Claims, should not have the authority to hear these types of cases. . . . By following the Constitution and using the power granted to the Congress by this document, we can restore freedom of conscience and the sanctity of human life." Rep. Ron Paul (R-TX), Congressional Record, 108th Cong., 1st sess., 2003, vol. 149, no. 52, E632 (1 Apr. 2003).

[463] It was presented to the President from Congress October 28, 2003. Public Law 108-105 (18 U.S. Code 1531). See Keith Perine, "Supreme Court Upholds Abortion Ban," CQ Weekly Online (April 23, 2007): 1204. http://library.cqpress.com/cqweekly/weeklyrep ort 110-000002494586 (accessed October 19, 2007).

[464] Keith Perine, "Supreme Court Upholds Abortion Ban," CQ Weekly Online (April 23, 2007): 1204-1204. http://library.cqpress.com/cqweekly/weeklyreport110-000002494586 (accessed October 19, 2007).

[465] 550 U.S. _____ (2007).

> vacuum the fast-developing brain of her unborn child, a child assuming the human form.[466]

In dissent, Justice Ginsburg wrote "[t]he court's hostility to the right *Roe* and *Casey* secured is not concealed." "In candor, the act, and the court's defense of it, cannot be understood as anything other than an effort to chip away at a right declared again and again by this court – and with increasing comprehension of its centrality to women's lives."[467]

According to one observer, "[t]he decision marks the first time the court has upheld a ban on a specific type of abortion. It is also the first time since the court's landmark 1973 abortion decision in *Roe v. Wade* that the court has upheld a restriction on abortion services that does not include an exception for procedures deemed necessary to preserve a woman's health."[468] While some felt the decision was "a faithful application of existing Supreme Court precedent,"[469] others disagreed, believing that "the Roberts Court has begun its march on abortion

---

[466] Keith Perine, "Supreme Court Upholds Abortion Ban," CQ Weekly Online (April 23, 2007): 1204. http://library.cqpress.com/cqweekly/weeklyreport110-000002494586 (accessed October 19, 2007).

[467] Keith Perine, "Supreme Court Upholds Abortion Ban," CQ Weekly Online (April 23, 2007): 1204. http://library.cqpress.com/cqweekly/

weeklyreport110-000002494586 (accessed October 19, 2007).

[468] Keith Perine, "Supreme Court Upholds Abortion Ban," CQ Weekly Online (April 23, 2007): 1204-1204. http://library.cqpress.com/cqweekly/weeklyreport110-000002494586 (accessed October 19, 2007).

[469] Law Professor Douglas Kmiec, "Equality's Defeat: How Abortion Disserves Equality," available at http://communities.justicetalking.org/blogs/day24/archive/2007/04/23/equality-s-defeat-how-abortion-disserves-equality.aspx. This sentence is the opening line of the article, which could not be found anywhere else. A similar quote can also be found at The Federalist Society Online Debate Series, "Partial-Birth Abortion Ban Act," available at http://74.125.47.132/search?q=cache:j4RMHnBIdIUJ:www.fed-soc.org/debates/dbtid.3/default.asp+Cherminsky+dramatic+change+in+the+law+of+abortion&cd=5&hl=en&ct=clnk&gl=us. Page 1 of the pdf file has Professor Kmiec's remark.

rights"[470] and that the case was "a dramatic change in the law of abortion."[471] Thus, participants in this debate may have helped stake out new constitutional ground in abortion jurisprudence. Congress may have helped to "construct" new areas of abortion jurisprudence through its deliberation and dialogue with the other branches. If Dawn Johnsen's fears are realized, it may be that while *Roe* is left intact, due to the developments in *Gonzales*, other means are found to restrict abortion procedures while leaving the actual constitutional right alone.[472] It may also mean that supporters of abortion in Congress use the example of *Gonzales* to buttress the abortion right by clarifying their own language in potential legislation.[473]

---

[470] Professor Susan Estrich speaking in the Los Angeles Daily Journal. "If you can dream of a way to limit abortion rights, and get it enacted, they'll uphold it." Quoted in John C. Eastman, "Justice Kennedy's Partial Birth Abortion Decision Invites Long-Overdue Dialogue," available at http://www.claremont.org/publications/pubid.712/pub_detail.asp.

[471] Professor Erwin Chemerinsky. The quote can be found at The Federalist Society Online Debate Series, "Partial-Birth Abortion Ban Act," available at http://74.125.47.132/search?q=cache:j4RMHnBId IUJ:www.fed-soc.org/debates/dbtid.3/default.asp+Cherminsky+dramatic+change+in+the+law+of+abortion &cd=5&hl=en&ct=clnk&gl=us. Page 4 of the pdf file has Professor Chemerinsky's remark.

[472] Dawn Johnsen, "The hollowing out of Roe v. Wade," Slate.com (January 25, 2006).

[473] As George Thomas writes, [g]iven the persistent conflict over abortion rights, it would be difficult to call *Roe* 'authoritatively settled.' The Court's own opinions have evolved on the matter, with the justices themselves squabbling over the meaning of precedents [*Stenberg v. Carhart* 530 U.S. 914 (2000). See especially the exchange between Justices O'Connor (at 947) and Kennedy (at 957) over the meaning of *Casey*]. If there is a consensus that women ought to have a constitutional right to terminate a pregnancy in the early months, the evidence suggests this is based on social and political understandings and not derived from the Court's constitutional reasoning." George Thomas, "Recovering the Political Constitution: The Madisonian Vision," The Review of Politics 66, no. 2 (spring 2004): 254. See Jeffrey

Given the relevant political regime and presence of an affiliated age, first, in addition to extreme amounts of symbolic speech and partisan behavior, we see an underlying "settled" value in which members were not eager to mention, much less even discuss, important precedents in the history of abortion jurisprudence, the most important being the initial cases in 1965 and more prominently 1973. Instead, members of Congress and their affiliated president, trying to satisfy their coalition without alienating any coalition members within, or close to joining, that coalition, chose to work with their perceived Court majority, which was to be expected if the majority of the justices were aligned with the previous reconstructive president, and ignore the more fundamental issue and instead focus on a new, somewhat separate, narrower issue, by which, no doubt, they sought to shift public opinion.[474] Also, in non-reconstructive eras, elected leaders are willing to give the Court room to express their supremacy since the members seek to lessen the degree to which they can be held directly accountable. In this case, we see both sides deferring to the Court and using the Court as their non-arbitrary anchor for what is or is not constitutional and proper in a system of checks-and-balances, a deference that has not always been a reality.

Rosen, "Worst Choice: Why We'd be Better off Without Roe," The New Republic, February 24, 2003.

474 "Their goals can necessarily therefore be quite ambitious, and the expectations placed on them by their supporting coalition can be quite high. They are expected to advance the coalition's inherited agenda in favorable circumstances. Within the context of their particular agenda and historical period, affiliated presidents are expected to be activists. . . . The relationship of an affiliated president with the Court is one of partnership." Keith E. Whittington, "The Political Foundations of Judicial Supremacy," in Sotirios A. Barber and Robert P. George, eds., Constitutional Politics: Essays on Constitution Making, Maintenance, and Change (Princeton: Princeton University Press, 2001), 276-277.

CHAPTER 4

The Habeas Corpus Restoration Act of 2007

I believe in a strong, robust executive authority, and I think that the world we live in demands it. . . .[In wartime, the president] needs to have his constitutional authority unimpaired.[475]

Much took place between the events of September 11, 2001 and Congress' debate over the Habeas Corpus Restoration Act of 2007. More than 600 suspected terrorists were detained after the initial attacks and the issue of habeas was immediately controversial.[476] In fact, according to Jonathan Alter

> [w]hen Attorney General John Ashcroft sent the secret first draft of the antiterrorism bill to Capitol Hill in October, it contained a section explicitly titled: 'Suspension of the Writ of Habeas Corpus.' . . . GOP Rep. James Sensenbrenner, who chair[ed] the House Judiciary Committee, remember[ed] how

---

[475] Vice-President Dick Cheney, quoted in, Peter Baker and Jim VandeHei, "Clash is Latest Chapter in Effort to Widen Executive Power," The Washington Post, 21 Dec. 2005, p. A1.

[476] David Masci and Patrick Marshall, "Civil Liberties in Wartime," CQ Researcher Online 11, no. 43 (14 Dec. 2001): 1017-1040, available at http://library.cqpress.com/cqresearcher/cqresrre2001121400 (accessed October 17, 2007).

> 'that stuck out like a sore thumb. It was the first thing [he crossed] out.'[477]

That bill, the United and Strengthening America by Providing Appropriate Tools Required to Intercept and Obstruct Terrorism Act of 2001, passed Congress October 26th, 2001[478] and on October 30th new Department of Justice rules limiting the attorney-client privilege for certain criminal defendants were issued. Fourteen days later, rather than relying on civilian courts, President Bush issued an Executive Military Order authorizing military tribunals or military commissions by "executive fiat" to try suspected terrorists.[479] In his announcement, he stated, "[t]hese are extraordinary times. And I would remind those who don't understand the decision I made that Franklin Roosevelt made the same decision in World War II. Those were extraordinary times, as well."[480]

In January of the following year, the first detainees were sent to the U.S. Naval Station at Guantánamo Bay, Cuba, which, "[u]nlike, say,

---

477 Jonathan Alter, "Keeping Order in the Courts," Newsweek (10 Dec. 2001): 48.

478 The PATRIOT ACT. 115 Stat. 172 (2001).

479 Military Order of Nov. 13, 2001-Detention, Treatment, and Trial of Certain Non-Citizens in the War Against Terrorism, 9 C.F.R. 918 (2002), reprinted in 8 U.S.C. § 801 (2006). See also, Stuart Taylor, Jr., "Terror: We Need New Laws," National Journal (2 Aug. 2008); Elizabeth A. Palmer and Adriel Bettelheim, "War and Civil Liberties: Congress Gropes for a Role," CQ Weekly Online (1 Dec. 2001): 2820-2827, available at http://library.cqpress.com/cqweekly/weeklyreport107-000000348 017 (accessed October 20, 2008).

480 Masci, David and Patrick Marshall. "Civil Liberties in Wartime." CQ Researcher Online 11, no. 43 (14 Dec. 2001): 1017-1040, available at http://library.cqpress.com/cqresearcher/cqresrre2001121400 (accessed October 17, 2007). Brad Berenson, a White House lawyer who worked on the Commissions in the fall of 2002, said, "[w]e relied on the same language in FDR's order, the same congressional statute that FDR did, and we had a unanimous Supreme Court decision on point. . . . As a lawyer advising a client, it doesn't get much better than that." Jack Goldsmith, The Terror Presidency: Law and Judgment Inside The Bush Administration (New York: W. W. Norton, 2007), 109.

Afghanistan or Iraq . . . was completely secure. . . . [A] 1903 treaty with Cuba gives the U.S. total, permanent jurisdiction and control. But because Cuba technically retains 'sovereignty,' Guantánamo -- unlike prisons in the U.S. -- seemed beyond the reach of any court."[481] In February, Sen. Arlen Specter (PA) introduced the Military Commission Procedures Act. It had a sole co-sponsor and was legislatively inert.[482] Also early in 2002, President Bush said Geneva Conventions did not apply to Guantánamo detainees because they were stateless terrorists.[483]

During these first several years post-9/11 individuals transported to and held at Guantánamo quickly began to challenge their detentions in court, several of which reached the Supreme Court. On June 28th, 2004, the Supreme Court issued three momentous rulings in response, stipulating that legal challenges to detainee detentions were acceptable,

---

[481] Stuart Taylor, Jr., "Ending Bush's War on Due Process," National Journal (1 Dec. 2007).

[482] Toobin recounts, "'[t]he whole idea never really went anywhere,' Specter told me. 'Nobody was much interested in it.' On a trip to Guantanamo, [Sen.] Lindsey Graham told David Addington, counsel to Vice-President Cheney, that 'You really need to come over and draft some legislation with us, and, if you do that, the Supreme Court will be much more likely to uphold what we do. It would be better to work in concert with each other when it comes to wartime decision-making about how you try and interrogate a prisoner.' 'I remember Dave had a copy of the Constitution he carried around with him,' 'He took it out, and he said the Administration didn't need congressional authorization for what it was doing. The President had the inherent authority to handle the prisoners any way he wanted.' And I said, 'That may be a good legal argument, but it's not a good political argument. The more united the nation, the better it is for everyone.' But Dave said, 'Thanks but no thanks.' 'And after that we never had much dialogue.'" Jeffrey Toobin, "Killing Habeas Corpus: Arlen Specter's about-face," The New Yorker (4 Dec. 2006).

[483] Agreements ostensibly binding U.S. policy were the Geneva Convention Relative to the Treatment of Prisoners of War, adopted August 12, 1949, 6 U.S.T. 3317 ("GPW") and the Geneva Convention Relative to the Protection of Civilian Persons in Time of War, adopted August 12, 1949, 6 U.S.T. 3516 ("GC").

detainees had access to federal courts, and that habeas corpus does extend to Guantánamo. In *Rasul v. Bush*, "the U.S. Supreme Court held that U.S. courts have jurisdiction pursuant to 28 U.S.C. § 2241 to hear legal challenges on behalf of persons, including non-citizens, detained at the U.S. Naval Station in Guantánamo Bay, Cuba, in connection with the war against terrorism."[484] Writing for a 6-3 majority, Justice John Paul Stevens quoted from Justice Jackson: "[e]xecutive imprisonment has been considered oppressive and lawless since John, at Runnymede, pledged that no free man should be imprisoned, dispossessed, outlawed, or exiled save by the judgment of his peers or by the law of the land. The judges of England developed the writ of habeas corpus largely to preserve these immunities from executive restraint."[485] The majority found that "Congress, by *statute*, had intended to give habeas rights to alien enemy combatants."[486]

> Rasul's lawyers did not argue and the Court did not rule on whether Rasul had a constitutional right to habeas – that particular issue was deferred for the moment. The Court relied

---

[484] *Rasul v. Bush*, 542 U.S. 466 (2004). See Jennifer K. Elsea and Kenneth R. Thomas, Legislative Attorneys, American Law Division, Enemy Combatant Detainees: *Habeas Corpus* Challenges in Federal Court CRS Report for Congress (updated January 28, 2008), available at http://www.policyarchive.org/handle/10207/bitstreams/2654_Previous_Version_2008-01-28.pdf; "Summary: Key Moments in the Detainee Rights Battle," CQ Weekly Online (10 Dec. 2007): 3637, available at http://library.cqpress.com/cqweekly/weeklyreport110-000002638876 (accessed October 20, 2008); Keith Perine, Keith, "Supreme Court Hands Congress the Lead in Rewriting Terror Suspect Detention Rules," CQ Weekly Online (3 Jul. 2004): 1628-1629, available at http://library.cqpress.com/cqweekly/weeklyreport108-000001233692 (accessed October 20, 2008).

[485] Opinion of Justice John Paul Stevens in *Rasul v. Bush*, 542 U.S. ___, 5-6 (2004), citing, Robert H. Jackson, *Shaughnessy v. United States ex rel. Mezei*, 345 U.S. 206, 218-219 (1953) (dissenting opinion).

[486] William J. Quirk, Courts & Congress: America's Unwritten Constitution (New Brunswick (U.S.A.): Transaction Publishers, 2008), 73, citing, *Rasul v. Bush*, 542 U.S. 466 (2004). Emphasis in original.

on the fact the habeas statute did not specify that it was limited to citizens. So, reasoned the Court, the statute applies to alien enemy combatants picked up in Afghanistan and held in Guantánamo. The Court further held the habeas statute extended to aliens held at Guantánamo because, although the detainees themselves were beyond the Court's jurisdiction, the Court had jurisdiction over the detainees' custodians, *i.e.*, the U.S. Government, and that was sufficient for subject matter jurisdiction.[487]

In *Hamdi v. Rumsfeld,_* the Court ruled that Yaser Esam Hamdi, a U.S. citizen (Hamdi was born in the United States but had lived most of his life in Saudi Arabia) captured in Afghanistan allegedly taking part in hostile action against U.S. forces, must be tried and could not be held indefinitely.[488] The "Court ruled . . . the president had the authority to detain him under the law, enacted just after the Sept. 11 terrorist attacks, that authorized the use of military force in Afghanistan, but that he was entitled to challenge the basis of his detention before 'a neutral decision-maker.'"[489] Justice O'Connor stated

> We have long since made clear that a state of war is not a blank check for the President when it comes to the rights of the Nation's citizens. . . . Whatever power the United States Constitution envisions for the Executive in its exchanges with other nations or with enemy organizations in times of conflict, it most assuredly envisions a role for all three branches when individual liberties are at stake. . . . Absent suspension [of

---

[487] William J. Quirk, Courts & Congress: America's Unwritten Constitution (New Brunswick (U.S.A.): Transaction Publishers, 2008), 73-74. Emphasis in original.

[488] 542 U.S. 507 (2004).

[489] Jacob Freedman, "Different Circumstances, Different Rights for Detainees," CQ Weekly Online (21 Nov. 2005): 3117, available at http://library.cqpress.com/cqweekly/weeklyreport109-000001975392 (accessed October 20, 2008).

> habeas corpus] by Congress, a citizen detained as an enemy combatant is entitled to this process.[490]

Nine days after these rulings, the Department of Defense issued new guidelines creating Combatant Status Review Tribunals to identify more precisely "enemy combatants."

In October of the next year, after almost four years and initial resistance from the Administration, Congress took substantive action by passing the Detainee Treatment Act.[491] It was designed to overrule *Rasul* by eliminating statutory habeas jurisdiction for detainees at Guantánamo in federal courts. It stipulated that "no court, justice or judge shall have jurisdiction to . . . consider . . . an application for . . . habeas corpus filed by or on behalf of an alien detained by the Department of Defense at Guantanamo." [492] The Act only allowed for limited review of final tribunal decisions by the D.C. Circuit Court.

---

[490] *Hamdi v. Rumsfeld*, 542 U.S. ___, 29 (2004). Keith Perine, Keith, "Supreme Court Hands Congress the Lead in Rewriting Terror Suspect Detention Rules," CQ Weekly Online (3 Jul. 2004): 1628-1629, available at http://library.cqpress.com/cqweekly/weeklyreport108-000001233692 (accessed October 20, 2008). Freedman adds, "Hamdi was deported to Saudi Arabia last year after he agreed to renounce his U.S. citizenship and never return." Jacob Freedman, "Different Circumstances, Different Rights for Detainees," CQ Weekly Online (21 Nov. 2005): 3117, available at http://library.cqpress.com/cqweekly/weeklyreport109-000001975392 (accessed October 20, 2008). The final decision emerging from the Court in June 2004 involved Jose Padilla, a U.S. citizen arrested within the United States and charged with being an enemy combatant. In *Rumsfeld v. Padilla*, the Court ruled that because the Secretary of Defense was not Jose Padilla's "immediate custodian" the habeas corpus petition had been improperly filed (542 U.S. 426 (2004)). See Freedman, "Different Circumstances, Different Rights for Detainees," 3117.

[491] The Act, Detainee Treatment Act of 2005 (DTA), Pub. L. No. 109-148, 119 Stat. 2739 (codified as amended in scattered sections of 1, 5, 10, 15, 16, 28, 37, 41, 42, and 50 U.S.C.), was actually an amendment to the 2006 Department of Defense Authorization Bill.

[492] 28 U.S.C. § 2241(e)(1)(2006).

Nine months later, on the 29th of June 2006, the Supreme Court issued their ruling in *Hamdan v. Rumsfeld*, a military tribunal case. Hamdan, a Yemeni national fighting in Afghanistan, had been captured in November 2001 after allegedly having worked for Osama Bin Laden as a bodyguard and driver.[493] He was transported to Guantánamo in June 2002 and in July of the next year President Bush declared Hamdan eligible for trial by military commission. After over two-and-a-half years of detention, Hamdan was formally charged with conspiracy in July 2004 but the District of Columbia District Court determined Hamdan could not be tried by a military commission not specifically approved by Congress and that the commission procedures were inconsistent with the Uniform Code of Military Justice. On appeal, the District of Columbia Circuit Court reversed the decision of the District Court, concluding Congress *had* authorized the military commissions and Hamdan was required to exhaust the military remedies available.

In June 2006, the Supreme Court, in a 5-3 vote, reversed the Court of Appeals, finding that the procedures and structure of the military commissions in fact violated the Geneva Conventions, the Uniform Code of Military Justice, and remanded the case "for further proceedings."[494] The Court held the stripping provision of the Detainee Treatment Act was not retroactive and thus it had jurisdiction to hear the pending habeas petitions.[495] In addition, "[w]ith respect to the authority to create the military commissions,_ the Court held that any power to create them must flow from the Constitution and must be among those 'powers granted jointly to the President and Congress in time of war.'"[496]

---

493 William J. Quirk, Courts & Congress: America's Unwritten Constitution (New Brunswick (U.S.A.): Transaction Publishers, 2008), 79; Jennifer K. Elsea and Kenneth R. Thomas, Legislative Attorneys, American Law Division, Enemy Combatant Detainees: *Habeas Corpus* Challenges in Federal Court, CRS Report for Congress (updated January 28, 2008): 11.

494 *Hamdan v. Rumsfeld*, 548 U.S. 557 (2006).

495 548 U.S. 557 (2006).

496 Jennifer K. Elsea and Kenneth R. Thomas, Legislative Attorneys, American Law Division, Enemy Combatant Detainees: *Habeas Corpus* Challenges in Federal Court, CRS Report for Congress (updated January 28, 2008): 13,

Four months later, Congress responded to *Hamdan v. Rumsfeld* by passing the Military Commissions Act of 2006.[497] After debate on September 27th and 28th, the bill passed the Senate 65-34. It passed the House 250-170 the very next day and President Bush signed it into law on October 17, 2006.[498] The Act repudiated *Hamdan* by specifically authorizing military commissions to try those who engage in or materially support hostilities against the United States or its allies, allowed for more relaxed rules for bringing detainees to trial, created a new appellate body, the Court of Military Commission Review, and explicitly said there was no right of habeas corpus for Guantánamo detainees within federal court jurisdiction, *including* pending cases. Only a D.C. Circuit Court review was allowed.[499] An amendment sponsored by Sens. Arlen Specter and Patrick Leahy to preserve habeas corpus was defeated by three votes. At the very end of the 109th Congress, S. 4081, the Habeas Corpus Restoration Act, was introduced in the Senate.[500]

---

citing, *Hamdan*, slip op. at 27 (citing Congress's powers to "declare War . . . and make Rules concerning Captures on Land and Water," Art. I, §8, cl. 11, to "raise and support Armies." Id., cl. 12, to "define and punish . . . Offences against the Law of Nations," Id., cl. 10, and "To make Rules for the Government and Regulation of the land and naval Forces," Id., cl. 14.).

[497] PL 109-366.

[498] At least one member of the Senate felt the vote on the Military Commissions Act was deliberately and hastily scheduled right before the midterm election. See Sen. Patrick Leahy (D-VT), Congressional Record, 110th Cong., 1st sess., 2007, vol. 153, no. 1, S180 (4 Jan. 2007).

[499] Military Commissions Act of 2006 § 7(a), 28 U.S.C.A. § 2241(e)(1)(Supp. 2009), which stated "No court, justice, or judge shall have jurisdiction to hear or consider an application for a writ of habeas corpus filed by or on behalf of an alien detained by the United States who has been determined by the United States to have been properly detained as an enemy combatant or is awaiting such determination." See also, William J. Quirk, Courts & Congress: America's Unwritten Constitution (New Brunswick (U.S.A.): Transaction Publishers, 2008), 81.

[500] Sen. Specter (R-PA) introduced it on December 5, 2006.

LEGISLATIVE HISTORY

At the beginning of the 110th Congress, S. 185, "A bill to restore habeas corpus for those detained by the United States," was introduced again by Sen. Specter, this time with 31 other co-sponsors.[501] Specter again made introductory remarks, the bill was read twice, and then referred to the Senate Judiciary Committee. The bill language stipulated that it

> [r]epeals provisions of the Military Commissions Act of 2006 that eliminated the jurisdiction of any court to hear or consider applications for a writ of habeas corpus filed by aliens who have been determined by the United States to have been properly detained as enemy combatants (or who are awaiting such determination) and actions against the United States relating to the detention of such aliens and to military commissions (thus restoring habeas corpus rights existing prior to the enactment of such Act). Allows courts to hear or consider legal challenges to military commissions only as provided by the Code of Military Justice or by a habeas corpus proceeding.[502]

In February, the D.C. Court of Appeals upheld the Military Commission Act's restrictions on habeas for detainees.[503] On June 7th, 2007, the Senate Judiciary Committee ordered the Habeas bill to be

---

501 S. 185 was introduced on January 4th, 2007. Five different House bills were also listed as being related to S. 185 by THOMAS: H.R. 267, H.R. 1189, H.R. 1416, H.R. 2543, and H.R. 2826. All but one received no further attention than introduction and referral. H.R. 2826 did receive one respective subcommittee consideration.

502 Located on THOMAS (Library of Congress), available at http://thomas.loc.gov.

503 *Boumediene v. Bush*, 476 F.3d 981 (D.C. Cir. 2007) (consolidated appeal of *Kalid v. Bush* and *In re Guantanamo Detainee Cases*). Jennifer K. Elsea and Kenneth R. Thomas, Legislative Attorneys, American Law Division, Enemy Combatant Detainees: Habeas Corpus Challenges in Federal Court, CRS Report for Congress (updated January 28, 2008): 9-10, 25.

reported favorably without amendment and on June 26th the bill was reported without amendment with written report No. 110-90 and additional majority and minority views filed. Sen. Specter was the only Republican to vote for the bill and in the report, "five of the panel's GOP members said the legislation could force the government to choose between revealing secret intelligence sources and methods and releasing committed terrorists."[504] That same day, the bill was placed on the Senate Legislative Calendar (Calendar No. 220) under General Orders. Finally, the bill was placed as an amendment to the fiscal 2008 defense authorization bill, considered in July. Majority Leader Harry Reid then pulled the bill due to a Republican filibuster.[505]

In 2001, the Patriot Act passed Congress virtually unopposed.[506] At that time, one member of the Senate said he did not "believe there [was] anything in the administration's bill that the Supreme Court would conclude violates the Constitution of the United States."[507] Another said the Act "raises none of the great constitutional issues that have confronted the country in prior wars."[508] While these statements were made solely in relation to that specific piece of legislation, that view would change as it applied to detainees in the "war on terror."

---

[504] Keith Perine, "Fall Agenda: Habeas Corpus for Detainees," CQ Weekly Online (3 Sept. 2007): 2554, available at http://library.cqpress.com/cqweekly/weeklyreport110-000002576956 (accessed October 19, 2007).

[505] The filibuster was related to a separate amendment on Iraq. Keith Perine, "Fall Agenda: Habeas Corpus for Detainees," CQ Weekly Online (3 Sept. 2007): 2554, available at http://library.cqpress.com/cq weekly/weeklyreport110-000002576956 (accessed October 19, 2007).

[506] The vote in the House of Representatives was 357-66. The vote in the Senate was 98-1.

[507] Sen. Orrin Hatch (R-UT), Congress, Senate, Committee on the Judiciary, Subcommittee on the Constitution, Federalism, and Property Rights, Protecting Constitutional Freedoms in the Face of Terrorism, hearing, 107th Cong., 1st sess., 3 Oct. 2001 (Washington, D.C.: GPO, 2001), 5.

[508] Sen. Jeff Sessions (R-AL) Congress, Senate, Committee on the Judiciary, Subcommittee on the Constitution, Federalism, and Property Rights, Protecting Constitutional Freedoms in the Face of Terrorism, hearing, 107th Cong., 1st sess., 3 Oct. 2001 (Washington, D.C.: GPO, 2001), 7.

DELIBERATION

GENERIC EXPRESSION

Surrounding the 2007 Act, members sometimes made an appeal to authority through an expression of, acknowledgement to, or belief about, the Constitution, the constitutional text, or their constitutional prerogative with no citation to text or constitutional reasoning. For example, during debate over the Detainee Treatment Act, a senator remarked, "[s]o I am pleased to support the amendment. . . . I hope the military will . . . continue to gather intelligence in dealing with these terrorist networks . . . but do it in a way that is consistent with the intent, the principle, and the philosophy of our Constitution."[509] After passage of that same bill, another simply stated a refrain that would often be repeated: "[t]here has never been a constitutional right for that [granting habeas to enemy combatants]."[510] During debate over the Military Commissions Act of 2006, one member asserted:

> This is a constitutional issue. The debate today will undoubtedly go down in the annals of our country as being one that stands out as a study in constitutional law and duty thereunder. Our duty as Members of Congress is to uphold the Constitution. That is what I intend to do in my speech and in my vote. . . . But also it is our duty to pass legislation that is constitutional. I have serious questions as to whether this is constitutional or not.[511]

Another declared: "[e]very one of us has sworn an oath to uphold the Constitution. In order to uphold that oath, I believe we have a duty to vote . . . against this irresponsible and flagrantly unconstitutional bill. That is what I will do. . . . Th[is] Senator . . . answers to the

---

[509] Sen. John Sununu (R-NH), Congressional Record, 109th Cong., 1st sess., 2005, vol. 151, pt. 128, S11068 (5 Oct. 2005).

[510] Sen. Lindsey Graham (R-SC), Congressional Record, 109th Cong., 1st sess., 2005, vol. 151, pt. 150, S12732 (14 Nov. 2005).

[511] Rep. Ike Skelton (D-MO), Congressional Record, 109th Cong., 2nd sess., 2006, vol. 152, pt. 123, H7536 (27 Sept. 2006).

Constitution and to his conscience. . . . not . . . to political pressure."[512] While another followed by stating, "[h]abeas, which is also known as the Great Writ, is one of the most fundamental protections against arbitrary governmental power. This right dates back to the Magna Carta of 1215, and is enshrined in Article I, section 9, clause 2 of the U.S. Constitution."[513]

Members also frequently expressed that restricting habeas was wrong but not articulate the basis for that judgment: "[t]here are numerous constitutional challenges regarding this legislation. . . . [one being] [t]he provisions that strip the Federal courts of jurisdiction over habeas corpus."[514] Or, as was most common, they might simply state their belief about the issue in non-constitutional rhetoric. The following argument was emblematic of many used by those opposed to granting habeas to detainees:

> What is going on here is our body politic, the people, are under attack from foreigners, a different people. They are trying to impose their will on us and kill us. In that situation, the very notion of the judiciary backing off and playing some role as a neutral arbiter between the people of the United States and a foreign adversary is ludicrous and perverse. The idea that we can fight a war with the same degree of perfection we try to impose on our law enforcement system, which is to say we will not tolerate any collateral damage in law enforcement and we have to be absolutely mistake-free—to try to use those rules and impose them on a war-fighting machine, to say it has to be absolutely perfect and we can't hold anyone in detention and they have all kinds of due process—the idea that a foreign person that our troops believe is a combatant is going to be held, you know, and we are going to turn the earth upside down and turn our army into

---

[512] Sen. Patrick Leahy (D-VT), Congressional Record, 109th Cong., 2nd sess., 2006, vol. 152, pt. 123, S10359 (27 Sept. 2006).

[513] Sen. Jeff Bingaman, (D-NM), Congressional Record, 109th Cong., 2nd sess., 2006, vol. 152, pt. 123, S10260-61 (27 Sept. 2006).

[514] Rep. Ike Skelton (D-MO), Congressional Record, 109th Cong., 2nd sess., 2006, vol. 152, pt. 123, H7536 (27 Sept. 2006).

> detectives to figure out whether it is true or not is ridiculous. We will lose wars. We will lose our freedom.[515]

OTHER VALUES

Other times, instead of stating simple declaratory views on the Constitution, a specific piece of legislation, or event related to habeas, members proclaimed all of the important "values" that would be either harmed or strengthened by pertinent behavior and action related to habeas corpus.

The writ of habeas corpus was described as "a *critical tenet* of our justice system. . . . [a] *basic tenet*[,] . . . [a] *critical individual right* against arbitrary arrest and imprisonment.[516] It was "a *cornerstone of American liberty* since the founding of this Nation,"[517] a "*fundamental protection*" and part of the then-necessary "revitaliz[ation of] our tradition of checks and balances."[518] Habeas was part of "the *very foundation* upon which our Nation was established."[519] Habeas rights were "*fundamental rights*"[520] and vital if we wish "to uphold our commitments to the rule of law."[521] It was argued that "the Constitution

---

[515] Former Attorney General, William P. Barr, Congress, Senate, Committee on the Judiciary, Detainees, hearing, 109th Cong., 1st sess., 15 June 2005 (Washington, D.C.: GPO, 2006), 62-63.

[516] Rep. Adam Schiff (D-CA), Congressional Record, 107th Cong., 2nd sess., 2002, vol. 148, pt. 91, H4403 (9 Jul. 2002). Emphasis added.

[517] Sen. Patrick Leahy (D-VT), Congressional Record, 110th Cong., 1st sess., 2007, vol. 153, no. 1, S180 (4 Jan. 2007). Emphasis added.

[518] Sen. Patrick Leahy (D-VT), Congressional Record, 110th Cong., 1st sess., 2007, vol. 153, no. 1, S180 (4 Jan. 2007). Emphasis added.

[519] Sen. Christopher Dodd (D-CT), during debate over the Military Commissions Act, Congressional Record, 109th Cong., 2nd sess., 2006, vol. 152, pt. 124, S10352-10353 (28 Sept. 2006). Emphasis added.

[520] Sen. Arlen Specter (R-PA), Congressional Record, 109th Cong., 1st sess., 2005, vol. 151, pt. 151, S12801 (15 Nov. 2005). Emphasis added.

[521] Sen. Patrick Leahy (D-VT), Congressional Record, 109th Cong., 1st sess., 2005, vol. 151, no. 151, S12801 (11 Nov. 2005).

doesn't protect just our citizens, it protects people"[522] and that "[w]e're losing the larger battle for ideas, which is, as I like to put it, means that somehow we found a way to lose a PR war to Osama bin Laden. *This is a piece of it, okay?*"[523]

A refusal to grant habeas to detainees would be a failure to "uphold American values and the rule of law."[524] Habeas restrictions would be "repugnant to our Nation's values"[525] and would "set back basic rights by some 900 years."[526] Thus, Congress should "work to preserve the principles of human rights and the rule of law upon which this Nation was founded."[527] Efforts to strip habeas were "wrong . . . .

---

[522] Rep. Roscoe E. Bartlett (R-MD), Congress, House, Committee on Armed Services, Upholding the Principle of Habeas Corpus for Detainees, hearing, 110th Cong., 1st sess., 26 July 2007 (Federal News Service, Inc., 2007), 11. This statements echoes Jefferson's earlier quote ("The Habeas Corpus secures every man here, alien or citizen, against everything which is not law, whatever shape it may assume") and it is surprising those in favor of granting habeas to detainees didn't use it more frequently. Jefferson does insert the word "here", but nevertheless, its employable historical rhetoric since one could argue, using Jefferson's statement, that habeas should not be prohibited from aliens.

[523] Rep. Adam Smith (D-WA), Congress, House, Committee on Armed Services, Upholding the Principle of Habeas Corpus for Detainees, hearing, 110th Cong., 1st sess., 26 July 2007 (Federal News Service, Inc., 2007), 13. Emphasis added.

[524] Rep. Benjamin Cardin (D-MD), during debate over the Military Commissions Act. Congressional Record, 109th Cong., 2nd sess., 2006, vol. 152, pt. 123, H7555 (27 Sept. 2006).

[525] Sen. Jeff Bingaman (D-NM), Congressional Record, 109th Cong., 1st sess., 2005, vol. 151, no. 167, S14310 (15 Nov. 2005).

[526] Sen. Arlen Specter (R-PA), during debate over the Military Commissions Act. Congressional Record, 109th Cong., 2nd sess., 2006, vol. 152, pt. 123, S10265 (27 Sept. 2006).

[527] Sen. Harry Reid (D-NV), Congressional Record, 109th Cong., 1st sess., 2005, vol. 151, pt. 151, p. S 12777 (15 Nov. 2005). S12803. For one other, among many over this time period, example of an appeal to human rights, see Sen.

unconstitutional . . . . and un-American."[528] To restrict habeas would be to "lower[] our moral standards in how we treat prisoners of war, [and to] . . . encourage other countries to do the same.[529] During debate over the Military Commissions Act, Rep. Jerry Nadler summed up this position:

> Mr. Speaker, this is how a nation loses its moral compass, its identity, its values, and ultimately its freedom to fear. . . . We rebelled against King George III for far less infringements on liberty than this 200 years ago, but we seem to have forgotten. This bill makes the President a dictator – for when someone can order people jailed forever without subject to any judicial review. That is dictatorial power. The President wants to exist in a law-free zone. He does not want to be bound by the law of war or by our treaty obligations. He does not want to answer to our Constitution, to the Congress or to the Courts.[530]

Sen. Leahy was especially aggrieved. He said:

> We have eliminated basic legal and human rights for the 12 million lawful permanent residents who live and work among us. . . . We have removed a vital check that our legal system provides against the government arbitrarily detaining people for life without charge. . . . We have removed the mechanism the Constitution provides to check government overreaching and lawlessness. . . . We should not outsource our moral, legal and constitutional responsibility to the courts. Congress must

---

Christopher Dodd (D-CT), Congressional Record, 110th Cong., 1st sess., 2007, vol. 153, no. 137, 11562-63 (17 Sept. 2007).

[528] Sen. Patrick Leahy (D-VT), Congressional Record, 109th Cong., 2nd sess., 2006, vol. 152, no. 132, S11199 (5 Dec. 2006).

[529] Rep. Jerry Costello (D-IL), during debate over the Military Commissions Act, Congressional Record, 109th Cong., 2nd sess., 2006, vol. 152, pt. 124, E1891 (28 Sept. 2006).

[530] Rep. Jerry Nadler (D-NY), Congressional Record, 109th Cong., 2nd sess., 2006, vol. 152, no. 123, H7550.

> be accountable for its actions and we should act to right this wrong. . . . It is from strength that America should defend our values and our Constitution. . . . In standing up for American values and security, I will keep working on this issue until we restore the checks and balances that are fundamental to preserving the liberties that define us as a nation. We can ensure our security without giving up our liberty.[531]

In March of that same year, Leahy would again take to the floor: "[a]bolishing habeas corpus for anyone who the Government thinks might have assisted enemies of the United States is unnecessary and morally wrong. It is a betrayal of the most basic values of freedom for which America stands. It makes a mockery of the administration's lofty rhetoric about exporting freedom across the globe.[532] In July 2007, Sen. Feinstein would echo these themes in debate over the proposed Habeas Restoration bill.

> The simple fact remains that Guantanamo violates our values and our traditions, including respect for the rule of law and for human rights. . . . We will fight terror with vigor and drive and purpose, but we must not forget who we are. We are a nation of laws. We are a nation of value and tradition. These values have been admired throughout the decades all over the world. . . . The world has looked at Guantanamo and made the judgment that it is wrong. I think it is time for the Senate to do something about it. The Senate has borne the burden of

---

[531] Sen. Patrick Leahy (D-VT), Congressional Record, 110th Cong., 1st sess., 2007, vol. 153, no. 1, S181 (4 Jan. 2007).

[532] Sen. Patrick Leahy (D-VT), Congressional Record, 110th Cong., 1st sess., 2007, vol. 153, pt. 41, S2963 (9 Mar. 2007). Leahy had already stated and would repeat these remarks several times over the next several months. See Sen. Patrick Leahy (D-VT), Congressional Record, 110th Cong., 1st sess., 2007, vol. 153, no. 1, S181 (4 Jan. 2007); Congressional Record, 110th Cong., 1st sess., 2007, vol. 153, pt. 41, S2962-63 (9 Mar. 2007); Congressional Record, 110th Cong., 1st sess., 2007, vol. 153, no. 109, S8908-8909 (10 Jul. 2007); Congressional Record, 110th Cong., 1st sess., 2007, vol. 153, no. 137, S11542-43 (17 Sept. 2007).

> Guantanamo for too long. The time has come to close it down.[533]

In September, Leahy concluded by saying:

> I hope all Senators will now join with us in restoring basic American values and the rule of law, while making our Nation stronger. . . . It is from strength that America should defend our values and our way of life. It is from the strength of our freedoms, our Constitution, and the rule of law that we shall prevail. I hope all in the Senate, Republicans and Democrats, will join us in standing up for a stronger America, for the America we believe in, and support the Habeas Corpus Restoration Act of 2007.[534]

Conversely, to affirmatively grant habeas to detainees would be to depart "from longstanding principles in our Anglo-American legal tradition" and to do "something . . . fundamentally drastic . . . [and] different from anything that has ever been done in the history of this Nation."[535] Sen. Graham summarized this view during debate over the Detainee Treatment Act. He said:

> If you want to give a Guantanamo Bay detainee habeas corpus rights as a U.S. citizen, not only have you changed the law of armed conflict like no one else in the history of the world, I think you are undermining our national security because the habeas petitions are flowing out of that place like crazy. There are 500-some people down there, and there are 160 habeas corpus petitions in Federal courts throughout the United States. Three hundred of them have lawyers in Federal court

---

[533] Sen. Dianne Feinstein (D-CA), Congressional Record, 110th Cong., 1st sess., 2007, vol. 153, no. 113, S9234-35 (16 Jul. 2007).

[534] Sen. Patrick Leahy (D-VT), Congressional Record, 110th Cong., 1st sess., 2007, vol. 153, pt. 137, S11543 (17 Sept. 2007).

[535] Rep. Dan Lungren (R-CA), Congressional Record, 110th Cong., 1st sess., 2007, vol. 153, no. 144, H10935-36 (26 Sept. 2007).

> and more to follow. We cannot run the place. . . . I want to end with this thought. Never in the history of military commissions where we have tried enemy combatants and spies have they appealed those convictions to Federal court. Never.[536]

ARTICLE I SECTION 8

Despite these aforementioned common and generic references, many members were more specific about Congress's specific constitutional powers, because, while the President has important Commander-in-Chief powers, by definition Congress cannot help but be involved in issues dealing with habeas corpus and foreign persons. They have specific textual authority.[537]

As early as two months after the attacks, some members believed Congress should take the initiative and constitute proper constitutional "rules" for handling this new terrorism-focused situation. During discussion of his proposed Military Commission Procedures Act of 2002, Sen. Specter said:

> it is a matter that I believe ought to be considered by the Congress, because under the Constitution the Congress has the authority to establish military courts and tribunals dealing with international law. . . . The Constitution provides that the Congress is empowered to define and punish violations of international law, as well as to establish courts with exclusive jurisdiction over military offenses. Under articles of war, enacted by Congress, and statutes, the President does have the authority to convene military commissions to try offenses against the law of war. Military commissions could be convened to try offenses, whether committed by U.S. service members, civilian U.S. citizens, or enemy aliens, and a state of war need not exist. So there has been a delegation of authority

---

[536] Sen. Lindsey Graham (R-SC), Congressional Record, 109th Cong., 1st sess., 2005, vol. 151, no. 149, S12656, S12665 (10 Nov. 2005).

[537] "The Congress shall have Power To . . . define and punish . . . Offences against the Law of Nations. . . . declare War . . . and make Rules concerning Captures on Land and Water[.]" U.S. Constitution, art. 1, sec. 8, cl. 10, 11.

> by the Congress. But under the Constitution it is the Congress that has the authority to establish the parameters and the proceedings under such courts.[538]

Sen. Durbin agreed, stating, "[u]nder the Constitution Congress must also accept responsibility, and under Article I, Section 8 of the Constitution, it is my belief that Congress has the sole authority to declare war."[539] Sen. Leahy also agreed, maintaining "[t]he Constitution entrusts the Congress with the power to 'define and punish . . . offenses against the laws of nations.'"[540] Sen. Specter referred to their attempt years later when he would again reference these powers:

> Shortly after 9/11, on February 13, Senator Durbin and I introduced legislation which would have dealt with the military commission procedures. This is pursuant to the provisions of article I, section 8, clauses 10 and 11 of the Constitution, which confers upon the Congress the power 'To define and punish . . . Offenses against the Law of Nations; . . .[and] make Rules concerning Captures on Land and Water.'[541]

In the House of Representatives, Rep. Zoe Lofgren and Rep. Jane Harman "introduced legislation . . . that would authorize the tribunals with the stipulation that suspects be guaranteed the habeas corpus right

---

[538] Sen. Arlen Specter (R-PA), Congressional Record, 107th Cong., 1st sess., 2001, vol. 147, pt. 158, S11888 (15 Nov. 2001).

[539] Sen. Richard Durbin (D-IL), Congress, Senate, Committee on the Judiciary, Department of Justice Oversight: Preserving Our Freedoms While Defending Against Terrorism, hearing, 107th Cong., 1st sess., 28 Nov., 4 Dec., 6 Dec., 2001 (Washington, D.C.: GPO, 2001): 151.

[540] Sen. Patrick Leahy (D-VT), Congress, Senate, Committee on the Judiciary, Department of Justice Oversight: Preserving Our Freedoms While Defending Against Terrorism, hearing, 107th Cong., 1st sess., 28 Nov., 4 Dec., 6 Dec., 2001 (Washington, D.C.: GPO, 2001): 3.

[541] Sen. Arlen Specter (R-PA), Congressional Record, 109th Cong., 1st sess., 2005, vol. 151, pt. 149, S12658 (10 Nov. 2005).

to challenge the government's right to hold them."[542] On December 12, 2001, Rep. Harman said:

> Today my colleague Zoe Lofgren and I are introducing legislation to authorize the President to use military tribunals to try foreign terrorists captured abroad. . . . The Administration's intention is to interview those who could provide information, and to prosecute the senior leadership. . . . This is a good strategy, and I support it. . . . But to execute that strategy consistent with Constitutional requirements, the use of those tribunals needs specific authorization from Congress.[543]

Rep. Harman would repeat this argument five years later during debate over the Military Commissions Act: "Mr. Speaker, I take a back seat to no one in my effort to understand the threats against us, find those who would cause us harm, and prevent them from harming us. I also believe strongly that Congress must act under article I, section 8 of the Constitution to regulate "captures on land and on water."[544]

In February 2002, during discussion of his proposed Military Commission Procedures Act of 2002, Sen. Specter emphasized the same clause:

> The President issued an order establishing generalized procedures for trying members of al-Qaida and the Taliban. It is my view . . . that Congress ought to consider what are the appropriate procedures pursuant to our authority under the Constitution, article I, section 8, which gives to the Congress

---

[542] Adriel Bettelheim, "Lawmakers Still Feeling Their Way On Whether to Intervene In Plan for Military Tribunals," CQ Weekly Online (15 Dec. 2001): 2984, available at http://library.cqpress.com/cqweekly/weeklyreport107-000000356326 (accessed October 20, 2008).

[543] Rep. Jane Harman (D-CA), Congressional Record, 107th Cong., 1st sess., 2001, vol. 147, pt. 173, E2284-85 (13 Dec. 2001).

[544] Rep. Jane Harman (D-CA), Congressional Record, 109th Cong., 2nd sess., 2006, vol. 152, pt. 123, H7538 (27 Sept. 2006).

> the responsibility and authority 'To define and punish . . . Offenses against the Law of Nations.'[545]

In July 2002, Rep. Adam Schiff would too rely on Article 1, Section 8 in offering his own Military Tribunals Act, explaining that:

> Article I, section 8 of the Constitution provides that it is the Congress that has the power to constitute tribunals inferior to the Supreme Court to define and punish offenses against the law of nations. . . . Some would argue, not implausibly, that despite the clear language of article I, section 8, congressional authorization is not necessary; that as President and commander in chief, he has the authority, all the authority he needs, to regulate the affairs of the military, and this power extends to the adjudication of unlawful combatants. Ultimately, if the Congress fails to act, any adjudications of the military tribunals will be challenged in court on the basis that the tribunals, having been improperly constituted, the sentences cannot stand.[546]

Three years later (after the three important cases had been handed down in June 2004), Chairman Specter began hearings over detainees by stating that "[t]he starting point of this issue is the Constitution of the United States. Under Article I, section 8, clauses 10 and 11, the Constitution explicitly confers upon Congress the power ''to define and punish offenses against the laws of nations'' and ''to make rules concerning captures on land and water.''[547] During that same hearing, Sen. Feinstein remarked:

---

[545] Sen. Arlen Specter (R-PA), Congressional Record, 107th Cong., 2nd sess., 2002, vol. 148, pt. 13, S733-34 (13 Feb. 2002).

[546] Rep. Adam Schiff (D-CA), mentioned in relation to his proposed Military Tribunals Act of 2002, Congressional Record, 107th Cong., 2nd sess., 2002, vol. 148, pt. 91, H4402-4403 (9 Jul. 2002).

[547] Sen. Arlen Specter (R-PA), Congress, Senate, Committee on the Judiciary, Detainees, hearing, 109th Cong., 1st sess., 15 June 2005 (Washington, D.C.: GPO, 2006), 1-3.

> It has been my view that Congress has both the power and the responsibility to take on the issue of detentions and interrogations, specifically pursuant to two clauses of section 8, to make rules concerning captures on land and water, and to make rules for the government and regulation of the land and naval forces. . . . What is clear to me is that we have the legal responsibility to make the rules and I think we ought to do that.[548]

In October 2005, during debate over the Detainee Treatment Act, Sen. Lamar Alexander said:

> So for the longer term, the people should set the rules. That is why we have an independent Congress. That is our job. In fact, the Constitution says quite clearly that is what Congress should do. Article I, section 8, of the Constitution says that Congress and Congress alone shall have the power to make 'Rules concerning Captures on Land and Water.' So Congress . . . has a responsibility to set clear rules here.[549]

Sen. Leahy[550] and Sen. Feinstein[551] both agreed, as did Sen. McCain who stated:

> All my career I have supported the rights and prerogatives of the Commander in Chief. . . . [but] I would like to point out the Congress not only has the right but the obligation to act. Article I, section 8 of the Constitution of the United States, clause 11: To declare War, grant Letters of Marque and

---

[548] Sen. Dianne Feinstein (D-CA), Congress, Senate, Committee on the Judiciary, Detainees, hearing, 109th Cong., 1st sess., 15 June 2005 (Washington, D.C.: GPO, 2006), 59-60.

[549] Sen. Lamar Alexander (R-TN), Congressional Record, 109th Cong., 1st sess., 2005, vol. 151, pt. 128, S11067 (5 Oct. 2005).

[550] Sen. Patrick Leahy (D-VT), Congressional Record, 109th Cong., 1st sess., 2005, vol. 151, pt. 128, S11070 (5 Oct. 2005).

[551] Sen. Dianne Feinstein (D-CA), Congressional Record, 109th Cong., 1st sess., 2005, vol. 151, pt. 128, S11071 (5 Oct. 2005).

> Reprisal, and make Rules concerning Captures on Land and Water[.] . . . I repeat: . . . make Rules concerning Captures on Land and Water[.] . . . Someone is going to come down to the floor and say that applied back in the time of the Framers of the Constitution; it didn't apply to today. At least from my point of view, unless there is an overriding need to change the Constitution of the United States_if that clause of the Constitution no longer applies, then lets amend the Constitution and remove it; otherwise, lets live by it. . . . The Congress has the responsibility: To declare War, grant Letters of Marque and Reprisal, and make Rules concerning Captures on Land and Water[.][552]

THE SUSPENSION CLAUSE

More directly, the Suspension Clause[553] was quite prominent in habeas discourse. In 2001, during her discussion of the proposed Military Commissions bill, Rep. Harman was adamant: "we make clear that habeas corpus is not waived. Article 1, Section 9 of the Constitution requires action by Congress to suspend this right: a President cannot waive it by military order.[554] Rep. Lofgren followed:

> We are a nation of laws. The most important, our original law, is our Constitution. . . . Article 1, Section 9 provides that the writ of Habeas Corpus may only be suspended when the public safety may require it and then only in cases of rebellion or invasion. Suspension require Congress to act. It is not the President's prerogative. Even President Lincoln, who felt the need to suspend Habeas during the civil war, had to seek and

---

[552] Sen. John McCain (R-AZ), Congressional Record, 109th Cong., 1st sess., 2005, vol. 151, pt. 128, S11071-72 (5 Oct. 2005).

[553] "The Privilege of the Writ of Habeas Corpus shall not be suspended, unless when in Cases of Rebellion or Invasion the public Safety may require it." U.S. Constitution, art. 1, sec. 9, cl. 2.

[554] Rep. Jane Harman (D-CA), Congressional Record, 107th Cong., 1st sess., 2001, vol. 147, pt. 173, E2284-85 (13 Dec. 2001).

> obtain approval from Congress to do so. We have expressly preserved habeas corpus in our bill.[555]

In December of that year, Sen. Specter reminded a witness: "there is a provision in the Executive Order which essentially says that no one can have any redress to the Federal courts or any other court. And that runs directly in conflict with the constitutional provision which says that the writ of habeas corpus may not be suspended except in time of invasion or rebellion."[556] In support of his Military Commission Procedures Act of 2002, Sen. Specter reminded his colleagues: "[i]n the President's order, there was a provision that there could be no appeal from any order of the military tribunal. But that, on its face, was inconsistent with the Constitution, which preserves the right of habeas corpus unless there is rebellion or invasion, neither of which had occurred here."[557] During debate over the Military Commissions Act, Rep. Zofgren reminded her House colleagues:

> We all took an oath to defend and uphold the Constitution of the United States, and here is what article I, section 9 says: 'the privilege of the writ of habeas corpus shall not be suspended unless when in cases of rebellion or invasion the public safety may require it.' . . . Congress may not suspend the great writ of habeas corpus and limit the checks and balances whenever it wants to. Congress may do so only in cases of rebellion and invasion, neither of which is present today.[558]

---

[555] Rep. Zoe Lofgren (D-CA), Congressional Record, 107th Cong., 1st sess., 2001, vol. 147, pt. 173, E2285 (13 Dec. 2001).

[556] Sen. Arlen Specter (R-PA), Congress, Senate, Committee on the Judiciary, Department of Justice Oversight: Preserving Our Freedoms While Defending Against Terrorism, hearing, 107th Cong., 1st sess., 28 Nov., 4 Dec., 6 Dec., 2001 (Washington, D.C.: GPO, 2001): 149.

[557] Sen. Arlen Specter (R-PA), Congressional Record, 107th Cong., 2nd sess., 2002, vol. 148, pt. 13, S733-34 (13 Feb. 2002).

[558] Rep. Zoe Lofgren (D-CA), Congressional Record, 109th Cong., 2nd sess., 2006, vol. 152, pt. 123, H7548 (27 Sept. 2006).

Sometimes members began with the assumption the clause applied to all individuals within United States proper and custody, not just citizens, and were thus insistent upon a certain textual interpretation. In introducing the Habeas Act, Sen. Specter proclaimed:

> Mr. President, I will introduce legislation denominated the Habeas Corpus Restoration Act. Last year, in the Military Commissions Act, the constitutional right of habeas corpus was attempted to be abrogated. I fought to pass an amendment to strike that provision of the Act which was voted 51 to 48. I say 'attempted to be abrogated' because, in my legal judgment, that provision in the Act is unconstitutional. . . . It is hard to see how there can be legislation to eliminate the constitutional right to habeas corpus when the Constitution is explicit that habeas corpus may not be suspended except in time of invasion or rebellion, and we do not have either of those circumstances present, as was conceded by the advocates of the legislation last year to take away the right of habeas corpus.[559]

He would repeat these sentiments six months later by stating:

> There can be no doubt that habeas corpus is a constitutional mandate because the Constitution explicitly states that habeas corpus may be suspended only in time of invasion or rebellion, and no one contends that we have either invasion or rebellion. . . . It is true the statute was changed by the Congress of the United States, but the Congress of the United States, by statute, cannot change the constitutional mandate of habeas corpus.[560]

---

[559] Sen. Arlen Specter (R-PA), Congressional Record, 110th Cong., 1st sess., 2007, vol. 153, no. 1, S42 (4 Jan. 2007).

[560] Sen. Arlen Specter (R-PA), Congressional Record, 110th Cong., 1st sess., 2007, vol. 153, no. 109, S8910 (10 Jul. 2007).

During debate over the Military Commissions Act, Sen. Leahy and Sen. Byrd would both issue emphatic statements:

> I would assume the Bush-Cheney administration is not saying we are handling this question of terrorists so poorly that we are under invasion now. And I have no doubt this bill, which will permanently eliminate the writ of habeas corpus for all aliens within and outside the United States whenever the Government says they might be enemy combatants, violates that prohibition. . . . What are we doing? What is going on? That is outrageous. That is running scared. That is so wrong. Is he saying that for 5 years this administration has been allowing an ongoing invasion in the United States and we are not aware of it? Are we going to suspend the great writ on this basis? . . . The habeas provisions of this bill are wrongheaded. They are flagrantly unconstitutional.[561]

> I wonder whether those who drafted the provision in this bill to eliminate habeas corpus have read this clause of the Constitution. Inconceivably, the U.S. Senate is being asked to abolish a fundamental right that has been central to democratic societies, including our own, for centuries. . . . The provision in the bill before us deprives Federal courts of jurisdiction over matters of law that are clearly entrusted to them by the Constitution of the United States. The Constitution is clear on this point: The only two instances in which habeas corpus may be suspended are in the case of a rebellion or an invasion. We are not in the midst of a rebellion, and there is no invasion. It is notable that those who drafted the Constitution deliberately used the word 'suspended.' They did not say that habeas corpus could be forever denied, abolished, revoked, or eliminated. They said that, in only two instances, it could be

---

[561] Sen. Patrick Leahy (D-VT), Congressional Record, 109th Cong., 2nd sess., 2006, vol. 152, pt. 123, S10256-58 (27 Sept. 2006).

> 'suspended,' meaning temporarily. Not forever. Not like in this bill.[562]

After the MCA had passed, Sen. Specter hypothesized that:

> the Federal courts will strike down the provisions in the legislation eliminating Federal court jurisdiction for a number of reasons. One is that the Constitution of the United States is explicit that habeas corpus may be suspended only in time of rebellion or invasion. We are suffering neither of those alternatives at the present time. We have not been invaded, and there has not been a rebellion.[563]

Another House member remarked, "I think the meaning of the suspension clause of the Constitution is that absent some emergency, limited circumstances, this country will not be a party to a situation where any person can be held indefinitely without being confronted with the charges against him or her so there can be some fair and just resolution of those claims."[564] One member summed up the debate over the Clause well: "what divides this discussion . . . is whether or not you think an enemy combatant [who] was captured on a foreign battlefield, a person who has sworn to kill each and every one of us, is covered by the U.S. Constitution."[565]

---

[562] Sen. Robert Byrd (D-WV), Congressional Record, 109th Cong., 2nd sess., 2006, vol. 152, pt. 123, S10366 (27 Sept. 2006).

[563] Sen. Arlen Specter (R-PA), Congressional Record, 109th Cong., 2nd sess., 2006, vol. 152, pt. 132, S11196 (5 Dec. 2006). Sen. Specter had used this same argument previously during debate over the Military Commissions Act. See, Congressional Record, 109th Cong., 2nd sess., 2006, vol. 152, pt. 123, S10264 (27 Sept. 2006).

[564] Rep. Robert Andrews (D-NJ), Congress, House, Committee on Armed Services, Upholding the Principle of Habeas Corpus for Detainees, hearing, 110th Cong., 1st sess., 26 July 2007 (Federal News Service, Inc., 2007), 20.

[565] Rep. Thelma Drake (R-VA), Congress, House, Committee on Armed Services, Upholding the Principle of Habeas Corpus for Detainees, hearing, 110th Cong., 1st sess., 26 July 2007 (Federal News Service, Inc., 2007), 21.

How Many Writs?

During this congressional deliberation there was also a discussion over the content of habeas in the Constitution: whether it was fundamentally a constitutional right or whether the presence of the term in the Constitution confirmed the need for a statutory right which could naturally then be restricted.

There were competing definitions of the writ upon which members differed. One was given, for example, by the Senate Judiciary majority report on the Habeas Bill:

> The writ of habeas corpus protects individuals against unlawful exercises of state power. It provides the means for a person detained by the state to require that the government demonstrate to a neutral judge that there is a factual and legal basis for his or her detention. The writ has roots at least as far back as 16th century England, and beginning with Parliament's passage of the Habeas Corpus Act of 1679, this protection became known as the 'Great Writ.' . . . Habeas corpus has long been a cornerstone of Anglo-Saxon and American legal traditions. At English common law, courts exercised habeas jurisdiction not only within the Crown's formal territorial limits, but also over other areas which the Crown exercised sovereign control. The Great Writ was imported into the laws of all 13 American colonies, and it was one of the first subjects to which the first Congress turned its attention. The Judiciary Act of 1789 specifically empowered federal courts to issue writs of habeas corpus 'for the purpose of an inquiry into the cause of commitment.' . . . Habeas corpus is also the only common law writ mentioned in the Constitution. . . . Thus, the Founders clearly established their intention that habeas corpus serve as a bulwark of individual liberty.[566]

The other was expressed by the Chief Minority Counsel on the Subcommittee on the Constitution, Civil Rights, and Civil Liberties, House Judiciary Committee:

---

[566] Congress, Senate, Senate Report on the Habeas Corpus Restoration Act of 2007, 26 Jun. 2007, 1.

> The Constitution, in referring to the writ of habeas corpus, did not create it, and the writ is understood as being granted by statute, as enacted by the legislature.[567] Professor Erwin Chemerinsky, for example, has explained that '[t]he constitutional provision does not create a right to habeas corpus; rather, federal statutes [do so].'[568] . . . the Founders wrote Article I, Section Nine, Clause Two, in order to ensure that the federal government could not, absent cases of invasion and rebellion, trump state statutes establishing the writ.[569] . . . The Founders understood that the federal writ could be created and altered by statute. The first Congress enacted the first federal habeas corpus protections in the Judiciary Act of 1789,[570] and that Act explicitly prohibited the use of the writ of habeas corpus in certain circumstances.[571] If the Founders had understood that the Constitution created an absolute right to the writ in all circumstances, it would have been anomalous to enact only a partial creation of the writ by statute.[572]

---

567 Once the right is granted by statute, the Constitution requires that it be suspended only when "in Cases of Rebellion or Invasion the public Safety may require it." U.S. Const. art. 1, sec. 9, cl. 2.

568 Erwin Chemerinsky, Federal Jurisdiction, 4th ed. (2003), 864.

569 Id, at 868 ("[T]he Constitutional Convention prevented Congress from obstructing the state courts' ability to grant the writ, but did not try to create a federal constitutional right to habeas corpus.").

570 Judiciary Act of 1789, ch. 20, 1 Stat. 73 (1789).

571 See id. § 14, 1 Stat. at 81-82 ("[W]rits of habeas corpus shall in no case extend to prisoners in gaol [jail], unless where they are in custody, under or by colour of the authority of the United States, or are committed for trial before some court of the same, or as necessary to be brought into court to testify.").

572 See also *Lonchar v. Thomas*, 517 U.S. 314, 323 (1996) (stating that judgments about the proper scope of the writ are "normally for Congress to make"); *Ex parte Bollman*, 8 U.S. (4 Cranch) 75, 94 (1807) (confirming that the jurisdiction of federal courts to issue writs of habeas corpus is not inherent and that "the power to award the writ by any of the courts of the

Some members saw no distinction. For example, during debate over the Military Commissions Act, one member of the House exclaimed that "[t]his bill is flatly unconstitutional, for it repeals the Great Writ_Habeas Corpus. Not a statutory writ, but the Constitutional Great Writ."[573] Another member of the Judiciary Committee agreed, stating: "[an opposing member] keeps trying to tell us that there are two writs of habeas corpus. A wonderful idea, if it were only true."[574]

Others disagreed. One senator remarked that "[w]e have the statutory jurisdiction to write whatever kinds of laws we want. We clearly have the statutory jurisdiction to say it does not apply to foreign terrorists,"[575] while Rep. Lungren stated, "[w]e are not talking about the great writ that is found in the Constitution, the great writ of habeas corpus. We are talking about a statutory writ, which the Supreme Court has said time and time again Congress has the right to create, Congress has the right to constrict, Congress has the right to eliminate."[576] Rep. Sensenbrenner agreed, saying, "[t]here are two types of habeas corpus: one is the constitutional great writ. We are not talking about that here. We can't suspend that. That is in the Constitution, and we can't suspend that by law. . . . The other is statutory habeas corpus, which has been redefined time and time again by the Congress. That is what we are talking about here, and we have the constitutional power to redefine it."[577]

United States, must be given by written law"). Paul Taylor, "The Historical and Legal Norms Governing the Detention of Suspected Terrorists and the Risks Posed by Recent Efforts to Depart From Them," Texas Review of Law & Politics 12, no. 2 (Spring 2008): 223.

573 Rep. Jerold Nadler (D-NY), Congressional Record, 109th Cong., 2nd sess., 2006, vol. 152, pt. 123, H7555-56 (27 Sept. 2006).

574 Rep. John Conyers (D-MI), Congressional Record, 109th Cong., 2nd sess., 2006, vol. 152, pt. 125, H7941-42 (29 Sept. 2006).

575 Sen. Jon Kyl (R-AZ), Congressional Record, 109th Cong., 1st sess., 2005, vol. 151, pt. 149, S12659 (10 Nov. 2005).

576 Rep. Daniel Lungren (R-CA), Congressional Record, 109th Cong., 2nd sess., 2006, vol. 152, pt. 123, H7513 (27 Sept. 2006).

577 Rep. James Sensenbrenner (R-WI), Congressional Record, 109th Cong., 2nd sess., 2006, vol. 152, pt. 123, H7548 (27 Sept. 2006).

DIALOGUES

COOPERATION & COMMUNICATION

It would be peculiar for members of Congress to be apathetic toward their co-equal branches of government, particularly the Supreme Court. They have a vested interest in knowing the current constitutional milieu in relation to individual cases and issues and what previous rulings have said as well as what precedents are considered at least minimally important. While we do have three distinct branches of government, the Supreme Court is given great deference in today's political environment. Thus, these types of inquiries and examples would be expected, but are still important to note given their constitutional implications.[578]

Many members of Congress spoke of the need for cooperation and communication between Congress and Court, or Congress and the Executive Branch. They believed there were specific benefits to such interactions or normative reasons for encouraging such behavior. Sometimes members interpreted Court language to indict their peers for failure to act. Here, Sen. Graham asserts the Court is asking Congress for further clarification on their intentions:

> The Supreme Court has been shouting to us in Congress: Get involved. . . . Habeas corpus rights have been given to Guantanamo Bay detainees because the location is under control of the United States, and Congress has been silent on how to treat these people. The Supreme Court has looked at section 2241, the habeas statute, and they are saying to us:

---

[578] For example, Sens. Kyl (R-AZ) and Specter (R-PA) have a long debate over how often the word "individual" and the word "citizens" appear in the *Hamdi* plurality decision. One could obviously infer this would be of no concern if the Court was inconsequential to members. Sen. Jon Kyl (R-AZ) and Sen. Arlen Specter (R-PA), Congressional Record, 109th Cong., 2nd sess., 2006, vol. 152, pt. 124, S10354-56 (28 Sept. 2006).

> Since you haven't spoken, we are going to confer habeas rights *until you act*.[579]

Four days later, he again said:

> The court in *Rasul* is asking the Senate and the House, do you intend for al-Qaida terrorists, enemy combatants, to have access to Federal courts under habeas rights to challenge their detention as if they were American citizens? The answer should be, no, we never intended that. That is what my amendment does. It says to the courts and to the world that an enemy combatant is not going to have the rights of an American citizen, and we are going to stop all these lawsuits undermining our ability to protect ourselves.[580]

Here, Sen. Leahy laments the lack of cooperation on the part of the Executive Branch:

> Some members of the Senate have argued that these prisoners should be tried in the military justice system. I think that we could all agree on such a course if the administration had worked with Congress from the start and established with our approval procedures that are fair and consistent with our tradition of military justice. . . . If the administration wanted to use military commissions to try detainees, it should have sought and obtained the explicit authorization of Congress. It did not do so.[581]

Often, members expressed the salutary effects of such cooperation between branches. Sen. Graham expressed that "[t]here is not enough

---

[579] Sen. Lindsey Graham (R-SC), Congressional Record, 109th Cong., 1st sess., 2005, vol. 151, pt. 149, S12656 (10 Nov. 2005). Emphasis added.

[580] Sen. Lindsey Graham (R-SC), Congressional Record, 109th Cong., 1st sess., 2005, vol. 151, pt. 150, S12732 (14 Nov. 2005).

[581] Sen. Patrick Leahy (D-VT), Congressional Record, 109th Cong., 1st sess., 2005, vol. 151, pt. 167, S14245 (21 Dec. 2005).

buy-in by the Congress to what is going on at Gitmo"[582] and that "[w]hen it comes time to keep people off the battlefield, with this amendment we are stronger as a nation because Congress will have blessed what the administration has done."[583]

As Sen. Specter pointed out, many felt the Administration oddly initially ignored Congress.[584] Echoing one witness's comments about cooperation right after the attacks,[585] Sen. Leahy offered similar thoughts:

> But stepping back for a moment from who is right or who is wrong . . . Wouldn't it have made more sense—we are giving you all this extra authority, anyway—at the time when you were asking us for all these things, but apparently not telling us that you were thinking about military commissions, would it not have made some wisdom to come here and say, look, why don't you put in another section authorizing under—as has been done in the past, giving us specific authorization for the President as Commander-in-Chief to set up military

---

[582] Sen. Lindsey Graham (R-SC), Congress, Senate, Committee on the Judiciary, Detainees, hearing, 109th Cong., 1st sess., 15 June 2005 (Washington, D.C.: GPO, 2006), 22.

[583] Sen. Lindsey Graham (R-SC), Congressional Record, 109th Cong., 1st sess., 2005, vol. 151, pt. 128, S11074 (5 Oct. 2005).

[584] Specter said, "The President promulgated his order without consultation with Congress. This legislation is a starting point for what we believe ought to be consideration by the Judiciary Committee." Sen. Arlen Specter (R-PA), during debate over the Military Commission Procedures Act of 2002, Congressional Record, 107th Cong., 2nd sess., 2002, vol. 148, pt. 13, S733-34 (13 Feb. 2002).

[585] "From the standpoint of both constitutional law and democratic legitimacy, it is far better if the President and Congress act in concert. As a general rule, the executive branch stands on the firmest ground if it acts pursuant to clear congressional authorization." Prof. Cass Sunstein, Congress, Senate, Committee on the Judiciary, Department of Justice Oversight: Preserving Our Freedoms While Defending Against Terrorism, hearing, 107th Cong., 1st sess., 28 Nov., 3 Dec., 6 Dec., 2001 (Washington, D.C.: GPO, 2001): 181.

> commissions, thus removing the legal debate now going on in this country about whether you have the authorization to do so or not?[586]

Sen. Lugar agreed, stating, "the administration appears to be adamant about going it alone and risking a bad court decision on the underlying legality of the military commission. Why take a chance that the punishment meted out to terrorists by a military commission will not stick due to a constitutional infirmity in the commission's jurisdiction?"[587]

Other members were aware of Justice Jackson's three-pronged analysis of presidential power and felt that the respective branches should share authority.[588] Rep. Schiff summarized this view:

> Through this bill, we can remove any legal cloud that would overhang these prosecutions. For one thing the Supreme Court

---

[586] Sen. Patrick Leahy (D-VT), Congress, Senate, Committee on the Judiciary, Department of Justice Oversight: Preserving Our Freedoms While Defending Against Terrorism, hearing, 107th Cong., 1st sess., 28 Nov., 3 Dec., 6 Dec., 2001 (Washington, D.C.: GPO, 2001): 16.

[587] Sen. Richard Lugar (R-IN), Congressional Record, 107th Cong., 1st sess., 2001, vol. 147, pt. 174, S13276 (14 Dec. 2001).

[588] In one example, it was argued, signaling led to outright literal cooperation, as Sen. Graham (R-SC) explained: "[w]hat is going on at Guantanamo Bay is called the Combat Status Review Tribunal, which is the Geneva Conventions protections on steroids. It is a process of determining who an enemy combatant is that not only applies with the Geneva Conventions and then some, it also is being modeled based on the O'Connor opinion in *Hamdi*, a Supreme Court case, where she suggested that Army regulation 190-8, sections 1 through 6, of 1997, would be the proper guide in detaining people as enemy prisoners, enemy combatants. That regulation is "Enemy Prisoners of War, Retained Personnel, Civilian Internees, and other Detainees." We have taken her guidance. We have the Army regulation 190-8, and we have created an enemy combat status review that goes well beyond the Geneva Conventions requirements to detain someone as an enemy combatant." Sen. Lindsey Graham (R-SC), Congressional Record, 109th Cong., 1st sess., 2005, vol. 151, pt. 149, S12655-56 (10 Nov. 2005).

> has made abundantly clear is that the power of the executive when it acts in concert with the Congress is at its greatest ebb. But there is another reason, an even more compelling reason, for Congress to act, and that is the separation of powers. . . . No single branch should have the authority on its own to establish jurisdiction for a tribunal, to determine the charges, to determine indeed what defendants should be brought before that tribunal, to determine process, and to serve as judge, jury and potential executioner.[589]

Sen. Feingold saw a direct power connection between the branches and warned: "[i]f the legislative body signals to the executive branch that they are going to be intimidated, they are going to receive more of the same."[590] Whether the Court was asking for it or not, some members believed the Court needed to hear what Congress's true intentions were in restricting habeas petitions from detainees. As Rep. Lungren succinctly stated:

> we already made this decision in this Congress a year ago. What this does is say to the Supreme Court, we meant what we said when we passed the law a year ago which said this should apply to people already in Guantanamo. That was our intent. Unfortunately, the Supreme Court believed it not to be found in the language. This makes it clear that what we said a year ago we say again, only we say to the Supreme Court, 'This time we really mean it. Please follow it.'[591]

---

[589] Rep. Adam Schiff (D-CA), during debate over the Military Tribunals Act of 2002, Congressional Record, 107th Cong., 2nd sess., 2002, vol. 148, pt. 91, H4402-4403 (9 Jul. 2002).

[590] Elizabeth A. Palmer and Adriel Bettelheim, "War and Civil Liberties: Congress Gropes for a Role," CQ Weekly Online (1 Dec. 2001): 2820-2827, available at http://library.cqpress.com/cqweekly/ weeklyreport107-000000348017 (accessed October 20, 2008).

[591] Rep. Daniel Lungren (R-CA), Congressional Record, 109th Cong., 2nd sess., 2006, vol. 152, pt. 123, H7513 (27 Sept. 2006).

CHECKS & BALANCES

Similarly to the examples just described, habeas corpus also came up in congressional deliberation under the umbrella of checks and balances. Many members felt as if Congress had done a poor job of checking an overly-assertive Executive Branch. Sen. Byrd professed that "[w]hile the President grabbed the wheel and the Congress dozed, the Court stepped in to remind us of the separation of powers and the constitutional role of each branch, thank God. Yes, thank God for the separation of powers envisioned by our forefathers. Thank God for the Supreme Court. Yes, I said this before; I say it again: Thank God for the Supreme Court."[592] One day later he would proclaim:

> This flagrant attempt to deny a fundamental right protected by the Constitution reveals how White House and Pentagon advisers continue to chip away at the separation of powers. They relentlessly pursue their dangerous goal of consolidating power in the hands of the Executive at the expense of the Congress, the judiciary, and, sadly, the People. How can we even contemplate such an irresponsible and dangerous course as this de facto canceling of the writ of habeas corpus."[593]

During debate over the Military Commissions Act, Sen. Leahy said:

> The Supreme Court said, you abused your power. And they [the Bush Administration] said we will fix that. We have a rubberstamp Congress that will set that aside and give us power that nobody – no king or anyone else setting foot in this land – had ever thought of having. . . . With this bill, the Congress will have completed the job of eviscerating its role as a check and balance on the administration. . . . It is not a

[592] Sen. Robert Byrd (D-WV), Congressional Record, 109th Cong., 2nd sess., 2006, vol. 152, pt. 123, S10385 (27 Sept. 2006).

[593] Sen. Robert Byrd (D-WV), Congressional Record, 109th Cong., 2nd sess., 2006, vol. 152, no. 124, S10366 (28 Sept. 2006).

> check on the administration but a voucher for future wrongdoing.[594]

When he spoke on behalf of the re-introduced Habeas bill in January 2007, Sen. Leahy again stated:

> The conservative Supreme Court, with seven of its nine members appointed by Republican Presidents, has been the only check on this Administration's lawlessness. Certainly the last Congress did not do it. With passage of the Military Commissions Act, the Republican Congress completed the job of eviscerating its role as a check and balance on the Administration. . . . In standing up for American values and security, I will keep working on this issue until we restore the checks and balances that are fundamental to preserving the liberties that define us as a nation. We can ensure our security without giving up our liberty.[595]

Other members described how in addition to being important as an individual right in and of itself, habeas was also important as a means to the end of inter-branch balance. During debate over the Military Commissions Act, Sen. Levin articulated this view:

> Over the last 2 days, we have debated the habeas corpus provision in the bill. Most of that debate has focused on the writ of habeas corpus as an individual right to challenge the lawfulness of detention. The writ of habeas corpus does serve that purpose. . . . But the writ of habeas corpus has always served a second purpose as well: for its 900-year history, the writ of habeas corpus has always served as a means of making the sovereign account for its actions. By depriving detainees of the opportunity to demonstrate that they were detained in

---

[594] Sen. Patrick Leahy (D-VT), Congressional Record, 109th Cong., 2nd sess., 2006, vol. 152, S11199.

[595] Sen. Patrick Leahy (D-VT), Congressional Record, 110th Cong., 1st sess., 2007, vol. 153, no. 1, S181 (4 Jan. 2007).

> error, this bill not only deprives individuals of a critical right deeply embedded in American law, it also helps ensure that the administration will not be held to account for the illegal or abusive treatment of detainees.[596]

THE FINAL ARBITER

In a three-branch system of government with an established practice of judicial review, perhaps it is not striking that members would discuss the possibility of a particular congressional action standing up to Court scrutiny. Thus, common observations, such as the following reflect the overall importance of the Court: "[w]e have seen in past years a number of U.S. Supreme Court decisions invalidating acts of Congress because there has not been a sufficient deliberative process. The Supreme Court says they have the authority to declare acts of Congress unconstitutional when, in effect, they are not thought through."[597] Similarly, "[i]f I understand the Supreme Court decision correctly, detainees do have habeas corpus rights. They do have a right to be brought before a process."[598] Chairman Specter commented:

> As I said at the outset . . . we are looking at the procedures here. The Committee is taking up about 15 Supreme Court opinions—one plurality, two five-person opinions, and a bunch of concurring opinions, and a bunch of dissenting opinions, and then three district court opinions. And it is a genuine crazy quilt to try to figure out where the due process

---

[596] Sen. Carl Levin (D-MI), Congressional Record, 109th Cong., 2nd sess., 2006, vol. 152, pt. 124, S10418.

[597] Sen. Arlen Specter (R-PA) Congress, Senate, Committee on the Judiciary, Subcommittee on the Constitution, Federalism, and Property Rights, Protecting Constitutional Freedoms in the Face of Terrorism, hearing, 107th Cong., 1st sess., 3 Oct. 2001 (Washington, D.C.: GPO, 2001), 64.

[598] Sen. Dianne Feinstein (D-CA), Congress, Senate, Committee on the Judiciary, Detainees, hearing, 109th Cong., 1st sess., 15 June 2005 (Washington, D.C.: GPO, 2006), 29.

> rights lie. The Supreme Court has said there are due process rights.[599]

It was also not uncommon to view the Court as a check, which, again, would be expected in a system of governmental which includes judicial review. As Sen. Levin exclaimed:

> The substance of the ruling in *Hamdan* establishes that the President, acting alone, lacks the power to unilaterally determine the legal rights of detainees at Guantanamo Bay, Cuba. Only Congress and the President, acting together, have the power to make such a determination, the Court ruled. Today's decision demonstrates once again the vital constitutional role of the Supreme Court as a check on the actions of the executive and legislative branches of Government.[600]

Rep. Jackson-Lee stated that "Congress should pass legislation that will . . . . also respond to the United States Supreme Court's ruling in the *Hamdan* case and withstand judicial scrutiny, or it may not serve its other purposes."[601] Sen. Specter said the "procedures in Guantanamo . . . do not satisfy the requirements of the Supreme Court of the United States in having a collateral proceeding which is adequate to protect the rights of someone who is in detention."[602] Sen. Feinstein exclaimed, "[t]here are serious questions about whether this provision will withstand a court test. . . . From this case, we will find out whether the military commissions law, which prevents full appeals, in fact, can

---

599 Sen. Arlen Specter (R-PA), Congress, Senate, Committee on the Judiciary, Detainees, hearing, 109th Cong., 1st sess., 15 June 2005 (Washington, D.C.: GPO, 2006), 38-39.

600 Sen. Carl Levin (D-MI), Congressional Record, 109th Cong., 2nd sess., 2006, S6773 (29 Jun. 2006).

601 Rep. Jackson-Lee (D-TX), Congressional Record, 109th Cong., 2nd sess., 2006, vol. 152, pt. 123, H7559 (27 Sept. 2006).

602 Sen. Arlen Specter (R-PA), Congressional Record, 110th Cong., 1st sess., 2007, vol. 153, pt. 109, S8908-8911 (10 Jul. 2007).

stand the court test.[603] Sen. Hatch defended the President's constitutional prerogatives and acknowledged the Court's role in judicial review:

> Finally, there have been many alarmist and misleading statements about the potential use of military commissions. Most glaring is the claim by some of my colleagues this past weekend that military tribunals are 'unconstitutional.' The Supreme Court has repeatedly upheld the constitutionality of using military commissions to prosecute individuals charged with crimes under the law of war.[604]

---

[603] Sen. Dianne Feinstein (D-CA), Congressional Record, 110th Cong., 1st sess., 2007, vol. 153, pt. 113, S9233-9235 (16 Jul. 2007).

[604] Sen. Hatch then mentions *Ex Parte Quirin* and *In re Yamashita*. Sen. Orrin Hatch (R-UT), Congress, Senate, Committee on the Judiciary, Department of Justice Oversight: Preserving Our Freedoms While Defending Against Terrorism, hearing, 107th Cong., 1st sess., 28 Nov., 3 Dec., 6 Dec., 2001 (Washington, D.C.: GPO, 2001): 7. Later, in the same hearing, Hatch would add: "some of my colleagues still question whether military tribunals are, in fact, permitted by the Constitution. The fact is that the Supreme Court has repeatedly upheld the constitutionality of using military commissions to prosecute individuals charged with crimes under the law of war. As the Supreme Court has explained, '[s]ince our Nation's earliest days, such commissions have been constitutionally recognized agencies for meeting many urgent governmental responsibilities related to war.' Furthermore, contrary to recent suggestion, military tribunals can be—and have been—established without further congressional authorization. Because the President's power to establish military commissions arises out of his constitutional authority as Commander-in–Chief, an act of Congress is unnecessary. Presidents have used this authority to establish military commissions throughout our Nation's history, from George Washington during the Revolutionary War to President Roosevelt during World War II. Congress, for its part, has repeatedly and explicitly affirmed and ratified this use of military commissions. Article 21 of our Code of Military Justice, codified at section 821 of Title 10 of the United States Code, expressly acknowledges that military commissions have jurisdiction over offenses under the law of war. 125."

Some members exerted, if not departmentalist views, at least a willingness *not* to rely on the Court but to assert necessary congressional views. For example, one month after the initial attacks, Sen. Feingold said, "[a]nd this is a job that only the Congress can do. We cannot simply rely on the Supreme Court to protect us from laws that sacrifice our freedoms. We took an oath to support and defend the Constitution of the United States. In these difficult times that oath becomes all the more significant."[605] In July 2007, Sen. Leahy said, "[w]e should not have to be bucking this to the Supreme Court for them to decide. We should correct the error here."[606] Six months earlier he had flatly admitted that:

> Some Senators uneasy about the Military Commissions Act's disastrous habeas provision took solace in the thought that it would be struck down by the courts. Instead, the first court to consider that provision, a federal court in the District of Columbia, upheld the provision. We should not outsource our moral, legal and constitutional responsibility to the courts. Congress must be accountable for its actions and we should act to right this wrong.[607]

Sometimes, views became a little more ambiguous. On the same day he expressed his previously noted view of the Suspension Clause, Sen. Specter said "[w]e have had Supreme Court decisions which have made it plain that habeas corpus is available to noncitizens and that habeas corpus applies to territory controlled by the United States, specifically,

---

[605] Sen. Russell Feingold (D-WI). Congressional Record, 107th Cong., 1st sess., 2001, vol. 147, pt. 136, S10570 (11 Oct. 2001). Emphasis added.

[606] Sen. Patrick Leahy (D-VT), Congressional Record, 110th Cong., 1st sess., 2007, vol. 153, no. 109, S8910 (10 Jul. 2007).

[607] Sen. Patrick Leahy (D-VT), Congressional Record, 110th Cong., 1st sess., 2007, vol. 153, no. 1, S181 (4 Jan. 2007).

including Guantanamo."[608] Six months later, Sen. Specter seemed to put constitutional fidelity above court deference.[609]

> To read the opinion of the Court of Appeals . . . is impossible to understand. I think a fair reading of the circuit opinion, simply stated, is that they flagrantly disregarded the holding of the Supreme Court of the United States, which under our system of laws they are obligated to uphold. They analyzed *Rasul* and said *Rasul* was based on the statute providing for habeas corpus and not on the constitutional mandate that habeas corpus is a part of the Constitution of the United States. . . . There can be no doubt that habeas corpus is a constitutional mandate because the Constitution explicitly states that habeas corpus may be suspended only in time of invasion or rebellion, and no one contends that we have either invasion or rebellion. . . . Now, it is true there is also a statute which provides for a writ of habeas corpus. The Court of Appeals said the portion of Justice Stevens' opinion as to the constitutional basis for habeas corpus was dictum and that the holding involved the statute. The Court of Appeals says since the holding involved the statute, the statute could be changed. It is true the statute was changed by the Congress of the United States, but the Congress of the United States, by statute, cannot change the constitutional mandate of habeas corpus. . . . For the Court of Appeals for the District of Columbia to say the constitutional basis for habeas corpus in *Rasul* was not the holding but only the statute was the holding is, simply stated, ridiculous.[610]

---

[608] Sen. Arlen Specter (R-PA), Congressional Record, 110th Cong., 1st sess., 2007, vol. 153, no. 1, S42 (4 Jan. 2007).

[609] Although here he is criticizing a Court of Appeals opinion and not the Supreme Court directly.

[610] Sen. Arlen Specter (R-PA), Congressional Record, 110th Cong., 1st sess., 2007, vol. 153, no. 109, S8910 (10 Jul. 2007).

Some members thought it important to pass "judicial scrutiny"[611] and "the scrutiny of the Supreme Court."[612] Others, like Rep. Conyers, went even further. Here, he seems to be asserting that Court opinions are all that matters when it comes to not only elucidating constitutional texts, but also in taking the initiative to propound constitutional law or applicable precedents.

> Recognizing the Supreme Court's concerns about judicial independence in cases such as *City of Boerne v. Flores* and *United States v. Morrison*, we have underscored that Congress is not attempting to settle any constitutional question that is the proper province of the federal courts. Thus . . . we have made clear, out of an abundance of caution, that we not purport to decide any constitutional question that remains within the proper bailiwick of the federal courts pursuant to Article III of the Constitution. Thus, this provision does not speak to the constitutionality of the military commissions or the old CSRTs. *We leave it to the courts to decide these questions.*[613]

Similarly, it is one thing to desire legislation that will not be overturned by a court or the Court. It is entirely another to claim the Constitution requires Congress to pass such qualified legislation. As Rep. Conyers stated, "Mr. Speaker, Congress has an obligation under the Constitution to enact legislation that creates fair trials for accused terrorists that will be upheld by the courts.[614] Sen. Specter also frequently alluded to a view of judicial supremacy: "[w]hen you have an issue of constitutionality, how can constitutionality be determined

---

[611] Rep. George Miller (D-CA), Congressional Record, 109th Cong., 2nd sess., 2006, vol. 152, pt. 123, H7556 (27 Sept. 2006).

[612] Rep. Ike Skelton (D-MO), Congressional Record, 109th Cong., 2nd sess., 2006, vol. 152, pt. 123, H7513 (27 Sept. 2006).

[613] Rep. John Conyers (D-MI), Congressional Record, 109th Cong., 1st sess., 2005, vol. 152, pt. 169, E2654-2655 (30 Dec. 2005). Emphasis added.

[614] Rep. Benjamin Cardin (D-MD), Congressional Record, 109th Cong., 2nd sess., 2006, vol. 152, pt. 123, H7555 (27 Sept. 2006). Emphasis added.

and interpreted *except in the Court*? . . . [W]ho is going to interpret the Constitution if the Court does not have jurisdiction?[615] Thus, in "the face of the explicit language of the Supreme Court of the United States there is a constitutional requirement, and *it is fundamental that Congress cannot legislate in contradiction to a constitutional interpretation of the Supreme Court*. That requires a constitutional amendment . . . not legislation."[616] A House member observed, "[w]ell, of course . . . higher authorities . . . are going to litigate and decide that question, what the suspension clause means."[617] Sen. Graham seemed to agree: I do not know what the Court will decide, but if the Court does say . . . there is a constitutional right to habeas corpus by those detained at Guantanamo Bay, then . . . *We would have to make a different legal determination. We would have to make a different legal analysis.*[618]

However, this reliance on the Court is often tempered by criticism of the Court[619] and an acknowledgement that Congress needs to act, but often waits on the Court. As Sen. Specter exclaimed, "[t]he Congress of the United States has the express responsibility under article I, section 8 of the U.S. Constitution to establish rules governing people captured on land and sea. . . . But the Congress of the United States did not act after 9/11, and we had people detained at Guantanamo. . . . *Congress did not*

---

615 Sen. Arlen Specter (R-PA), Congressional Record, 109th Cong., 2nd sess., 2006, vol. 152, pt. 123, S10264 (27 Sept. 2006).

616 Sen. Arlen Specter (R-PA), Congressional Record, 109th Cong., 2nd sess., 2006, vol. 152, pt. 124, S10354-56 (28 Sept. 2006). Emphasis added.

617 Rep. Robert Andrews (D-NJ), Congress, House, Committee on Armed Services, Upholding the Principle of Habeas Corpus for Detainees, hearing, 110th Cong., 1st sess., 26 July 2007 (Federal News Service, Inc., 2007), 21.

618 Sen. Lindsey Graham (R-SC), Congressional Record, 109th Cong., 2nd sess., 2006, vol. 152, pt. 123, S10267 (27 Sept. 2006).

619 "This case [*Hamdan*] was a clear-cut example of, I believe, Supreme Court overreach. *They seemed determined to do something about this*. They wanted to do something about it. Apparently, they did not like it." Sen. Jeff Sessions (R-AL), during debate over the Habeas Corpus Restoration Act of 2007. Congressional Record 110th Cong., 1st sess., 2007, vol. 153, pt. 137, S11565-11568 (17 Sept. 2007).

act on it because it was too hot to handle. . . . Congress punted. It didn't act, left it to the Supreme Court of the United States.[620] Finally, in defense of congressional prerogatives, Court stripping was briefly discussed,[621] as were other departmentalist views,[622] and, as Pickerill

---

620 Sen. Arlen Specter (R-PA), during debate over the Military Commissions Act. Congressional Record, 109th Cong., 2nd sess., 2006, vol. 152, pt. 123, S10264 (27 Sept. 2006). Sen. Specter had echoed this theme over a year earlier: "The only unifying factor coming out of the multitude of opinions by the Supreme Court [in June 2004] of the United States was that it is really the job of the Congress. . . . [T]here is a real question as to why Congress has not handled it. *It may be that it is too hot to handle for Congress. It may be that it is too complex to handle for Congress. Or it may be that Congress wants to sit back as Congress, [as] we [] customarily do awaiting some action by the court no matter how long it takes, Plessy* v. *Ferguson* in 1896 to *Brown* v. *Board of Education* in 1954. But, at any rate, Congress has not acted. . . . Justice Scalia wrote in an opinion, joined by the Chief Justice and Justice Thomas, 'Congress is in session. If it had wished to change Federal judges' habeas jurisdiction from what this Court held that to be, it could have done so.' Which is certainly true. . . . We constantly complain that the Court makes the law, and here we are having sat back with our constitutional mandate pretty clear. In more circumspect language, Justice Stevens went on to make a point which is[:] . . . [H]e could not determine the 'Government security needs' or the necessity to 'obtain intelligence through interrogation,' concluding, 'It is far beyond my competence or the Court's competence to determine that, but it is not beyond Congress'. If civil rights are to be curtailed during wartime, it must be done openly and democratically, as the Constitution requires, rather than by silent erosion through an opinion of the Court." Sen. Arlen Specter (R-PA), Congress, Senate, Committee on the Judiciary, Detainees, hearing, 109th Cong., 1st sess., 15 June 2005 (Washington, D.C.: GPO, 2006), 1-3.

621 Sen. Lindsey Graham (R-SC) and Sen. Jon Kyl (R-AZ) discussed *Ex parte McCardle* and the issue of "stripping" in relation to only allowing habeas appeals in the D.C. Circuit. Congressional Record, 109th Cong., 1st sess., 2005, vol. 151, no. 167, S14263-64 (15 Nov. 2005).

622 "The Supreme Court created a mess and hurt the Global War on Terror with its unnecessary and unconstitutional opinion in the *Hamdan* case. The

would predict, congressional action prompted by the threat or reality of judicial review.[623]

CONCLUSION

In 2007, the U.S. Court of Appeals for the District of Columbia upheld the Military Commission's Act prohibition on lawsuits brought by enemy combatants at Guantánamo Bay, Cuba. However, the Supreme Court reversed it and granted certiori (after previously rejecting cert) for that particular slate of defendants. On June 12th, 2008, in *Boumediene v. Bush*, the Court, in a 5-4 decision, overturned the 1950 *Johnson v. Eisentrager* case and held that "aliens designated as enemy combatants and detained at Guantanamo Bay have the constitutional privilege of habeas corpus. The Court . . . found that [the Military Commissions Act] did not provide an adequate habeas substitute and therefore acted as an unconstitutional suspension of the writ of

---

Supreme Court had no authority to hear the *Hamdan* case. The Detainee Treatment Act gave the Court of Appeals for the District of Columbia Circuit exclusive jurisdiction over the validity of any final decision of an enemy combatant status review tribunal. The Supreme Court in *Hamdan v. Rumsfeld* ignored the provision of the DTA and a longstanding line of its own precedents which stood for the principle that Congress can limit jurisdiction in pending as well as future cases. . . . Because of our national security, Congress and the President jumped through a series of hoops set by the Court, rather than carry on a protracted power struggle over the Constitution with the Court. But, Mr. Speaker, *Congress concedes no power to the Court not defined in the Constitution or specified by statute.*" Rep. Steve King (R-IA), Congressional Record, 109th Cong., 2nd sess., 2006, vol. 152, pt. 123, H7549 (27 Sept. 2006). Emphasis added.

623 "The Supreme Court clearly made a mistake [in *Hamdan*]. I must admit I was disappointed in some of the rulings of the judges, but *it has forced our hand* to try to make it clear in the law and with the administration how we are going to deal with this question of interrogating these terrorists, how we are going to deal with some of the evidence that is acquired through that process." Sen. Trent Lott (R-MS), Congressional Record, 109th Cong., 2nd sess., 2006, vol. 152, pt. 123, S10238 (27 Sept. 2006). Emphasis added.

habeas."[624] Justice Anthony M. Kennedy writing for the majority, said "[t]he laws and Constitution are designed to survive, and remain in force, in extraordinary times" and that "[t]o hold the political branches have the power to switch the Constitution on or off at will[.] . . . [would] lead . . . to a regime in which Congress and the President, not this Court, say 'what the law is.'"[625] This majority opinion was not minimalistic in nature. As Stuart Taylor writes:

> Understandably determined not to be seen as putting its seal of approval on the gross denials of due process at Guantanamo, the Court could have administered cautious, modest rebukes to the Bush policy. Instead, in 2004 and 2006 as well as in the latest decision, the five more liberal justices . . . eviscerated a major 1950 precedent, *Johnson v. Eisentrager;* struck down major parts of the 2005 and 2006 laws; and asserted potentially sweeping, open-ended powers to oversee wartime polices traditionally deemed the exclusive province of the elected branches. . . . The elected branches' disrespect for constitutional values has put the Supreme Court in a difficult position. It has responded by appearing to arrogate to the judiciary powers that are, for good reason, unprecedented in Anglo-American history."[626]

This was the "fourth major legal defeat for the Bush Administration on the issue of rights for foreign detainees"[627] and was the first decision "in which the court has ever overturned . . . a law enacted by the President and Congress during what they deemed to be

---

[624] Jennifer K. Elsea Michael John Garcia, and Kenneth R. Thomas, Legislative Attorneys, American Law Division, Enemy Combatant Detainees: *Habeas Corpus* Challenges in Federal Court, CRS Report for Congress (updated September 10, 2008): Summary.

[625] *Boumediene v. Bush*, 553 U.S. _____, 35-36 (2008).

[626] Stuart Taylor, Jr., "Bush and the Justices Behaved Badly," National Journal (21 Jun. 2008).

[627] Adam Zagorin, "What the Gitmo Ruling Means," TIME (12 Jun. 2008).

war time about matters of war."[628] "The courts, at first slow to respond to arrogations of executive power after September 11, have pushed back." [629] Many felt that "[s]o much of the anger against the Bush administration could have been avoided if Bush had gone to Congress in the first place."[630]

The entire history of the habeas issue after September 11th, 2001 illustrates several important aspects of political regime and political cycle analysis. First, in relation to the underlying "settled" value in terms of war powers and foreign policy decision-making, the executive continues to dominate, at least in the initial stages of crises, and Congress is reluctant to take the lead. Initial efforts at passing legislation related to detainees failed and it was only after the summer 2004 cases were issued by the Court that Congress chose to respond. Secondly, and concurrently, members of Congress, while engaging in a dialogue with the other two branches, were very symbolic and brief in their deliberations about habeas. More importantly, while in the past it has been said that war powers have been considered the Constitution's clearest "textually demonstrable constitutional commitment" of authority to the political branches,[631] members were still operating under the assumption of judicial supremacy, even failing to adequately discuss the appropriate precedents for Court-stripping when attempting to do just that in the DTA and the MCA.

The Court, after three years of silence in the face of a seemingly dominant coalition,[632] and perhaps sensing a vacuum, given there

---

628 Stuart Taylor, Jr., "Briefing on U.S. Supreme Court Rulings," (2007-08 Term) Brookings Institute Symposium, 11, available at http://www.brookings.edu/events/2008/ 0627_supreme_court.aspx.

629 Stuart Taylor, Jr. and Evan Thomas, "Obama's Cheney Dilemma: Cheney pushed for expanded presidential powers. Now that he's leaving, what will come of his efforts? The new president won't have to wait long to tip his hand," Newsweek.com, 19 Jan. 2009 [magazine on-line]; accessed 29 Jan. 2009; available from newsweek.com/id/178855.

630 ibid.

631 *Baker v. Carr*, 369 U.S. 186, 217 (1962).

632 "An affiliated judiciary is unlikely to take actions that are not favored by a substantial segment of the dominant coalition." Keith E. Whittington, "The Political Foundations of Judicial Supremacy," in Sotirios A. Barber and

appeared to be now no dominant coalition on this issue, and a dual-branch threat to its supremacist legitimacy,[633] went against its previous collaborative effort and previous understanding of jurisdiction stripping in its *Boumediene* decision. This was a significant change from the *Hamdi* plurality, which suggested to Congress using Army Regulation 190-8 as a model for the level of procedural protections for an enemy combatant, which Congress then did, only to be rebuked by the Court.[634]

Robert P. George, eds., Constitutional Politics: Essays on Constitution Making, Maintenance, and Change (Princeton: Princeton University Press, 2001), 279.

633 "The president is in part an interpreter of the national heritage, of which the Constitution is a prominent part. In this effort, the judiciary is both a potential competitor and a potential ally." Keith E. Whittington, "The Political Foundations of Judicial Supremacy," in Sotirios A. Barber and Robert P. George, eds., Constitutional Politics: Essays on Constitution Making, Maintenance, and Change (Princeton: Princeton University Press, 2001), 267. As another scholar has written, "[t]ime and again, the Supreme Court has refused to bow to political forces – even ones with which they are otherwise largely sympathetic – that push for the elimination of their habeas jurisdiction." Justin J. Wert, Habeas Corpus in America: The Politics of Individual Rights (Lawrence, Kansas: University Press of Kansas, 2011), 200.

634 See *Boumediene v. Bush*, 553 U.S. _____, 1-28 (2008) (Roberts, C.J., dissenting). See, in particular, 9-11.

CHAPTER 5

Deliberation, Affiliation, and our Political System

Government officeholders and constitutional commentators often find themselves engaged in constructing constitutional meaning from an indeterminate text. In this context, the Constitution is often understood less as a set of binding rules than as a source of authoritative norms of political behavior and as the foundation of governing institutions.[635]

Keeping the definition of constitutional deliberation in mind,[636] the cumulative evidence from these case studies suggests that constitutional deliberation in Congress can best be understood through a political regime and cyclical analysis. More specifically, these cases, falling within reasonably the same contemporary era, demonstrate and illustrate the importance and effects of regime contestation: the

---

635 Keith E. Whittington, Constitutional Construction: Divided Powers and Constitutional Meaning (Cambridge: Harvard University Press, 1999), 8.

636 Legislative action, engaged in by Congress, considered as an institution, that has "proceeded through [the] complex set of organization structures" within Congress which make "substantive reference to the U.S. Constitution" as well as floor statements and interviews which are also substantive, not ones that are merely perfunctory. In addition, "constitutional debate among members or other relevant policy-makers and lawmakers, committee hearings that focus at some length on constitutional issues, language in a bill or a statute that reflects constitutional principles or judicial doctrines, or some other indication that constitutional issues played an important part when the legislation in question was considered." See footnote 81.

normative engagement and debate between competing national governing coalitions over the proper definition, scope, perception, and breadth of the state and of society. More specifically, they each are most fully explained by their place at an "affiliated" stage in "political time."

Operating within this regime and "time" construct and, consequently, in an era of divided government,_ Congress is a highly political institution functioning within a highly political environment encompassing both fundamental "settled" values and secondary "unsettled" values. Thus, its deliberation is for the most part symbolic and derivative in nature, acting under an umbrella of judicial supremacy and attempting to exert influence primarily on unsettled values reflecting members' regime preferences, by which fundamental regime shifts are sought. These cases belie the notion of "settled" law and a "settled" regime, yet, despite these deviations from an undiluted "republic of reasons,"[637] Congress plays an important representational role by acting, and, further still, continues and perpetuates an ongoing dialogue with the other branches which would arguably not take place without their agency.

REGIME, TIME & AFFILIATION

As Whittington writes, "[t]he political regime within which political time is played out is in part a constitutional regime, 'the constitutional baseline in normal political life.'"[638] Within this "baseline" the notion of political regimes "incorporates not only electorally dominant partisan coalitions, but also a set of dominant policy concerns and legitimating ideologies. A regime in this sense overarches contending policy orientations at lower levels such that even electorally successful

---

[637] J. Mitchell Pickerill, Constitutional Deliberation in Congress: The Impact of Judicial Review in a Separated System, 131.

[638] Keith E. Whittington, "The Political Foundations of Judicial Supremacy," in Sotirios A. Barber and Robert P. George, eds., Constitutional Politics: Essays on Constitution Making, Maintenance, and Change (Princeton: Princeton University Press, 2001): 266, citing, Bruce Ackerman, We the People, vol. 1, Foundations (Cambridge: Harvard University Press, 1991), 59.

oppositional figures can be forced to sustain the commitments of the dominant regime. A strong regime transcends partisanship."[639]

Within this framework, the Supreme Court plays an important part and "[f]or at least fifty years, prominent political scientists have traced the decisions of the U.S. Supreme Court to the policy and political commitments of governing partisan regimes." They have found that "justices have almost always acted in alliance with the governing coalition of which they themselves are generally members."[640] During these "ordinary" times, as Pickerill and Clayton write, "one expects the Court's decisions to reflect broader regime values."[641] While "historically, the Court rarely exercise[s] its power in opposition to the substantive interests and values of the 'national governing coalition,'"[642] "[u]nder some circumstances, the Court may stray quite

---

[639] Keith E. Whittington, "The Political Foundations of Judicial Supremacy," 264-265, in Sotirios A. Barber and Robert P. George, eds., Constitutional Politics: Essays on Constitution Making, Maintenance, and Change (Princeton: Princeton University Press, 2001), citing Stephen Skowronek, The Politics Presidents Make (Cambridge: Harvard University Press, 1993).

[640] Thomas M. Keck, "Party Politics or Judicial Independence? The Regime Politics Literature Hits the Law Schools," review of From Jim Crow to Civil Rights: The Supreme Court and the Struggle for Racial Equality, by Michael J. Klarman, The Most Democratic Branch? How the Courts Serve America, by Jeffrey Rosen, and A Court Divided: The Rehnquist Court and the Future of Constitutional Law, by Mark Tushnet, Law & Social Inquiry 32, no. 2 (spring 2007): 511-12. Dahl wrote, "[t]he fact is, then, that the policy views dominant on the Court are never for long out of line with the policy views dominant among the lawmaking majorities of the United States." 285. Robert A. Dahl, "Decision-Making in a Democracy: The Supreme Court as a National Policy-Maker," Journal of Public Law 6 (1957): 279-295.

[641] J. Mitchell Pickerill and Cornell W. Clayton. "The Rehnquist Court and the Political Dynamics of Federalism." Perspectives on Politics 2, no. 2 (June 2004): 236.

[642] J. Mitchell Pickerill and Cornell W. Clayton. "The Rehnquist Court and the Political Dynamics of Federalism." Perspectives on Politics 2, no. 2 (June 2004): 236, quoting Dahl, Robert. "Decision-Making in a Democracy: The Supreme Court as a National Policy-Maker." Journal of Public Law 6 (1957): 279-295.

far from some of the dominant regime's values, as long as it does not challenge core values and constituencies."[643]

In these cases, the regime within which they took place was one associated with President Reagan. As Skowronek writes, "[n]ot only did he confound the gloomy prognostications of the 1970s, but he also repudiated the priorities of fifty years of liberal government, reset the national agenda, and became the touchstone of legitimacy for a new politics that would revolve around conservative priorities through ensuing decades. Politically speaking, America is still working its way through the Reagan era."[644]

"Settled" Values

In the three cases studied here, despite competing governing coalitions, there were fundamental "core" values, policy concerns, and legitimating ideologies that went unchallenged and virtually unspoken

---

[643] J. Mitchell Pickerill and Cornell W. Clayton, "The Rehnquist Court and the Political Dynamics of Federalism." Perspectives on Politics 2, no. 2 (June 2004): 236, citing, Neal Devins, "The Federal-Rights Nexus: Explaining why Senate Democrats Tolerate Rehnquist Court Decision Making but not the Rehnquist Court," University of Colorado Law Review 73, no. 4 (2002): 1307-36, and Keith E. Whittington, "Taking What They Give Us: Explaining the Court's Federalism Offensive," Duke Law Journal 51, no. 1 (2001): 477-520. As Pickerill and Clayton wrote regarding the Rehnquist Court's federalism decisions, "[y]et the Court's decisions show little sign of challenging the core political values of the national governing regime." 240. As Fisher writes, "[t]he Court has the 'power' to declare presidential and congressional acts unconstitutional, but it can exercise that power effectively only by acknowledging its place within the political system." Louis Fisher, Constitutional Dialogues: Interpretation as Political Process (Princeton: Princeton University Press, 1988), 221.

[644] Stephen Skowronek, Presidential Leadership in Political Time: Reprise and Reappraisal (2nd ed., revised and expanded) (Lawrence, KS: University Press of Kansas, 2011), 4. For further delineation of the reconstructive, affiliated, preemptive, affiliated pattern emerging beginning with President Reagan, specifically see Chapters 3 ("The Politics of Leadership at the End of the Twentieth Century") and 4 (Leadership by Definition: First-Term Reflections on George W. Bush's Political Stance").

by both coalitions. They were reluctant to approach them until future elections or political factors changed the regime dynamics so that the then-current underlying consensus was less secure and a new consensus had emerged.

In the civil rights case, there was fundamental agreement that thirty years after the civil rights movement and accompanying legislative actions, there would be federal involvement in civil rights policy. There were no vestiges of the Southern Manifesto. The constitutionality of the 1964 Civil Rights Act was not mentioned. More importantly, *Griggs*, the case that established disparate-impact analysis, itself was not directly challenged. Its interpretation by the Court was criticized but an effort was not made to eliminate disparate-impact analysis or the 80% rule from Equal Employment Opportunity Commission guidelines.

In the case of partial-birth abortion, an attack on *Roe* was explicitly disavowed. *Griswold* was barely mentioned. No one introduced the Human Life Bill. There was only one direct reference to fetuses falling within the Equal Protection Clause. A commitment of some kind to privacy was at least acknowledged as the reining regime value. In the case of habeas corpus, there was at least a fundamental value of a congressional commitment to participation in foreign affairs-related policy. The President would not simply act completely without congressional input.

"UNSETTLED" VALUVES

Given they are operating within a political regime context, combined with the fact that they are unable and unwilling to directly address the values of the fundamental regime, we see members of Congress being very willing to try and influence their body, the other branches, and the political context by influencing perceptions, facts, and outcomes at a secondary regime value level. National coalition members are willing to fight over these secondary values. These include the demarcation between racial intents and racial effects in public policy, the exact contours of the right to privacy, and the limits of habeas corpus itself. These issues are not settled and thus were the subject of greater and more intense rhetorical and deliberative efforts.

AFFILIATION

Reconstructive presidents are presidents who have asserted an authority to ignore the Court's constitutional reasoning and act upon their own independent constitutional judgments.[645] We do not see this behavior in these three cases. Both President Bushes were affiliated with President Reagan and thus unwilling to believe they inhabited reconstructive space within which to challenge a collapsing regime and propose new understandings of fundamental regime commitments and values or of articulating the foundations for a new regime. Both had expectations of the Court, given they were expecting "to inherit an affiliated Court[] . . . whose personnel were largely selected and/or confirmed by his own political coalition. Moreover, the Court can be expected to be operating under the ideological assumptions of the constitutional vision established by the last reconstruction."[646] Affiliated leaders "interpret the inherited regime, not the constitutional order itself – that is, they interpret the interpretations of the previous reconstructive leader. They are the workaday practioners of constitutional politics, concerned with clarifying what the constitutional regime is rather than with specifying what it should be."[647]

In these cases, we see that "political actors are not unconcerned with constitutional meaning, but they have less direct investment in taking a leadership role in specifying its requirements. Under such

---

645 Keith E. Whittington, "The Political Foundations of Judicial Supremacy," in Sotirios A. Barber and Robert P. George, eds., Constitutional Politics: Essays on Constitution Making, Maintenance, and Change (Princeton: Princeton University Press, 2001), 271.

646 Keith E. Whittington, "The Political Foundations of Judicial Supremacy," in Sotirios A. Barber and Robert P. George, eds., Constitutional Politics: Essays on Constitution Making, Maintenance, and Change (Princeton: Princeton University Press, 2001), 276, citing, Howard Gillman, The Constitution Besieged (Durham: Duke University Press, 1993); Ackerman, We the People, 1:131-162.

647 Keith E. Whittington, "The Political Foundations of Judicial Supremacy," in Sotirios A. Barber and Robert P. George, eds., Constitutional Politics: Essays on Constitution Making, Maintenance, and Change (Princeton: Princeton University Press, 2001), 276.

circumstances, the Court can carve out a constrained, but autonomous, role for itself as the 'ultimate interpreter' of constitutional meaning, with the assistance and tolerance of other political actors."[648] Whereas a "reconstructive leader must shoulder aside the Court's claim to be the primary expositor of constitutional meaning and must shift constitutional discourse more explicitly into the political arena," an affiliated president will be much less inclined to do so, members of Congress will defer to the Court, and both will attempt incremental changes to slowly move the regime.[649]

This is what we see in these cases. In 1989, a newly empowered majority of the Court issued a striking array of rulings in a short span, a prerogative they inhabited given their slowly building alliance with Republican presidents, a President was unwilling to forcefully lead onto new constitutional ground, and members of Congress either expressed outrage from the minority or argued for a more moderate stance. In 2003, another affiliated President Bush was unwilling to lead an assault on *Roe*, but was willing to defer to the Court's precedents and merely seek new incremental ground by which to please his coalition, while members of Congress from both parties deferred to the Court, either to claim their mantle of what was constitutional as sacrosanct, or to demonstrate the adherence by which the new law failed to stray from precedent. In 2007, while the President could arguably be said to have tried to assert new, or reassert old, constitutional ground in favor of executive power, he retreated when this seemed to fail. Congress deferred to the Court for a period of time, and the Court sought for itself a constrained institutional role as the ultimate interpreter of the Constitution.

---

[648] Keith E. Whittington, "The Political Foundations of Judicial Supremacy," in Sotirios A. Barber and Robert P. George, eds., Constitutional Politics: Essays on Constitution Making, Maintenance, and Change (Princeton: Princeton University Press, 2001), 270.

[649] Keith E. Whittington, "The Political Foundations of Judicial Supremacy," in Sotirios A. Barber and Robert P. George, eds., Constitutional Politics: Essays on Constitution Making, Maintenance, and Change (Princeton: Princeton University Press, 2001), 270.

DIVIDED GOVERNMENT

Affiliated eras, while being compromised of a regime of settled and unsettled values, can nevertheless be composed of divided political and electoral coalitions, which fact thereof then elicits its own expectations, which we do see in these cases. While in 1957 Dahl "argued that the Court rarely exercises the power of judicial review in a way that is contrary to the interests of the governing coalition in the national political system,"[650] the era encompassing these three cases has been dominated by a relatively divided, or competing, governing coalition(s) and partisan environment.[651] This is evident in the partisan compositions of Congress over the past twenty to thirty years in which these cases and their antecedents inhabit.[652] As mentioned earlier, during times of divided government:

---

650 Cornell Clayton and David A. May, "A Political Regimes Approach to the Analysis of Legal Decisions," Polity 32, no. 2 (Winter 1999): 242.

651 As opposed to an era of realignment, as described by Fisher: "The judiciary is most likely to be out of step with Congress or the President during periods of electoral and partisan realignment, when the country is undergoing sharp shifts in political directions while the courts retain the orientation of an age gone by." Louis Fisher, Constitutional Dialogues: Interpretation as Political Process (Princeton: Princeton University Press, 1988), 201, citing, Richard Funston, "The Supreme Court and Critical Elections," American Political Science Review 69, no. 3 (1975): 795-811, and David Adamany, "Legitimacy, Realigning Elections, and the Supreme Court," Wisconsin Law Review 1973, no. 3 (1973): 790-846.

652 In the Senate, Democrats controlled the chamber during the 96th (58-41-1), 100th (55-45), 101st (55-45), 102nd (56-44), 103rd (57-43), 110th (49-49-2), and the 111th Congress (57-41-2). Republicans were in control of the 97th (53-46-1), 98th (55-45), 99th (53-47), 104th (52-48), 105th (55-45), 106th (55-45), 108th (51-48-1), and 109th (55-44-1). The 107th Senate was evenly divided. In the House, Democrats controlled the 96th (277-158), 97th (242-192-1), 98th (269-166), 99th (253-182), 100th (258-177), 101st (260-175), 102nd (267-167-1), 103rd (258-176-1), 110th (233-202), and the 111th (257-178). Republicans controlled the 104th (230-204-1), 105th (228-206-1), 106th (223-211-1), 107th (221-212-2), 108th (229-205-1), and 109th (232-202-1).

'regime' values will be less stable and more conflicted, since neither party enjoys consistent control over legislative institutions. It is true that even when a single party dominates the electoral system, regime values may conflict, as for instance in the conflict between blue-collar labor interests and the civil rights movement within the Democratic coalition of the 1960s. But such conflicts are more prevalent when the regime lacks a unifying party structure to harmonize those competing interests. Even modest alterations to existing legal doctrines may induce dire warnings from politicians as the parties become ideologically more polarized and face a growing incentive to exaggerate the importance of change in an effort to lure independent voters. Third, the electorate is unlikely to mobilize against the Court's positions. To some extent, the polarization within the elected branches reflects polarization within the electorate itself. Indeed, the 2000 election saw the highest level of straight party voting in fifty years of National Elections Studies surveys, and, according to public opinion polls, marked the high point of a thirty-year trend of partisan and ideological polarization. During such periods of division, the Court's decisions will always enjoy support from a significant portion of the public.[653]

---

[653] J. Mitchell Pickerill and Cornell W. Clayton, "The Rehnquist Court and the Political Dynamics of Federalism," Perspectives on Politics 2, no. 2 (June 2004): 242. Citations omitted. As Keck adds, "the governing coalition is so often divided on important matters that the justices will have multiple acceptable alternatives in most cases. The Court's decision in a given case may be supported by some members of the governing coalition, but if the opposite decision would have been supported by other members of the coalition, then the justices may well have significant room for independent action." Thomas M. Keck, "Party Politics or Judicial Independence? The Regime Politics Literature Hits the Law Schools," review of From Jim Crow to Civil Rights: The Supreme Court and the Struggle for Racial Equality, by Michael J. Klarman, The Most Democratic Branch? How the Courts Serve America, by Jeffrey Rosen, and A Court Divided: The Rehnquist Court and the Future of Constitutional Law, by Mark Tushnet, Law & Social Inquiry 32, no. 2 (spring 2007): 517.

This is what we find during this time period. The substantiation of which regime values are the most stable was contested in all three cases. Neither party had consistent control over the legislature, immune to strong coalitional divisions within its own ranks, which further exemplified the reality of divided and unsettled values. The electorate was unable to verifiably mobilize on behalf of one national governing coalition or the other.

Thus, due to the divided nature of the regime, the Court has more latitude to rule independently, possibly even on issues they would have not ruled on otherwise. During divided government the Court will always be able to count on strong support and, as a consequence, "dire warnings" at Court action threatening settled and fundamental regime values are issued because members realize that slight modifications may lead to greater effects on contested fundamental values. During these cases, members were outraged over what could be argued were minor changes in law. But, to them, even slight deviations from the status quo may have signaled a regime shift and this violated their fundamental regime preferences.

A Political Branch

These cases also demonstrate that members of Congress operate in an extremely political environment. They often "only have fifteen minutes to decide an issue"[654] and it is important to keep in mind what we already understand about members of Congress from previous studies. As mentioned earlier, Pickerill reminds us that:

> [w]e should not expect members of Congress to routinely or systematically consider, of their own volition, constitutional issues raised by legislation. . . . [M]embers of Congress are primarily motivated by the 'electoral connection,' notions of representation, and the desire to make good public policy, and the institution of Congress is designed to help achieve these goals efficiently. However, Congress does not operate in a vacuum, and it may sometimes need to consider the actions of the judiciary, the presidency, or other institutions. Likewise, the Court's actions may be viewed as having important effects

[654] Staff Interview, 2008.

on other institutions of government and on the broader lawmaking process. . . . Constitutional issues must compete with other factors that influence congressional decision making.[655]

---

[655] J. Mitchell Pickerill, Constitutional Deliberation, 3, 21-22; citing Douglass Arnold, The Logic of Congressional Action (New Haven: Yale University Press, 1990); Richard Fenno, "U.S. House Members in Their Constituencies: An Exploration," American Political Science Review 71 (1977): 883-917; Elizabeth Garrett and Adrian Vermeule, "Institutional Design of a Thayerian Congress," Duke Law Journal 50 (2001): 1277-1333; John Kingdon, Congressmen's Voting Decisions (Ann Arbor: University of Michigan Press, 1989); David R. Mayhew, Congress: The Electoral Connection (New Haven: Yale University Press, 1974); Kenneth A. Shepsle and Barry R. Weingast, eds. Positive Theories of Congressional Institutions (Ann Arbor: University of Michigan Press, 1995); Charles M. Cameron, Veto Bargaining: Presidents and the Politics of Negative Power (Cambridge: Cambridge University Press, 2000); William N. Eskridge, Jr., "The Judicial Review Game," Northwestern University Law Review 88 (1993): 382-95; Charles O. Jones, The Presidency in a Separated System (Washington: Brookings Institution, 1994); Mark A. Peterson, Legislating Together: The White House and Capitol Hill from Eisenhower to Reagan (Cambridge: Harvard University Press, 1990); Charles R. Shipan, Designing Judicial Review: Interest Groups, Congress and Communications Policy (Ann Arbor: University of Michigan Press, 1997); Bradley C. Canon and Charles A. Johnson, Judicial Policies: Implementation and Impact, 2d ed. (Washington: CQ Press, 1999); Louis Fisher, Constitutional Dialogues: Interpretation as Political Process (Princeton: Princeton University Press, 1988); Charles O. Jones, "A Way of Life and Law: Presidential Address, American Political Science Association," American Political Science Review 89 (1994): 1-9; Richard Fenno, Home Style: House Members in Their Districts (Boston: Little, Brown, 1978); Congressmen in Committees (Boston: Little, Brown, 1973); John E. Jackson and John Kingdon, "Ideology, Interest Group Scores, and Legislative Votes," American Journal of Political Science 36 (1992): 805-823; John Kingdon, Agendas, Alternatives and Public Policies, 2nd ed. (New York: Longman, 1995); Keith Krehbiel, Information and Legislative Organization (Ann Arbor: University of Michigan Press, 1991); Kenneth Shepsle, "Institutional Arrangements and Equilibrium in Multidimensional

PARTISANSHIP

Given the increase in party polarization and the divided nature of the national governing majority and the characteristics it brings, within a regime structure of fundamental and secondary values, we would expect the deliberations to elicit predictable partisan divisions and responses. That fact continued here. As pointed out in each case study, in 1991 and 2003, votes on final passage were virtually along party lines. In 2007, in the preceding time to the actual bill, we know that Republican supporters of the bill most likely did not want to challenge a sitting Republican President on a foreign policy issue and Democrats, fearing their electoral chances may suffer, may have withheld from speaking out too forcefully.

In the Civil Rights Act case, Republicans were more likely to argue for less race-conscious and more color-blind policies and interpretations of civil rights law. Democrats were more likely to invoke the virtue of race-conscious policies and interpretations of civil rights law. Each party even inserted numerous ad hoc "interpretive memos" at odds with one another stipulating what narrow interpretation would be counted as correct statutory instruction for the court system to use.[656] In the abortion case, Republicans were more likely to argue

---

Voting Models," American Journal of Political Science 23 (1979): 27-59; Barry Weingast, "A Rational Choice Perspective on Congressional Norms," American Journal of Political Science 23 (1979): 245-62; Robert A. Katzmann, ed., Judges and Legislators: Toward Institutional Comity (Washington: Brookings Institution, 1988), 7. Although this former member downplayed the role of re-election. "Almost all members base their votes on principle and their own careful analysis, drawing on staff research, testimony, scholarly data, anecdotal testimony from constituents and a variety of other sources. The belief that most members base their votes on a re-election calculus is poli sci nonsense – constituent concerns and preferences are included, properly, in the decision[-]making process, among a great number of factors." (Former Member of Congress, Interview, 2008).

[656] See "The Dole/Administration Interpretive Memorandum", "The Danforth and Kennedy Interpretative Analyses", "The Resolution to Clarify the Effective Date Provision Applicable to the Wards Cove Packing Company", "The Kennedy Analysis of S. 1745", "Rep. Edwards' and Rep. Hyde's Section-by-Section Analyses", and "Rep. Ford's Analysis of Disparate

against the procedure and invoke "life", while Democrats were more likely to invoke "choice" and the harms that would come from placing a restriction on abortion accessibility. In the habeas case, Republicans, as they did in the other two cases, were more likely to voice their support for a position their Republican President advocated and in favor of executive discretion in war-making, while Democrats, as they did also in the previous two cases, were opposed to a President of the opposite party and in disfavor of greater executive discretion in war-making.

Again, these divisions highlight the presence of and the importance thereto of dueling governing coalitions that have been battling over the definition of the regime. Instead of one national governing coalition being dominant, there have been competing coalitions, and while at various times and in various circumstances each has been successful to some extent, one has not been able to dominate the political landscape. Thus, drawing on Pickerill and Clayton's earlier description:

> [w]ithout taking a position in this debate, we simply note that in contrast to earlier periods of American history and previous constitutional regimes, the post-1960s American political system has been characterized by electoral dealignment, divided government, and a rise in partisan polarization. . . . Indeed, divided government has become the norm during this period; between 1968 and 2002, the same party controlled both the White House and both houses of Congress during only seven years. . . . The consequences of this political system for the role of the Court and judicial review are [that] during extended periods of divided government,_ a stronger form of judicial review becomes possible. Without a stable coalition controlling the elected branches, both parties have an incentive to turn to the courts to resolve political issues, while judges are less afraid of institutional retaliation if they make unpopular decisions. Unlike under unified government,

---

Impact Provisions", found in Douglas S. McDowell, ed. The Civil Rights Act of 1991: A Legislative History (Employment Policy Foundation, 1992), 10-12.

> presidents and legislators are unwilling or unable to coordinate an assault on judicial independence, and each party will fiercely defend the judiciary from encroachments by the other party.[657]

This is exactly what we find in these cases. Each occurred during an era of divided government and a rise in partisan polarization. A stronger form of judicial review was seen in these cases as justices were perhaps less afraid of making unpopular decisions. The Court, inexplicably, ruled on numerous civil rights related cases within a brief span, ruling to a point where the coalition-affiliated administration and party members in Congress were even willing to work toward the rejection of several of the decisions. In 2000, as it had in 1992, the Court again was willing to stake out a forceful position that it would seemingly not be in the same position to make were it not confident in its electoral viability.[658] By 2007, the Court had issued several rebukes of the Administration on detention policy, wading into an issue many did not expect it to address given the history of wartime-Court involvement. In each of these cases neither presidents nor legislators were able to coordinate an all-out assault on judicial independence, and as seen in the 2003 case, each party will defend the judiciary from perceived encroachments by the other party. As one current member commented, "[i]f you agree, of course you are going to say 'the Court has spoken.'"[659]

SYMBOLIC SPEECH

In addition, as one would predict in a politically partisan and predictable environment, constitutional deliberation as seen in these three cases points to the fact that much of what gets said in Congress

---

[657] J. Mitchell Pickerill and Cornell W. Clayton, "The Rehnquist Court and the Political Dynamic of Federalism," Perspectives on Politics 2, no. 2 (June 2004): 240-241.

[658] As one committee staffer conveyed, proponents of the bill specifically strategized how to comply with the *Stenberg* ruling. Committee Staff Interview, 2008.

[659] Member Interview, 2008.

can be called "symbolic speech" at the expense of the archeology of the specific issues. As Steven S. Smith writes, "much of the talk on the House and Senate floors has merely symbolic and theatrical purposes."[660] On one hand, much of it, by even fair estimation, would seem to be hyperbole or even vitriolic in nature. As shown, in these three cases there were accusations of outright allegiance with David Duke, Andrew Johnson, and Jim Crow-era segregation. An allegation was made that a particular administration was not enforcing the *13th* Amendment. Support for the majority-preferred bill in 1991 was equated with "quotas" and correlated with a business owner hanging a "help-wanted" sign requesting statistically proportionate numbers of job-seeking applicants.

This symbolic speech was present in all three cases, but most prevalent in the 2003 case study. This demonstrates the nature of discourse related to the issue of abortion. Given the perceived clarity of the issue by all involved, the comparatively high number of co-sponsors and plethora of floor statements, point to the "credit-claiming" role congressional deliberation often takes as members seek to profit from popular legislation or oppose prominent legislation important to key constituents or interest groups. The 2007 case, for example, had drastically less numbers both of co-sponsors and member statements about habeas corpus.

Secondly, we also see the rhetorical priority and reliance members place on the founding era, the Framers themselves, and the founding texts of our polity. In each case study this was done by opponents and supporters in an attempt to give authority to their positions. Appeals to the Declaration of Independence and the Constitution, in general, were made in each case, but most frequently about the 2003 bill. When members want to attempt to have the greatest emotional or rhetorical impact they turn to the documents and "values" related to these documents to articulate their generic or specific position.

Thirdly, and perhaps most importantly, we see the importance members place on, and how they place this "symbolic speech" and these Founding references in, what one might call "value narrative-

---

660 Steven S. Smith, Call to Order: Floor Politics in the House and Senate (Washington, D.C.: The Brookings Institute, 1989), 238.

arcs." In each case study, there was a "competition-of-narratives" in argumentation. This exemplifies the ways in which members (attempt to) understand our political history in the United States, the ways issues are framed for the general public, and the ways in which members of both parties choose to interpret the issues' respective histories, beliefs, and coherence, and the history, beliefs, and coherence of the perceived national narrative. Each respective position is equated with the true founding principles in fact or aspiration of the United States and narratives are drawn from them to the case study period with the "other" position framed as being on the "wrong side of history."

Thus, in 1991 we see a competition between "equal opportunity" and "quotas," between "civil rights" and "discrimination," between "equality," "justice" and "fairness," between "color-blindness" and "equal results." In 2003 there was a competition between "life," and "liberty" or "privacy," between competing conceptions of 'rights." In 2007, although members did have the benefit of having specific constitutional clauses with which to appeal, we nonetheless see a competition between "justice" and "law," between "American values" and "human rights," between safety and Executive aggrandizement, between citizens and "aliens," and between differing understandings of "sovereignty."

Again, this points to the way in which the circumstances on the Hill, the time limitations, the plethora of issues, the demands of modern campaigns, and the limits on debate all compress any such statements into consumable sound-bytes. In each case study members tried to frame the issue to some broader moral, theoretical, historical, or rhetorical narrative. Are these values, rhetoric, and narratives evidence of constitutional deliberation? Are the implicit statements alluding to constitutional values really explicit expressions of constitutional coherence? The answer is a qualified yes.[661] Each offers an opportunity but these opportunities were often missed.

---

[661] This discussion of symbolic speech, rhetoric, and narratives has not been aimed at diminishing such tools or such content. As Gaddis says, "[y]ou can't escape thinking about history [or issues deliberated upon in Congress] in moral terms. Nor, I believe, should you try to do so." Gaddis, The Landscape of History: How Historians Map the Past, 122. As representatives in a republican system deliberating on issues affecting our collective life, to

Thus, deliberation involving the Civil Rights Act of 1991 stayed at the value-laden broad level, with dichotomies drawn between "equal results" and "equal opportunity," and competing interpretations of "justice." *Griggs* was not mentioned frequently in specificity as to its constitutionality. The constitutional basis of the Civil Rights Act of 1964 was never discussed.[662] There was no mention of entire historical

---

not bring "moral" concerns to bear would seem to be impossible if not illogical.

662 As Professor Kmiec argued at the time, legislating against "impact" instead of "intent" led the constitutionality of the Act to exist in "travesty, rather than reality." Douglas W. Kmiec, "Foreword: The 1991 Civil Rights Act: A Constitutional, Statutory, and Philosophical Enigma," Notre Dame Law Review 68, no. 5 Symposium: The Civil Rights Act of 1991: Theory and Practice (1993): 915-917. Kmiec draws from an analogy using Father Theodore M. Hesburgh. "[O]fficial slavery coexisted with [Christianity] four hundred years after the death of Christ. When it reoccurred a millennium later, Christians were the best customers of the Arab traders. . . . Throughout the world, human dignity and human rights continued to exist in travesty rather than reality." Theodore M. Hesburgh, C.S.C., The Humane Imperative 25 (1974). Introducing a symposium, Kmiec explains, "All of the papers that follow assume the 1991 Act's constitutional validity. No one can fault either law professors or practitioners for this bit of practical legal realism. But being practical, does not make the proposition true. . . . the constitutionality of the 1991 Act . . . exists in travesty, rather than reality. . . . The two sources of constitutional power that the Act may be claimed to be premised upon seem unavailing. First, there is Congress' so-called section 5 authority to enforce the guarantee of equal protection. But, as already noted, the contours of equal protection are bounded by the necessity of showing discriminatory intent for its violation. True, former Justice Brennan claimed that Congress has the power to define equal protection in the Fourteenth Amendment differently than the Court. But a majority of the Court has never formally acceded to Brennan's view because it fundamentally displaces the Court's article III role to 'say what the law is.' And even if Congress has wide latitude to craft its own racial preference schemes, a narrowly affirmed federal liberality that still greatly divides the Court and does not extend to the states [Compare *Metro Broadcasting v. FCC*, 497 U.S. 547 (1990) with

eras (1873, 1875, 1883) and constitutional facts (the Privileges or Immunities Clause and Justice Harlan's dissent in the *Civil Rights Cases*, for example) that could have been narratively utilized. Congressionally empowering language in the Reconstruction Amendments was not mentioned. These historical facts could have grounded arguments for both sides and given them narrative solidity rather than staying at the mere "values" level.[663] Since the cases called

---

Richmond v. Croson, 488 U.S. 469 (1989)], the scope of Congress' authority to undertake such programs in its own right is arguably inapposite to its ability to define unintentional impacts to be discriminatory practices by private parties. . . . The alternative source of congressional power that may be claimed to underlie the 1991 Act is the power to regulate interstate commerce. The commerce power, of course, played an instrumental role in the validity of the 1964 Civil Rights Act [*Heart of Atlanta Motel v. United States*, 379 U.S. 241 (1964)]. But there, the assertion of authority made some sense. Congress was rightly concerned about removing impediments to the free flow of goods and persons that result from intentional racial discrimination. The Hesburgh Civil Rights Commission's difficulties in securing accommodations is illustrative. Admittedly, too, the Court's Commerce Clause cases hold that Congress may legislate against individual action under the analytically boundless 'cumulative effect' principle.[662] Yet, as broad as the commerce power is, it is hard to see how commerce is advanced by de facto racial employment quotas. In actual fact, commerce is very likely burdened, not advanced, by such social engineering. In all events, whatever the scope of the commerce power with respect to private parties, Congress should not disregard hornbook equal protection guarantees, at least with respect to public employers, and those again relate to intent, rather than impact. . . . For political reasons and others, these constitutional misgivings are not likely to be soon addressed in court. So disregard the constitutional muddle, if you will, and turn to the statute."

[663] They could have helped facilitate a more "informed and informative debate." "Both Republican and Democratic minorities have claimed that the especially tailored and usually restrictive special rules under which the House now considers most major legislation degrade floor deliberation, and a good many commentators have bought that argument. This contention is, I argue, based on a false premise; it is unrealistic to expect deliberation, as a great many people use the term, to take place on the floor of either chamber,

into question the 1971 case which "first grafted disparate-impact rules onto the 1964 Civil Rights Act,"[664] it would have been an opportune time to revisit the intent of the 1964 Act and even the meaning and intent of the 14th Amendment and its clauses, if necessary. Members could have discussed *Griggs*, what it meant, and why it was important.[665] After all, this broader debate had been going on throughout the entire decade.[666]

---

and certainly not in the House. If deliberation is defined as the process by which a group of people get together and talk through a complex problem, mapping the problem's contours, defining the alternatives, and figuring out where they stand, it is unrealistic to expect all of that to occur on the chamber floors. Deliberation in this sense is a nonlinear, free-form process that depends on strictly limiting the size of the group; sub-committees, other small groups, and possibly committees are the forums where this sort of deliberation might be fostered. Deliberation so defined certainly did not occur on the House floor before restrictive rules became prevalent. . . . What we can and should expect on the chamber floors in informed and informative debate and sound decision making. Restrictive rules can in fact contribute toward those goals. Rules can provide order and predictability to the consideration on the floor of complex and controversial legislation; they can be used to ensure that floor time is apportioned in a reasonable and sensible way for each bill, and that debate focuses on the major alternatives, not on minor or side issues." Barbara Sinclair, "Can Congress Be Trusted with the Constitution? The Effects of Incentives and Procedures," in Congress and the Constitution, 303.

664 Stuart Taylor, "Sotomayor And 'Disparate Impact,'" National Journal Magazine (30 May 2009), available at NationalJournal.com.

665 As Nicole Gueron writes, "The Supreme Court has interpreted Title VII of the Civil Rights Act of 1964 to prohibit not only intentional discrimination or 'disparate treatment,' but also unintentional discrimination that has a 'disparate impact' on protected class members. *See, e.g.*, *Griggs v. Duke Power Co.*, 401 U.S. 424 (1971). Disparate impact exists if facially neutral selection or promotion criteria, for example, operate to exclude or reduce the opportunities of protected class members at a disproportionate rate. id, at 431-32. Employers may argue as an affirmative defense to a disparate impact charge that the challenged criteria are a 'business necessity.' id, at 431. In

In the 2003 case, supporters of the ban did not offer detailed arguments of why the *Roe* and *Dalton* understanding was misguided. *Griswold* was in fact only mentioned twice.[667] A "pro-life" position

---

Wards Cove Packing Co. v. Atonio, 490 U.S. 642 (1989), the Court reinterpreted several aspects of disparate impact theory, thus raising numerous questions about the proper interpretation of business necessity doctrine. These issues included the extent to which business necessity would require that disputed hiring criteria be related to successful job performance, the location of the burden of proof of business necessity, and the specificity with which complaining employees or job applicants would have to pinpoint the employment practices that caused the disparate impact." Nicole L. Gueron, "An Idea Whose Time Has Come: A Comparative Procedural History of the Civil Rights Acts of 1960, 1964, and 1991," The Yale Law Journal 104, no. 5 (Mar. 1995): 1204.

[666] Between 1982 and 1988, Congress overruled seven Supreme Court decisions concerning interpretation of antidiscrimination provisions; in each instance, Congress increased the ability of plaintiffs to bring and prevail in suits compared to the rights recognized by the Court. See Abner J. Mikva and Jeff Bleich, "When Congress Overrules the Court," California Law Review 79, no. 3 Symposium: Civil Rights Legislation in the 1990s (May 1991): 740.

[667] Rep. King (R-IA) does mention it in his brief outline of the trajectory of abortion jurisprudence: "I am not a lawyer. I grew up in a cornfield and rode out on a bulldozer, but I can tell you I know this much about law. How did we get here to this point? I do not think anybody has referenced it now, and that is the case in 1965, *Griswold v. Connecticut*, right to privacy, when Connecticut outlawed contraceptives and the Supreme Court ruled that the State of Connecticut had no business getting into the privacy of the family and, therefore, found their law that outlawed contraceptives unconstitutional. That is the foundation for right to privacy. Just a few years later, 8 years later, along came *Roe v. Wade*. That was the piece that said, well, that right to privacy extends to the woman's womb and in our declaration where it defines life, liberty, pursuit of happiness, those rights are prioritized except that the right of the liberty of the pregnant female takes priority over the life of the unborn. And then *Roe v. Wade*, of course, outlawed, though it did not make an exception for, late-term post-viability abortions. But same day, concurrent decision, *Doe v. Bolton* gave that definition that I think we have

supporting a different principle of "privacy" was not offered. Opponents of the ban did not offer any explanation for how they might respond to a Court they were giving enormous deference, were that Court to start enforcing, as part of an unenumerated rights rubric, economic rights within a substantive due process understanding of 5th and 14th Amendment jurisprudence. Justice Black's dissent in *Griswold* was not mentioned. We did not see detailed discusses of constitutional first principles about "personhood" and the 14th Amendment.[668]

---

heard that addresses the health of the mother. It does not prohibit any abortion if in the medical judgment of the attending physician the abortion is necessary to preserve the life of the woman or to avert serious adverse health consequences to the woman, a hole you could drive a truck through. That is also what this amendment seeks to do, and that is another reason that I oppose it. *Planned Parenthood v. Casey* reaffirmed *Roe v. Wade*. That is what it looks like to this fellow who did not go to law school, but does read the cases." Rep. Steve King (R-IA), Congressional Record, 108th Cong., 1st sess., 2003, vol. 149, no. 81, H4943 (4 Jun. 2003). Using Lexis Nexis Congressional, only one other mention of "Griswold" relevant to partial-birth abortion entries can be found in the Congressional Daily Record & Rules during the 107th and 108th Congresses. Sen. Patty Murray (D-WA) quickly mentions it as a precedent for *Roe*. Congressional Record, 108th Cong., 1st sess., 149, no. 128, S11601 (17 Sept. 2003).

668 As for example, found in Nathan Schlueter and Robert H. Bork, "Constitutional Persons: An Exchange on Abortion," Human Life Review 29, issue 1 (Winter 2003): 17-33. This article first appeared in First Things (Jan. 2003). See also, for one such grounding, see Brief of Amici Curiae Professor Hadley Arkes and The Claremont Institute Center for Constitutional Jurisprudence In Support of Petitioner NO. 05-1382 In *The Supreme Court of the United States Alberto R. Gonzales, Attorney General, Petitioner, v. Planned Parenthood Fed. Of America, Inc., Et al., Respondents, On Writ of Certiorari to the United States Court of Appeals For the Ninth Circuit*. This amici curiae asked three main questions which seem pertinent here: "Whether the Partial-Birth Abortion Ban Act of 2003 is a valid exercise of Congress's authority under the Commerce Clause (either as originally understood or as presently interpreted)? Whether, apart from the Commerce Clause, Congress had the constitutional authority to enact the

In 2007, we did not hear supporters of the President's detention policies making forceful articulations and defenses of executive prerogative in foreign policy and war policy. Most defenses focused on the "rights" or non-rights of citizen and aliens or enemy combatants. They did not enter into prolonged discussions on the debate between declare and make war and the philosophical reasons why the executive needs a free hand in detention policy and war-making decisions. Virtually no members offered a robust explanation of the role of the Executive, of the Legislature, and of the Judiciary in war-time, in foreign affairs, and in war-related issues. No correlations were made to the philosophy behind an executive in republican government. We did not frequent or wide-ranging uses and references to *Ex parte Quirin* or *Johnson v. Eisentrager*, to *McCardle* to support Court-stripping,[669] to the *Prize Cases* to support congressional involvement, to *Ex parte Bollman* to support congressional suspension of the writ, or historical discussions of Article I, Sections 8 and 9, nor the discussions pertaining to habeas during the Constitutional Convention. In the frank assessment of one Senate staff member, "[f]oreign policy is driven by politics, not necessarily policy."[670]

ELECTIONS

Elections are obviously also important for members of Congress.[671] They are another factor, Pickerill argues, that enhance congressional

---

Partial-Birth Abortion Ban Act of 2003? Whether this Court's enunciation of an abortion right permits it to lay claim to the inherently legislative authority to determine the scope and weight to be given to that right?"

[669] As Whittington writes, the introduction of bills to restructure and rein in the judiciary is also periodic, with leadership support for such measures and their relative success most likely to come during these same reconstructive periods." Political Foundations of Judiciary Supremacy: The Presidency, the Supreme Court, and Constitutional Leadership in U.S. History, 81.

[670] Staff Interview, 2008.

[671] As one staffer commented, reaffirming the "electoral connection," "everything is about the next election." Staff Interview, 2009.

constitutional deliberation.[672] Keith Whittington writes, "elections seem to have the potential to encourage even greater discussion of constitutional matters, either because they have brought to power new legislative majorities with a new agenda to discuss or because incumbent legislators turn to constitutional issues in their quest to gain advantage in an upcoming electoral contest."[673] This was true in these three cases. As already mentioned, the upcoming congressional and presidential elections seemed to have a strong affect on the 1991 Civil Rights Act. Many argued the President switched his position at the last moment because of these elections. The 2003 Partial-Birth Abortion Ban Act was affected by the election of 2000, the 2002 midterm elections, and the upcoming elections in 2004. The election in 2000 allowed supporters to know they had a White House willing to sign the bill. The 2002 elections solidified majorities in both chambers supportive of the bill. Finally, it could be argued that the 2004 election constrained the supporters of the bill given that not knowing the outcome of the election, they stuck with a very confined bill rather than a more expansive one that may have been more controversial. The Military Commissions vote was scheduled right around the 2006 election. The Habeas Corpus Restoration Act of 2007 was affected by the election given that supporters simply didn't have the votes to pass the bill and thus the upcoming election allowed those opposed to the bill time to wait to see what direction the Court took next.

As previously discussed, Judge Mikva's dated observation is still relevant: many members who speak on the floor or in hearings may only be doing so to get their already predetermined views into the official record.[674] As one member stated lamenting the "lack of

---

[672] Keith E. Whittington, "Hearing about the Constitution in Congressional Committees," in Congress and the Constitution, 87-109.

[673] Keith E. Whittington, "Hearing about the Constitution in Congressional Committees," 105.

[674] Mikva wrote, "both houses are large, making the process of engaging in complex arguments during a floor debate difficult. For the most part, the speeches made on the floor are designed to get a member's position on the record rather than to initiate a dialogue. Because of the volume of legislation, the time spent with constituents, and the technical knowledge required to

understanding of the Constitution and what is constitutional," members have to be concerned with what "can . . . be put on a TV ad. . . . Most members don't deal with it [the Constitution] as an everyday issue. . . . Some people don't care about the words or phrases. You try to make it relevant but to some people it's just not relevant."[675]

Nevertheless, arguments to the contrary, judging from the partisan votes, predictable words, symbolic gestures, and missed opportunities, this evidence affirms what we know Congress to be: a very political institution.[676] In fact, for example, in 1991 they ducked the "business

---

understand the background of every piece of legislation, it is infrequent that a member considers the individual merits of a particular bill. Often a vote is determined by a thumbs up-or-down sign by the party leader, or by a political debt that needs to be repaid. While it is true . . . that a majority of the members of Congress are lawyers, they have not kept up-to-date on recent legal developments. In fact, most Supreme Court opinions never come to the attention of Congress. Unlike judges, the Representatives and Senators are almost totally dependent on the recommendations of others in making constitutional judgments." Abner J. Mikva, "How Well Does Congress Support and Defend the Constitution?," North Carolina Law Review 61 (1983): 609. A former House Parliamentarian reminds us of the importance of television. "It should be remembered that on March 19th, 1979, television first came into the House. As a former Parliamentarian describes, "there was a downside. 'Once television was in place,' 'members were less willing to take on their opponents and to potentially be embarrassed, preferring, instead, to have prescripted speeches and then sit down. And that's virtually all you see now.' Today, rarely, if ever, does a speech on the House floor change a single vote. Members are more likely to direct their remarks at an unseen television audience, not their colleagues." Robert V. Remini, The House: The History of the House of Representatives (Collins: Smithsonian Books, 2006), 461, quoting, Charles Johnson, Parliamentarian of the House from 1994-2004, to the author, March 9, 2005.

[675] The same member added, "[i]f 1% of the bill you find unconstitutional that's probably not enough to make you vote against it." Member Interview, 2008.

[676] When asked about Congress' constitutionally deliberative capacities, one former member commented: "[T]here are premises in your questions that seem to envision a kind of deliberation that is not common to the legislative process. The Congress is neither a court nor a law school. The discussions

necessity" issue.[677] They avoided the retroactivity issue and wanted no part in re-discussing *Runyon*.[678] They were intentionally statutorily

involved in legislation center on policy preferences and, as a part of that process, different perceptions of fact and differing assessments of likely outcomes. Legislation is always carefully drafted to meet constitutional standards, but of course lawyers and even Supreme Court justices disagree about what is constitutional. And of course the courts are not the sole arbiters of constitutionality, although in practice we let the Supreme Court make the final call. If a member believes a piece of proposed legislation violates the Constitution, he or she will make that point in debate – as I did on both term limits and [the] line item veto – and the bill's proponents will contend, believing it to be so, that the bill has been drawn to meet constitutional standards. Opponents will make their case in subcommittee, in committee, on the floor, in op[-]eds, in letters to other members, etc. But there will never be a debate about constitutionality as there will be in court. The civil rights act of 1991 was probably seen by most members not as a constitutional question but as a policy question. If a question is raised re constitutionality, some proponents will argue that the criteria have been met while others may say that they believe the criteria have been met, but if not, the courts will deal with the matter (a position I personally find troubling). But a last question is bothersome. Almost all members base their votes on principle and their own careful analysis, drawing on staff research, testimony, scholarly data, anecdotal testimony from constituents and a variety of other sources. The belief that most members base their votes on a re-election calculus is poli sci nonsense – constituent concerns and preferences are included, properly, in the decision[-]making process, among a great number of factors." Member Interview, 2008.

677 "Instead, Congress left that issue to future litigation, and delegated to the Court the power to breathe life into the defense of 'business necessity' – to either narrow its protective umbrella or expand it. It was Congress, not the Court, that created a vacuum and invited the judiciary to fill it. Congress could have overturned, modified, or elaborated on the *Wards Cove* test for 'business necessity,' but it did not do so. The only reason that the buck stops with the Supreme Court on this issue is that Congress chose to pass the buck." Ronald D. Rotunda, "The Civil Rights Act of 1991: A Brief Introductory Analysis of the Congressional Response to Judicial

ambiguous,[679] they curiously exempted themselves,[680] and they even excluded Wards Cove itself, the central entity the legislation was

---

Interpretation," Notre Dame Law Review 68, no. 5 Symposium: The Civil Rights Act of 1991: Theory and Practice (1993): 937. The definition of "business necessity" was changed from some disputed action by necessity being "essential to effective job performance" to that action "bear[ing] a substantial and demonstrable relationship to effective job performance."

[678] Likewise, in preparing to hear *Patterson*, the Supreme Court apparently touched a political nerve when it requested that the parties brief for reconsideration the decision in *Runyon v. McCrary*. In response, Congress filed an amicus brief signed by 66 Senators and 118 Representatives urging the Court to reaffirm its *Runyon* holding. The brief stated candidly that the members of Congress wished to avoid the political heat of having to decide *Runyon* itself. Their brief stated that 'the legislative effort necessary to restore [*Runyon*] would likely be fractious and divisive, since corrective legislation would, in all likelihood, compel the Congress to address numerous peripheral questions concerning the scope and application of Section 1981.' Brief of Amici Curiae in Support of Petitioner at 2, *Patterson*, 491 U.S. 164 (1989) (No. 87-107).

[679] "[T]he 1991 Act is a case of 'planned ambiguity' and that '[t]he inherent result of [this] planned ambiguity in the Civil Rights Act is unnecessary make-work for lawyers' as well as increased and burdensome litigation for employers and employees." Douglas W. Kmiec, "Foreword: The 1991 Civil Rights Act: A Constitutional, Statutory, and Philosophical Enigma," Notre Dame Law Review 68, no. 5 Symposium: The Civil Rights Act of 1991: Theory and Practice (1993): 915-917, citing Ronald D. Rotunda, "The Civil Rights Act of 1991: A Brief Introductory Analysis of the Congressional Response to Judicial Interpretation," Notre Dame Law Review 68, no. 5 Symposium: The Civil Rights Act of 1991: Theory and Practice (1993): 927.

[680] As Nelson Lund wrote two years later, "[d]uring the Senate's debate on the Civil Rights Act of 1991, its Members had occasion to exercise that responsibility in response to demands that the employment discrimination laws be extended to cover the Senate. The content of that debate, however, suggests Congress can be trusted to discern the limits of its own constitutional rights to about the same degree it can be trusted to police its own compliance with the laws against employment discrimination. . . . In reviewing the Senate's debates, it is important to keep in mind the difference

between reasoned interpretation of the Constitution, an undertaking that transcends persons and interests, and self-serving policy judgments masquerading as 'separation of powers' arguments that are untethered to any specific constitutional provision. . . . The Civil Rights Act of 1991 resulted from a compromise between the Bush administration and Senate supporters of a bill that had been vetoed by the President the previous year. A bill embodying this compromise, which was reached late in the 1991 session, was taken directly to the floor of the Senate, without committee consideration. The compromise bill did not include provisions addressing the congressional coverage issue. Because the Senate bill was considered by the House of Representatives under a closed rule, and passed out of the House without amendment, the legislative history of the congressional coverage provisions is contained entirely in the Senate debates. . . . The congressional exemption from the laws against employment discrimination has persisted since those laws were first enacted. Those who framed our Constitution considered such exemptions pernicious, and the Constitution neither encourages nor requires them. The Framers also recognized, however, that natural human selfishness would incline any legislature to create special privileges for itself, and the Constitution does not prevent this from happening. . . . One feature of the Constitution – arming the President with the legislative power that his veto provides – might be expected to help control the congressional appetite for special privileges. That device received a revealing test during the struggle that culminated in the Civil Rights Act of 1991. Faced with a President who said he favored applying the law to Congress and who had expressed strong opposition to many of the regulatory burdens that the new statute imposes on other employers, Congress nonetheless managed both to preserve its own exemption from the law and to impose significant new burdens on other employers. In the unusual circumstances that led to the enactment of the Civil Rights Act of 1991, it appears that greater presidential resolve might very well have forced the elimination of the longstanding congressional exemption. . . . Had Congress been brought under the law in 1991, the other revisions of the employment discrimination laws might also have been quite different. The new statute creates significant new legal impositions and uncertainties, and there is scant evidence they were ever measured carefully against the public benefits that may accrue from imposing them. Those who voted for this statute – and there was almost no opposition in either chamber to the final bill – might not supposed to address. In 2003, it held but one hearing on the issue and in 2007, Congress was routinely and loudly criticized for not legislating enough.

ALWAYS A BRANCH

DIALOGUES

Participatory members do deserve credit for doing so because this meets the minimal standard of informing their constituents where they stand on an issue and allowing for a collective parliamentary rule-bound discussion to take place. As Gutmann and Thompson write

> [i]n its strongest form, constitutional democracy tells representatives to consider how the Constitution should be interpreted, not simply to accept how the courts have so far interpreted it. Deliberative democracy goes further. To satisfy its demands, a representative . . . must consider, and encourage his constituents to consider with him in public discussion, what basic liberties should be protected by the Constitution. Without engaging in deliberation about this question, neither he nor his constituents can regard their conclusions about constitutional liberties as warranting the respect of their fellow citizens. They may be convinced that they are right – they may even be right – about what the Constitution requires or should require. But if they are deliberative democrats, they will submit their constitutional conclusions to the critical scrutiny of their fellow citizens, conducted in accord with principles of reciprocity and publicity. They will regard the capacity to survive such scrutiny as a necessary condition and a

---

have been nearly so ready to impose these burdens and uncertainties on private employers if they themselves had expected to have to live with them." Nelson Lund, "Congressional Self-Exemption from the Employment Discrimination Laws: A Rational Choice Analysis of the Civil Rights Act of 1991," Louisiana Law Review 54 (1993-1994): 1583-84, 1602-03.

> substantial reason for making their conclusions the law of the land.[681]

As Mayhew writes, "[*t*]aking *stands* is one of the fundamental activities that members of Congress engage in."[682] Thus, members can be commended for going on the record and whatever their motive, registering their public position on these controversial issues. "Looked at one way, politics is an unending sequence of contributions to a national conversation – an often crankly and contentious one, to be sure."[683]

It is important to understand the branches in the reality in which they exist. As Whittington argues, "[a]n examination of the political considerations of presidents sheds light on how constitutions are constructed and maintained in politically fractious environments. For constitutions and institutions like judicial review to exist in historical reality as more than imagined moral abstractions, powerful social actors must have political reasons to support them over time."[684] Thus, in relationship to the Court:

---

681 Amy Gutmann and Dennis Thompson, Democracy and Disagreement (Cambridge: Harvard University Press, 1996), 163-164. Also, as cited earlier, Garrett and Vermeule write, "[i]t seems indisputable that on balance, some congressional deliberation on constitutional questions is better than none at all." Elizabeth Garrett and Adrian Vermeule, "Institutional Design of a Thayerian Congress," in Congress and the Constitution, 248.

682 See David R. Mayhew, America's Congress: Actions in the Public Sphere, James Madison to Newt Gingrich (Binghamton, NY: Vail-Ballou Press, 2000), 90-102.

683 David R. Mayhew, "Actions in the Public Sphere," in Paul J. Quirk and Sarah A. Binder, eds. The Legislative Branch (Oxford: Oxford University Press, 2005), 76.

684 Keith E. Whittington, "The Political Foundations of Judicial Supremacy," in Sotirios A. Barber and Robert P. George, eds., Constitutional Politics: Essays on Constitution Making, Maintenance, and Change (Princeton: Princeton University Press, 2001), 263.

> the presidency is perhaps the most significant competitor with the Court for constitutional authority. The president is a highly visible institutional representative with numerous political and constitutional resources and functions that could easily lead him into conflicts with the judiciary. The president and the Court are, therefore, likely to compete for the right to authoritatively determine constitutional meaning. If the Court is to establish its authority as the ultimate interpreter of constitutional meaning, and thus secure judicial independence, it will have to contend with presidential challenges. Judicial success in this competition . . . depends crucially on the incentives facing the president. The president has the formal tools to defeat the Court. The interesting question is whether he has the will or political support needed to successfully challenge the Court for constitutional leadership. Generally, he does not, creating a politically sustainable place for autonomous judicial action.[685]

Nevertheless, the fact that Congress was acting is important because it continues the process of dialogue between the branches, informs the electorate and citizenry where they stand, and provides means by which that electorate can now receive new information and cues with which to then decide before the next election how well they are pleased with the status quo or attempt to change it through other means.

More importantly, these cases and this analysis highlight the importance of the understanding of inter-branch dialogues. Because affiliation assumes the presence of dialogue, since a reconstructive leader is neither present nor strong enough to shift regime changes in the political arena alone, it is important Congress view its deliberation as an important part of the inter-branch conversation.

---

[685] Keith E. Whittington, "The Political Foundations of Judicial Supremacy," in Sotirios A. Barber and Robert P. George, eds., Constitutional Politics: Essays on Constitution Making, Maintenance, and Change (Princeton: Princeton University Press, 2001), 264.

VETO BARGAINING

An important aspect of these relationships is a "veto bargaining" mechanism whereby Congress and presidents negotiate compromises and solutions through institutional "bargaining."[686] As Whittington writes, "[a] president's authority to lead is partly determined by his relationship to the dominant political 'regime' and the relative strength of that regime. . . . The authority for a president to act is structured largely by the expectations of other political actors, which help define 'what is appropriate for a given president to do.' 'A president's authority hinges on the warrants that can be drawn from the moment at hand to justify action and secure the legitimacy of the changes affected.'"[687]

This can very clearly be seen in 1991. President Bush very publicly vetoed the Civil Rights Act of 1990 and it was debated between the White House and Congress for two full years. In addition, given President Bush's reliance on and success with his anti-quota position and rhetoric, the House leadership added specific language to the final bill explicitly banning any use of quotas in employment, thereby attempting to allow supporters cover from the "quota" charge.

This is less the case in 2003 and 2007. In 2003, what had changed from the 1990s inter-branch debates was a change in administration. Thus, a majority in Congress and the President agreed on the issue, thereby lessening the need for bargaining. In the Habeas case, the President had for five years congressional majorities opposing habeas rights for detainees, and that position may have been strengthened by

---

686 "[T]he president may use actual vetoes not only to block legislation, but to shape it. . . . In most cases Congress and the president find their way to an agreement that reflects the preferences of both parties." Charles M. Cameron, Veto Bargaining: Presidents and the Power of Negative Bargaining (Cambridge: Cambridge University Press, 2000), 9, 176.

687 Keith E. Whittington, "The Political Foundations of Judicial Supremacy," 264-265, in Sotirios A. Barber and Robert P. George, eds., Constitutional Politics: Essays on Constitution Making, Maintenance, and Change (Princeton: Princeton University Press, 2001), quoting Stephen Skowronek, The Politics Presidents Make (Cambridge: Harvard University Press, 1993), 18.

the fact that a veto was likely if it did pass. Nevertheless, by asserting such unilateral executive power, President Bush probably misread the regime within which he was operating. By interpreting a "weak" regime for a strong one, he acted as if his regime was stronger than it actually was.[688] The President clearly emerging weaker, especially considering that "in fact most legal issues of executive branch conduct related to war and intelligence never reach a court, or do so only years after the executive has acted."[689] As Jack Goldsmith writes:

> The Military Commission Act was a victory for it [the Bush Administration] only against the baseline of expectations established by the Supreme Court a few months earlier. Measured against the baseline of what it could have gotten from a more cooperative Congress in 2002-03, the administration had lost a lot. If it had earlier established a legislative regime of legal rights on Guantanamo Bay, it never would have had to live with the Court's Common Article 3 holding, or with the War Crimes Act. If the administration had simply followed the Geneva requirement to hold an informal 'competent tribunal,' or had gone to Congress for support on their detention program in the summer of 2004, it probably would have avoided the more burdensome procedural and judicial requirements that became practically necessary under the pressure of subsequent judicial review._ It surely could have received an even more accommodating military commission system if they had made the push in Congress in 2002-2003 instead of the fall of 2006.[690]

---

688 As Dahl wrote, "[i]t is to be expected, then, that the Court is least likely to be successful in blocking a determined and persistent lawmaking majority on a major policy and most likely to succeed against a 'weak' majority; e.g., a dead one, a transient one, a fragile one, or one weakly united upon a policy of subordinate importance." Robert A. Dahl, "Decision-Making in a Democracy: The Supreme Court as a National Policy-Maker," Journal of Public Law 6 (1957): 286.

689 Jack Goldsmith, The Terror Presidency: Law and Judgment Inside The Bush Administration (New York: W. W. Norton, 2007), 32.

690 ibid, 139-140.

JUDICIAL BARGAINING

Similarly, Pickerill and many others have written extensively about veto bargaining in the judicial realm.[691] Pickerill found that

> legislation may be modified after judicial review to accommodate the Court and reflect the preferences of both institutions. That is, when the Court strikes down legislation as unconstitutional, Congress may choose to make concessions to the Court by modifying the law to comply with the Court's constitutional interpretation while maintaining the basic statutory policy. Veto-like bargaining between Congress and the Court will surely be different from that between Congress and presidents. Congress and presidents can negotiate directly, face to face. Communication between the Court and Congress is indirect at best.[692]

The Habeas Restoration Act does seem to provide an example of judicial veto bargaining.[693] Preceding it were numerous inter-branch

---

[691] Charles M. Cameron, Veto Bargaining: Presidents and the Politics of Negative Power (Cambridge: Cambridge University Press, 2000); J. Mitchell Pickerill, "Congressional Responses to Judicial Review," in Congress and the Constitution, eds. Devins and Whittington (Durham: Duke University Press, 2005), 151-172; J. Mitchell Pickerill, "(Judicial) Veto Bargaining Between Congress and the Supreme Court," in "Congress, the Constitution, and the Courts," Extensions: A Journal of the Carl Albert Congressional Research and Studies Center Fall 2008; J. Mitchell Pickerill, Constitutional Deliberation in Congress: The Impact of Judicial Review in a Separated System (Durham: Duke University Press, 2004).

[692] J. Mitchell Pickerill, "Congressional Responses to Judicial Review," in Congress and the Constitution, 154. Also, Constitutional Deliberation in Congress, 34-35. "When more is at stake for a majority in Congress, members will be more likely to explore ways to respond to the Court." 38.

[693] The term comes from Pickerill, Constitutional Deliberation in Congress: The Impact of Judicial Review in a Separated System. Given the habeas-related efforts at jurisdiction-stripping and the Court's declarations culminating in *Boumediene*, it might appear there was not much

developments. During the first several years after 9/11 Congress was unwilling to pass any substantive legislation dealing with habeas corpus and detainees at Guantánamo. Then, in reaction to the three major Court rulings in 2004, *Rasul*, *Hamdi*, and *Padilla*, Congress actively debated and deliberated over the Detainee Treatment Act in 2005. After *Hamdan* was issued in 2006 Congress debated and deliberated over the Military Commissions Act. Some in Congress tried to pass the 2007 Act. The Court issued *Boumediene* a year later, after previously declining to take the case. Various members in Congress responded again with the Military Commissions Act of 2009,[694] the

---

"bargaining" taking place. However, if one approaches the Act through the lens and context of the entire inter-branch "terror" dialogue and environment, one can make a strong case for bargaining taking place, of which habeas is perhaps its proxy, over what branch will be allowed what role over detainee policy in general and who will be allowed maximum leverage to define the overall nature of the "war on terror" as it relates to that policy. The Court in affect "stays in the game" by initially allowing detention but attempting to circumscribe it, recommending a path forward (Army Regulation 190-8), ruling that the DTA was not in fact retroactive, then reversing themselves to take cert in *Boumediene*. Congress, after failing to act, responds within these confines by twice legislating its own detainee procedural and review processes, nonetheless always without ambiguity about its position on habeas, as habeas, it can be argued, and many members may have felt, cuts to the heart of the "terror" dilemma: what is the ultimate identity of the enemy and who gets to so define it?

[694] Section XVIII of the Department of Defense Authorization for Fiscal 2010, H.R. 2647. The Military Commissions Act of 2009 amended the Military Commission Act of 2006. The 2009 Act is Title XVIII of the National Defense Authorization Act for Fiscal Year 2010, H.R. 2647, Public Law 111-84, enacted October 28, 2009. It placed restrictions on coerced testimony, hearsay evidence, and provided greater resources to defense counsels. According to CRS, the Act: "Amends the Uniform Code of Military Justice (UCMJ) to conform procedures for offenses triable by military commissions to procedures governing trials by military courts-martial (as necessitated by the Supreme Court's ruling in *Hamdan v. Rumsfeld*, 548 U.S. 557.) Includes among such changes: (1) replacing the term 'unlawful enemy combatant' with 'unprivileged enemy belligerent;' (2)

Enemy Belligerent Interrogation, Detention, and Prosecution Act of 2010, and the Terrorist Detention Review Reform Act of 2010[695] in an

---

making subject to military commissions any alien unprivileged enemy belligerent who engaged in or supported hostilities against the United States or its coalition partners; (3) requiring the Secretary to prescribe regulations for the appointment and performance of defense counsel in capital cases before military commissions; (4) requiring that statements obtained by the use of torture or cruel, inhuman, or degrading treatment, whether or not under color of law, be inadmissible in a trial by a military commission; (5) specifically requiring procedures and rules of evidence applicable to trials by general courts-martial to apply in trials by military commissions, except when necessitated by the unique circumstances of the conduct of military and intelligence operations during hostilities or other practical need; (6) the accused's right to the suppression of evidence that is not reliable or probative; (7) specific limitations on the use of hearsay evidence not otherwise admissible under rules of evidence applicable in trials by general courts-martial; (8) specific procedures for the treatment and protection of classified information; (9) appeal rights with respect to classified information; and (10) adding contempt and perjury and obstruction of justice as triable offenses. Directs the Secretary to report to the defense committees: (1) setting forth revised rules for military commissions as amended by this section; and (2) annually on any trials conducted by military commissions during the preceding year. Expresses the sense of Congress that: (1) the fairness and effectiveness of the military commission system will depend to a significant degree on the adequacy of defense counsel and associated resources for individuals accused, particularly in capital cases; and (2) defense counsel in such cases should be fully resourced to perform such duties."

695 See Josh Gerstein, "Graham quietly files Gitmo habeas bill," Politico 11 Aug. 2010, available at http://www.politico.com/news/stories/0810/40968.html. Sen. Lindsey Graham filed the Terrorist Detention Review Reform Act on August 4, 2010. As Gerstein writes, "Graham . . . may have concluded that filing formal legislation was the best way to pressure the administration into a position on the politically sensitive issue. . . . The bill would apply to anyone whom the federal government seeks to detain as an 'unprivileged enemy belligerent' – including U.S. citizens. It could also apply to anyone apprehended on U.S. soil, since there is no geographic

effort at continued negotiation, as the previous institutional actions can be understood to be as well, in effect, over the specific contours of detention policy and the desire to assert and defend the relevance of one's institutional participation.

The data points are less frequent but we can see the same framework in the 2003 case. For half-a-decade bills were introduced in Congress and vetoed by the President, never reaching the Court. However, the Court did overrule a state statute that was in effect a proxy for what congressional majorities had been trying to do. Congress responded to the Court by specifically operating within the Court-delineated jurisprudential confines of the issue, rather than attempting a more sweeping piece of legislation. The Court upheld the response, giving the parties what Whittington calls a "win-win,"[696] a

---

limitation. . . . Asked whether the bill has missed its political moment, [Brookings Institution scholar Benjamin] Wittes said he doesn't know whether it ever had one, because Graham 'is the only voice for something that really should be a matter of political consensus.' "'The administration hasn't been able to get its act together to give a serious response,' Wittes said. Republicans, he added, 'have been too busy demagoguing the issue to engage seriously and the Democrats have just abandoned the field.'" Also, Justice Kennedy recently endorsed civilian courts for detainees, saying the "attack on the rule of law [military tribunals]" has failed." See "Kennedy favors civilian courts in terrorism cases." Available at http://news.yahoo.com/s/ap/20100820/ap_on_re_us/us_judicial_conference_kennedy.

[696] See Keith E. Whittington, "Review: James Madison Has Left the Building," Review of Constitutional Deliberation in Congress: The Impact of Judicial Review in a Separated System by J. Mitchell Pickerill University of Chicago Law Review 72 (summer 2005): 1146. He is referring to Pickerill's discussion on 34-38 in Constitutional Deliberation in Congress, where he discusses how often the Court, operating on a constitutional dimension will get to "keep" its constitutional framework, while Congress, operating on a policy aim, will adjust their stricken-down statute to accomplish the same goal. Also, here Congress engaged in "anticipatory obedience." "A legislature engages in anticipatory obedience when it predicts what a court would say about the constitutionality of a proposal were it to be enacted, and adapts the proposal to ensure that it will survive judicial scrutiny." Mark Tushnet,

situation in which the Court has kept important parts of its institutional and jurisprudential prerogative, while Congress has participated coordinately and added important contributions.[697]

The 1991 case is more difficult to assess. While it may not have been thought of as "bargaining," the Court, by taking so many civil-rights cases, appeared to have been sending a message to Congress. In fact, the most important question was never answered: why did the

---

"Evaluating Congressional Constitutional Interpretation: Some Criteria and Two Informal Case Studies," in Congress and the Constitution, 271.

697 Pickerill also reminds us that "Other scholars have shown that legislative responses to *Roe v. Wade* (1973) indicate challenges to the Court's decision establishing abortion rights for women. While Congress did not ignore or successfully override *Roe*, it did, along with state legislatures, pass legislation that made it more difficult for women to obtain abortions, often with the avowed intent of discouraging and reducing the number of abortions. [Pickerill cites Susan R. Burgess, Contest for Constitutional Authority: The Abortion and War Powers Debates (Lawrence: University Press of Kansas, 1992) and Neal Devins, Shaping Constitutional Values: Elected Government, the Supreme Court, and the Abortion Debate (Baltimore: Johns Hopkins University Press, 1996) while adding, "[t]his does not mean that members of Congress did not try to override *Roe* by constitutional amendment or other legislative means, but only that successful congressional enactments did not ultimately rise to the level of an override."] Congress passed legislation limiting the availability of federal funding for abortions, and state legislatures passed numerous regulations intended to discourage and reduce abortion. While not an instance of an override, coordinate constructionists view the abortion saga as evidence of both legislative authority and the ability to engage in constitutional construction, influence the course of constitutional law, and reject the notion that the Court's exercise of judicial review is the final say in a constitutional matter." Pickerill, Constitutional Deliberation, 32-33. Thus, after all these years, we still have a vast milieu of permissible and impermissible regulations. See Louis Fisher and David Gray Adler, American Constitutional Law, Vol. 2 Constitutional Rights: Civil Rights and Civil Liberties, 911.

Court agree to take so many civil-rights cases in a single term?[698] What were the motivating factors for this decision? No explanation has been found.[699] Obviously, the new Court majority (with the then-addition of Justice Kennedy) may have been trying to send a message to Congress. If so, it may have been surprised at the reaction, resulting in the 1991 Act.[700]

---

698 As Mikva and Bleich write, the "Court contributed to the perception of activism by agreeing to decide so many questions concerning that policy area within a relatively brief period of time, and in particular by abandoning the Court's general policy against revisiting its statutory precedents." Abner J. Mikva and Jeff Bleich, "When Congress Overrules the Court," California Law Review 79, no. 3 Symposium: Civil Rights Legislation in the 1990s (May 1991): 745, citing, Eskridge, "Overruling Statutory Precedents," Georgetown Law Journal 76 (1988): 1361.

699 Mikva and Bleich offer their own partial explanation: "[t]hree lessons can be drawn from the New Deal experience that appear applicable to the present relationship between the Court and Congress. First, when either branch quibbles with the language of a statute, it risks unsettling its legitimate objectives. When Congress tries to avoid a difficult issue by including vague language, it may only promote antagonism and, ultimately, more intense scrutiny of the issue by the Court and the public. Likewise, when the Court quibbles with the language of Congress, it may only entrench contrary congressional opinion and reduce the healthy deference that Congress ought to give to the Court's decisions. Second, parties who seek to win in the Court what they lost in Congress must be wary of what they pray for. Frequently, these parties win the battle but lose the war by galvanizing congressional forces to overrule the Court and advance to an even higher policy ground."Abner J. Mikva and Jeff Bleich, "When Congress Overrules the Court," California Law Review 79, no. 3 Symposium: Civil Rights Legislation in the 1990s (May 1991): 730.

700 The Court had no immediate response, but did rule two years later the Act did apply retroactively, a policy supporters of the Act desired. *Landgraf v. USI Film Products*, 511 U.S. 244 (1994); *Rivers v. Roadway Exp. Inc.*, 511 U.S. 298 (1994).

DIVIDED GOVERNMENT

As mentioned earlier, these cases all occurred within an era of divided government. While it may be true that "[w]hen bargaining among multiple institutions results in a more comprehensive justification for law and policy, the normative preference for a republic of reasons has been more fully realized,"[701] divided government complicates the bargaining task. As noted before, and as expected under divided government, we also see the importance and prevailing umbrella of judicial supremacy that members were operating under as one would expect given competing national majorities look to shield the Court from their counterpart when necessary to protect their regime values. In all three cases, but more forcefully in 2003 and 2007, we see members arguing that the Supreme Court is the final arbiter in constitutional questions. A departmentalist perspective was rarely mentioned. During the 1991 debate, there were few 14th Amendment Section 5 orations on congressional enforcement power related to civil rights laws. As one staffer commented about congressional constitutional prerogative, "environmental issues . . . have been settled,"[702] and settled obviously by the Court. Members often "defer[] to the Supreme Court" on constitutional matters.[703] An inter-branch scholar lamented that over the "last 20-25 years, members don't have a clue. . . . Members have no interest in educating constituents and lose interest quickly when you talk to them" about constitutional issues or values. "Everybody is looking to the Court." [704] Many members think that "if something is important it must be constitutional."[705] As Whittington writes, "[e]lected officials have an incentive to bolster judicial authority not only to encourage the judiciary to take independent action but also to

---

[701] J. Mitchell Pickerill, Constitutional Deliberation in Congress, 60.

[702] Staff Interview, 2008.

[703] Staff Interviews, 2008.

[704] Interview with Louis Fisher, 2008.

[705] Member Interview, 2008.

weaken the voter's ability to trace responsibility back to elected officials."[706] Therefore:

> Affiliated presidents are powerful, but they operate under constraints. The twin imperatives of pursuing their substantive goals and maintaining their political coalition are increasingly in tension. Moreover, the ideological constraints of the inherited regime limit the options of affiliated presidents. These characteristics of affiliated politics favor judicial independence and power in constitutional interpretation. When constitutional politics is primarily interpretive rather than creative, the Court can claim a larger space of operations, and affiliated leaders have strong incentives to bolster judicial authority. An independent judiciary helps secure regime commitments and solve problems of coalitional maintenance.[707]

We do see greater calls for cooperation with the Court in the habeas case, perhaps being attributable to its more unsettled nature historically, thereby allowing more room for maneuvering. Members were also not only looking to the Court as the final arbiter of constitutional matters but of devising controversial detainee policy. In July 2008, even after his party had gained control of both chambers of Congress and appeared to have a more than plausible shot at winning the White House, Sen. Patrick Leahy

> essentially said that Congress trusts the courts, not the White House, to come up with solutions to these issues. 'The courts have a long history of considering habeas petitions and of

---

[706] Keith E. Whittington, "The Political Foundations of Judicial Supremacy," in Sotirios A. Barber and Robert P. George, eds., Constitutional Politics: Essays on Constitution Making, Maintenance, and Change (Princeton: Princeton University Press, 2001), 279.

[707] Keith E. Whittington, "The Political Foundations of Judicial Supremacy," in Sotirios A. Barber and Robert P. George, eds., Constitutional Politics: Essays on Constitution Making, Maintenance, and Change (Princeton: Princeton University Press, 2001), 280-281.

> handling national security matters, including classified information,' he said. 'The administration made this mess by seeking to avoid judicial review at all costs, causing years of delay and profound uncertainty.'[708]

His counterpart in the House, Rep. Jerrold Nadler (NY), when asked the chances Congress would enact the kind of laws then-Attorney General Michael Mukasey was advocating after the *Boumediene* decision was announced, answered "'[z]ero. . . . We don't have to pass anything.' 'Let the courts deal with it.' 'Most of them [the detainees] are guilty of nothing.'"[709] This reflects an earlier sentiment expressed by the new majority after the 2006 mid-term elections. "'This is definitely not going to be the first thing out of the box for us,' one Democratic Senate staffer said. 'We make fun of Specter, but we're basically leaving it up to the Courts, too.'"[710] This may all reflect the fundamental fact of political reality faced by those in Congress, as best expressed by Sen. Specter four years ago:

> The Supreme Court finally took the bull by the horns and came down with the three decisions in June of 2004 because the Congress had not acted. It didn't know what to do. It didn't know quite how to approach it. And perhaps it was too hot to handle. But the Congress frequently is inactive in the face of assertions by the executive of the need to defer to Presidential power.[711]

---

[708] Michael Isikoff and Mark Hosenball, "Mocking Mukasey," Newsweek Web Exclusive (23 Jul. 2008).

[709] Michael Isikoff and Mark Hosenball, "Mocking Mukasey," Newsweek Web Exclusive (23 Jul. 2008).

[710] Jeffrey Toobin, "Killing Habeas Corpus: Arlen Specter's about-face," The New Yorker 4 Dec. 2006 [magazine on-line]; accessed 27 March 2009; available from http://www.newyorker.com/archive/ 2006/12/04/ 061204fa_fact.

[711] Sen. Arlen Specter (R-PA), Congressional Record, 109th Cong., 1st sess., 2005, vol. 151, pt. 149, S12659 (10 Nov. 2005).

We also do not see members of Congress arguing on the floor or in committee hearings that the Court is completely wrong and should be challenged, ignored, or overruled. Morgan's insight into the change the New Deal era wrought seems to have held up in these three cases.[712]

CONCLUSION

Despite this highly political and predictable context, congressional action and deliberation is still important due to this regime nature of our inter-branch and political environment. These cases illustrate the unsettled nature of these three issues and thus the importance of congressional involvement in these "dialogues."[713] Were we to witness silence by Congress and an abdication to judicial monopoly of these issues, then it could be said Congress' deliberative actions were of no

---

[712] As mentioned earlier, Donald Morgan, "examin[ed] a wide range of cases that traced congressional responsibility for constitutional interpretation over the course of American history." He argued that Congress changed during the New Deal and he was "particularly distressed to find a decline in the acceptance of such congressional responsibility and the rise of 'judicial monopolism' by which the 'legislative function could receive definition solely in relation to policy' while the Constitution was understood to be 'technical, and too abstruse for any but lawyers in the courtroom and judges on the bench to discuss with sense." Neal Devins and Keith E. Whittington, "Introduction," in Congress and the Constitution, eds. Neal Devins and Keith E. Whittington (Durham: Duke University Press, 2005), 5, citing, Donald G. Morgan, Congress and the Constitution (Cambridge: Harvard University Press, 1966), 334-35.

[713] This may also be an example of adhering to the "Madisonian Constitution." See George Thomas, The Madisonian Constitution (Baltimore: The John Hopkins University Press, 2008). Thomas argues that "[w]hile sustaining the ultimate sovereignty of the text . . . Madison designed a constitution that calls forth institutions that each have the equivalent responsibility for articulating explanations of what the Constitution means. As a result, constitutional meaning can never be settled, as each branch properly asserts its own interpretation." Douglas C. Dow, Review of The Madisonian Constitution by George Thomas Law & Politics Book Review 19, no. 1 (Jan. 2009): 28-31.

import, something our tripartite representational system did not anticipate.[714]

Instead, the employment-related civil rights issues were home to numerous inter-branch movements, an ongoing dialogue in affect. Congress passed the Civil Rights Act in 1964. The Court issued *Griggs* in 1971. Congress passed the Equal Employment Amendments in 1972. The Court and Congress went back and forth over civil rights laws throughout the 1980s. The Court ruled in these cases in 1989. Congress acted in 1990 and 1991 to respond to the Court and to a regime largely committed to imposing color-blind policies. Yet, disparate impact analysis is still part of Equal Employment Opportunity Commission guidelines and our employment laws, and has recently returned to prominence with the 2007 *Ricci* case and the new "strong basis-in-evidence" standard.[715]

---

[714] "No one doubts the right of Congress to pass legislation that overturns what it considers to be judicial misinterpretations of statutes. But even when the courts render a constitutional interpretation, it is usually only a matter of time before Congress prevails if it wants to. Through changes in the composition of courts or adjustments in the attitudes of judges who continue to sit, a determined majority in Congress is likely to have its way. At some point, a similar statute, struck down in the past as unconstitutional, will find acceptance in the courts. If Congress fails to act, judicial policy (as with child labor and the definition of federal commerce) can dictate national policy for decades." Louis Fisher, Constitutional Dialogues: Interpretation as Political Process (Princeton: Princeton University Press, 1988), 229, citing, Charles A. Johnson and Bradley C. Canon, Judicial Policies: Implementation and Impact (Washington, D.C.: CQ Press, 1984), 230-236. Also citing Robert A. Dahl, "Decision-Making in a Democracy: The Supreme Court as a National Policy-Maker," Journal of Public Law 6 (1957): 279-295, and Jonathan D. Casper, "The Supreme Court and National Policy Making," American Political Science Review 70, no. 1 (1976): 50-63.

[715] In *Ricci*, Justice Scalia pointed out the discrepancy between the Court's strict scrutiny for race-related policies and its disparate impact holdings.

Abortion jurisprudence continues to evolve with a fifty-year dialogue continuing to take place,[716] and while in 2003, the legislation and subsequent Court validation did break new ground, it was not that far outside already tilled ground, stemming from *Akron*, *Thornborough*, *Webster*, and even *Casey*, where the Court wrote that state considerations of the value of human life is a worthy consideration. As mentioned at the end of the case study, despite the Court carving out room for its jurisprudential prerogative, the partial-birth abortion bill also fits within a recent trio of abortion-related measures passed since *Stenberg*,[717] that may speak to a pro-life "determined majority" at least able to pass incremental measures.[718] In 2007, Congress helped stop a

---

716 *Poe v. Ullman* (1961); *Griswold v. Connecticut* (1965); *Eistadt v. Baird* (1972); *Roe v. Wade* (1973); *Doe v. Bolton* (1973); *Planned Parenthood of Missouri v. Danforth* (1976); Hyde Amendment (1976); *Bellotti v. Baird* (1979); *Harris v. McRae* (1980); *Akron v. Akron Center for Reproductive Health* (1983); *Thornburgh v. American College of Obst. & Gyn.* (1986); *Webster v. Reproductive Health Services* (1989); *Planned Parenthood v. Casey* (1992); *Stenberg v. Carhart* (2000).

717 The Born-Alive Infants Protection Act (2002); The Partial Birth Abortion Protection Act (2003); the Unborn Victims of Violence Act (2004).

718 "No one doubts the right of Congress to pass legislation that overturns what it considers to be judicial misinterpretations of statutes. But even when the courts render a constitutional interpretation, it is usually only a matter of time before Congress prevails if it wants to. Through changes in the composition of courts or adjustments in the attitudes of judges who continue to sit, a determined majority in Congress is likely to have its way." Citing Robert A. Dahl, "Decision-Making in a Democracy: The Supreme Court as a National Policy-Maker." Journal of Public Law 6 (1957): 279-295, and Jonathan D. Casper, "The Supreme Court and National Policy Making," American Political Science Review 70, no. 1 (1976): 50-63. At some point a similar statute, struck down in the past as unconstitutional, will find acceptance in the courts. If Congress fails to act, judicial policy (as with child labor and the definition of federal commerce) can dictate national policy for decades." Louis Fisher, Constitutional Dialogues: Interpretation as Political Process (Princeton: Princeton University Press, 1988), 229, citing, Charles A. Johnson and Bradley C. Canon, Judicial Policies: Implementation and Impact (Washington, D.C.: CQ Press, 1984), 230-236.

determined President. They possibly encouraged the Court in now believing the consequences of overturning *Eisentrager* were minimal, which may have helped lead to *Boumediene*.

We can also say Congress partook in a serious constitutionally deliberative process if for no other reason than that they also responded relatively quickly to Court action. Pickerill argues that the average congressional response time to a judicial review action by the Supreme Court is four years.[719] Overall, these three cases would indicate a quicker response time from Congress, perhaps indicating the three issues' salience to members. The civil rights related cases struck down by the Court were in the 1988-89 term with deliberation over the responding Act immediately following during the next two years. The Court case to which the Partial-Birth bill responded was in 2000, with the Act passed within three years. The Habeas Act, while not passed, was proposed and debated soon after *Hamdan* was announced.

In all three cases, they kept the discussion going despite the apparent regime divisions. Thus, even though Congress' deliberation was often rhetorical, symbolic, and operates in a political environment, because these actions radiate back to other malleable entities within our political culture, they affect both more secondary levels of regime values and can affect the fundamental regime values that guide actors within their eras.

This is important. If there were to be no dialogue, then Congress would be ceding the legislative and policy fields to the other two branches. If, in fact, we are living in an entire era dominated by judicial supremacy and the lack of reconstructive presidents willing to aggressively assert constitutional prerogative,[720] then it is vital that Congress engage the other branches of our system, the national polity, and the competing national governing coalitions within itself, which have support within coalitions and composite parts of the other actors as well. If it does not, its part of the conversation, and its perspective on the constitutional issue, ceases to be heard.

---

[719] Pickerill, Constitutional Deliberation in Congress, 42-43.

[720] Keith E. Whittington, Political Foundations of Judicial Supremacy: The Presidency, the Supreme Court, and Constitutional Leadership in U.S. History (Princeton: Princeton University Press, 2007).

Again, deliberation is, it can be argued, even more important during era of affiliation. For it is during those times when there are competing national governing coalitions that other citizens, other voters, other actors, can be influenced, in ways both large and small, both permanent and temporary, in an attempt to cement reality to a given norm, a certain constitutional interpretation, or policy pronouncement. Thus, congressional actors should always value their deliberative means and ends.

The fact that the congressional deliberation is circumscribed, or confined, by the political regime within the political time in which it operates, may not be a surprise to many. Yet, this empirical reality does help us better understand the nature of the arguments we do here or may not be hearing when listening to Congress' collective voice. This reality may also help us decipher the maneuvers and actions of the respective branches, and the majoritarian or plurality-driven factions, within those branches.

As previously mentioned, David Currie described members of Congress during an earlier period in our history as "center[ing] on the task of determining [the Constitution's] meaning."[721] In recent times, by contrast, it may simply be that "[u]ltimately, with fundraising,

---

[721] David P. Currie, The Constitution in Congress: The Federalist Period 1789-1801 (Chicago: The University of Chicago Press, 1997), 116-117. As noted in Chapter 1., here Currie writes, during the First Congress, "[r]espect for the Constitution . . . went far beyond ritualistic acknowledgement of its authority; a remarkable proportion of the debate centered on the task of determining its meaning. At the outset Madison admonished the House, as Washington had admonished him, that constitutional issues should be given 'careful investigation and full discussion' because '[t]he decision that is at this time made, will become the permanent exposition of the [C]onstitution' [Annals of Congress, 1st Cong., 1st sess., H514 (17 June 1789)]. Constitutional questions cropped up in the House and Senate every time somebody sneezed, and one proposal after another was subjected to intensive debate to determine its compatibility with relevant constitutional provisions. Members of Congress plainly thought it necessary to demonstrate that the Constitution supported their actions, and thus everything they did as well as everything they said helps to inform our understanding of particular constitutional provisions."

constituent service, and other demands, members of Congress cannot pursue knowledge for knowledge's sake."[722] Nevertheless, if it is true that "the original constitutional understanding [was] that the Court *and* the President *and* the Congress would determine statutory policy,"[723] then these Congresses succeeded.

It has also been said that "[c]onstitutional scholarship today tends to focus on yesterday's Supreme Court decision and tomorrow's pending case, ignoring, to our detriment, the more fundamental shaping of the Constitution through great historical events in favor of the study of the latest doctrinal ripples in Supreme Court decisions of middling importance."[724] This may be true. It may also be true that contemporary congressional scholarship minimizes Congress's overall relationship to the Constitution and constitutional structure as well as the important role it has played in proposing, debating, stifling, influencing, ignoring, and grabbling with the issues which have defined our history. Nevertheless, it is important to not encourage legislative supremacy at the detriment of the other branches and actors. As Paulsen writes, "[t]he text designates 'this Constitution' – the document itself – as the supreme law of the land, and not the interpretations of any specific actor or body."[725] After all, if George Thomas is correct, "[t]he 'settlement' of constitutional issues is not an essential feature of our constitutional system and, thus, constitutional politics with overlapping

---

[722] Neal Devins, "Congressional Fact Finding," in Congress and the Constitution, 225.

[723] William N. Eskridge, Jr., "Reneging on History? Playing the Court/Congress/President Civil Rights Game," California Law Review 79, no. 3 Symposium: Civil Rights Legislation in the 1990s (May 1991): 617. Emphasis in original.

[724] Michael Stokes Paulsen, "The Civil War as Constitutional Interpretation," review of Lincoln's Constitution, by Daniel Farber, The University of Chicago Law Review 71, no. 2 (spring 2004): 693.

[725] Michael Stokes Paulsen, "The Civil War as Constitutional Interpretation," review of Lincoln's Constitution, by Daniel Farber, The University of Chicago Law Review 71, no. 2 (spring 2004): 711.

views, discontinuities, and essentially unsettled meanings are inherent features of the Madisonian Constitution."[726]

Do these deliberations fall short of a republican ideal of debate and the authentic exchange of ideas grounded in reasoned arguments or are they merely interest-group and permanent-campaign based exhibits in vacuous partisanship? Were he still with us and writing on this era instead, would David Currie describe with great admiration for how serious and constitutionally deliberative members of Congress were in these three cases? Possibly not. We know that many of the statements are often mere assertions, are the translation of talking points meant to

---

[726] "Indeed, the Constitution itself, by dividing power between institutions, calls forth debate about constitutional meaning and the proper ordering of constitutional values. . . . Constitutional meaning may be settled over time and in ways that cannot be divorced from politics. Such settlements are likely to depend upon the political forces of the day, suggesting that a particular constitutional vision may only be as stable as the political forces which support it, leaving open the possibility that there is no such thing as 'authoritative settlement' in the long run – whether judicial or otherwise." George Thomas, "Recovering the Political Constitution: The Madisonian Vision," The Review of Politics 66, no. 2 (spring 2004): 233. "Madison's constitutionalism suggests that constitutional politics is an ordinary part of our constitutional system. As a polity we may give primacy to the Court in determining constitutional meaning. But even if this is true – and it is an empirical question that is under investigated – the Court's role is subject to change over time and thus is historically contingent. Patterns of constitutional development depend upon what all of the branches of government are doing. While judicial supremacy may be accepted at one moment – suggesting a political basis to judicial power even at these moments – this acceptance may well be contingent on the very actions of the judiciary. This draws our eye toward important constitutional issues and developments that are not, properly speaking, legal but political." George Thomas, "Recovering the Political Constitution: The Madisonian Vision," The Review of Politics 66, no. 2 (spring 2004): 256. See also, Jeffrey Rosen, "What's a Liberal Justice Now?" New York Times Magazine 26 May 2009, discussing a new movement of "democratic constitutionalism" among progressive legal scholars and espousing sentiments potentially shared by the President.

frame issues and shield members from difficult votes or having to explain their position in any substantive detail.

We should be thankful for our constitutional system. After all, "[t]hough there may be a long gap between our present ideals and practice of democracy and those at the birth of the republic . . . that gap is nothing compared to the gulf that separated the founding generation from any that had come before or that lived anywhere else in the world during the late eighteenth century."[727] Eight years ago, one scholar wrote that the "Thirteenth, Fourteenth, and Fifteenth Amendments to the Constitution were a great national interpretation and implementation of the Republican Form of Government and Privileges and Immunities Clauses of Article IV of the Constitution, and a repudiation of the Supreme Court's decision in *Dred Scott* – major interpretive victories won in a bloody civil war fought over constitutional meaning.[728] Thirty-one years ago, another scholar stated that the federal government had a "crisis of legitimacy" and that Congress "is not the deliberative body it was designed to be and that modern democracy requires."[729] These three cases no doubt do not rise to the level of Civil War and Reconstruction-era Amendments, and no doubt, deliberative problems still remain in Congress. Nevertheless, these three cases do demonstrate the *possibility* of constructive deliberation taking place in the legislative branch of our tripartite governmental system.

Given that the national governing coalition has been divided and thus unable to mobilize against the Court, it has had room to act with marked independence, which, while maintaining its institutional

---

[727] Keith E. Whittington, "Clothed with the Legitimate Authority of the People," review of America's Constitution: A Biography, by Akhil Reed Amar, Virginia Law Review 91, no. 7 (Nov. 2005): 2026. Whittington is describing Amar's opening discussion of the Constitution's Preamble.

[728] Michael Stokes Paulsen, "The Civil War as Constitutional Interpretation," review of Lincoln's Constitution, by Daniel Farber, The University of Chicago Law Review 71, no. 2 (spring 2004): 692.

[729] Joseph M. Bessette, "Is Congress a Deliberative Body?," in The United States Congress: Proceedings of the Thomas P. O'Neill, Jr. Symposium on the U.S. Congress, ed. Dennis Hale (Chestnut Hill, MA: Boston College, 1981), 4.

legitimacy, allows one of the national governing coalitions to respond with concomitant outrage. Congress, while operating under an umbrella of judicial supremacy and often articulating little more than symbolic rhetoric, is nevertheless able to participate in an ongoing, and at this point continuous, dialogue with the Court and the President, which continue to affect the status of issues by which we collectively live.

Whittington writes that "[c]onstitutional meaning emerges from the interplay of multiple actors, rather than through the abstracted reasoning of an isolated judiciary."[730] Those actors, including Congress, operate within a political regime, and in these cases during an affiliated age. It thus will seek to avoid settled values,_ incrementally shift lesser-settled values, avoid responsibility for approaching those settled values, seek to maintain its coalition, issue dire warnings about minor precedential shifts, and participate in dialogue with the other two branches. Being a very political and partisan institution within this regime and time, its deliberations may be lacking in substance. Normatively, given the frequency of elections, of changes in partisan composition, of shifts in national coalitions and values, as well as the presence of constitutionally functional mechanisms like judicial review and inter-branch dialogues and bargaining, Congress would seem to be well served to not further diminish their deliberations, less, among other important consequences, their institutional respect continue to decline. Has James Madison "left the building"?[731] Let us hope not.

---

[730] Keith E. Whittington, "The Political Foundations of Judicial Supremacy," in Sotirios A. Barber and Robert P. George, eds., Constitutional Politics: Essays on Constitution Making, Maintenance, and Change (Princeton: Princeton University Press, 2001), 267, citing, Louis Fisher, Constitutional Dialogues (Princeton: Princeton University Press, 1988); Neal Devins, Shaping Constitutional Values (Baltimore: John Hopkins University Press, 1996).

[731] See Keith E. Whittington, "Review: James Madison Has Left the Building," Review of Constitutional Deliberation in Congress: The Impact of Judicial Review in a Separated System by J. Mitchell Pickerill University of Chicago Law Review 72 (summer 2005): 1137-1158.

Bibliography

Alter, Jonathan. “Keeping Order in the Courts,” *Newsweek* 138, no. 24 (12/10/2001): 48.

Barber, Sotirios A. and Robert P. George, eds. *Constitutional Politics: Essays on Constitution Making, Maintenance, and Change.* Princeton, NJ: Princeton University Press, 2001.

Beermann, Jack M. “The Supreme Court’s Narrow View on Civil Rights.” *The Supreme Court Review* 1993 (1993): 199-243.

Bell, Derrick. “Foreword: The Final Civil Rights Act.” *California Law Review* 79, no. 3 Symposium: Civil Rights Legislation in the 1990s (May 1991): 597-611.

Bettelheim, Adriel. "Abortion Politics: Sound and Fury, But Signifying What?" *CQ Weekly Online* (July 25, 2005): 2032-2037. Available at http://library.cqpress.com/cqweekly/weeklyreport109-000001792272 (accessed October 12, 2007).

__________. “Lawmakers Still Feeling Their Way On Whether to Intervene In Plan for Military Tribunals,” *CQ Weekly Online* (December 15, 2001): 2984-2984. http://library.cqpress.com/cqweekly/weeklyreport107-000000356326 (accessed October 20, 2008).

Biskupic, Joan. “Expected Bush Veto Looming Over Civil Rights Measure.” *CQ Weekly Online* (October 20, 1990): 3518-3519. Available at http://library.cqpress.com /cqweekly/WR101401693 (accessed October 23, 2007).

__________. "PROVISIONS: Civil Rights Act of 1991,” *CQ Weekly Online* (December 7, 1991): 3620-3622. Available at http://library.cqpress.com/cqweekly/WR102405603 (accessed October 12, 2007).

__________. “Rights Bill Is Almost Ready After Long Delay, Debate.” *CQ Weekly Online* (November 11, 1989): 3055-3059. Available at http://library.cqpress.com/cqweekly/WR101407818 (accessed October 23, 2007).

"Black America Long March for Equality." CQ Electronic Library, *CQ Researcher Online*, cqresrre1985111500. Originally published in *Editorial Research Reports 1985*, vol. II (Washington: CQ Press, 1985). Available at http://library.cqpress.com/cqresearcher/cqresrre1985111500 (accessed October 12, 2007).

Burgess, Susan R. *Contest for Constitutional Authority: The Abortion and War Powers Debates*. Lawrence, KS: University Press of Kansas, 1992.

"Bush on Job Rights Bill." CQ Electronic Library, *CQ Historic Documents Series Online Edition*, hsdc91-0000911038. Originally published in *Historic Documents of 1991* (Washington: CQ Press, 1992). Available at http://library.cqpress.com/historicdocuments/hsdc91-0000911038 (accessed October 23, 2007).

Cameron, Charles M. *Veto Bargaining: Presidents and the Politics of Negative Power*. New York: Cambridge University Press, 2000.

Carey, Mary Agnes. "Abortion Rights Supporters On Defensive Again as House Votes To Ban 'Partial Birth' Procedure." *CQ Weekly Online* (April 8, 2000): 839-840. http://library.cqpress.com/cqweekly/weeklyreport106-000000060933 (accessed October 12, 2007).

__________. "ABORTION: Roe v. Wade's Challenge at 25: Hang On to the Votes." *CQ Weekly Online* (January 17, 1998): 127-128. http://library.cqpress.com/cqweekly/WR19980117-03ABORTION001 (accessed October 12, 2007).

__________. "ABORTION: Senate Heads for Showdown On Controversial Procedure." *CQ Weekly Online* (May 17, 1997): 1137-1138. http://library.cqpress.com/cqweekly/WR10519970517-20ABORTION001 (accessed October 12, 2007).

Clayton, Cornell and David A. May. "A Political Regimes Approach to the Analysis of Legal Decisions." *Polity* 32, no. 2 (Winter 1999): 233-252.

Clegg, Roger. "Epilogue: Civil Rights in the Eighties and Nineties." *Louisiana Law Review* 54, no. 6 *The Civil Rights Act of 1991: A Symposium* (1993-1994): 1605-1617.

__________. "Introduction: A Brief Legislative History of the Civil Rights Act of 1991." *Louisiana Law Review* 54, no. 6 *The Civil Rights Act of 1991: A Symposium* (1993-1994): 1459-1471.

Cohodas, Nadine. “Argument Over Reach of the Bill: Echoes From Past Punctuate Grove City Debate.” *CQ Weekly Online* (March 12, 1988): 677-678. Available at http://library.cqpress.com/cqweekly/WR100402849 (accessed October 23, 2007).

__________. “Ignoring Reagan, House Passes Grove City Bill.” *CQ Weekly Online* (March 5, 1988): 563-565. Available at http://library.cqpress.com/cqweekly/WR100402807 (accessed October 23, 2007).

__________. “The Post-Bork Civil Rights Agenda: Sponsors Plan Early 1988 Push For Grove City, Housing Bills.” *CQ Weekly Online* (January 23, 1988): 160-163.Available at http://library.cqpress.com/cqweekly/WR100402525 (accessed October 23, 2007).

Cooper, Mary H. “Racial Quotas.” *CQ Researcher Online* 1 (May 17, 1991): 277-300. Available at http://library.cqpress.com/cqresearcher/cqresrre1991051700 (accessed October 12, 2007).

Currie, David P. *The Constitution in Congress: The Federalist Period, 1789-1801*. Chicago: University of Chicago Press, 1997.

__________. *The Constitution in Congress: The Jeffersonians, 1801-1829*. Chicago: University of Chicago Press, 2001.

__________. *The Constitution in Congress: Democrats and Whigs, 1829-1861*. Chicago: University of Chicago Press, 2005.

__________. *The Constitution in Congress: Descent into the Maelstrom, 1829-1861*. Chicago: University of Chicago Press, 2005.

Dahl, Robert. “Decision-Making in a Democracy: The Supreme Court as a National Policy-Maker.” *Journal of Public Law* 6 (1957): 279-295.

Devins, Neal. “Reagan Redux: Civil Rights Under Bush.” *Notre Dame Law Review* 68, no. 5 *Symposium: The Civil Rights Act of 1991: Theory and Practice* (1993): 955-1001.

Devins, Neal and Keith Whittington, eds. *Congress and the Constitution*. Durham, North Carolina: Duke University Press, 2005.

Donnelly, John M. "Bush Yields on Detainee Accord." *CQ Weekly Online* (September 25, 2006): 2554-2555. http://library.cqpress.com/cqweekly/weeklyreport109-000002377083 (accessed October 12, 2007).

__________. “Detainee Treatment Debate Simmering,” *CQ Weekly Online* (November 14, 2005): 3064-3064. http://library.cqpress.com/cqweekly/weeklyreport109-000001962036 (accessed October 20, 2008).

__________. "Senate Vote 259: Establishment of Military Tribunals." *CQ Weekly Online* (January 1, 2007): 71-71. http://library.cqpress.com/cqweekly/weeklyreport109-000002421999 (accessed October 12, 2007).

__________. "2006 Legislative Summary: Military Tribunal Standards." *CQ Weekly Online* (December 18, 2006): 3342-3342. http://library.cqpress.com/cqweekly/weeklyreport109-000002418330 (accessed October 12, 2007).

Dumas, Kitty. "A Habeas Corpus Primer." *CQ Weekly Online* (February 22, 1992): 412-412. http://library.cqpress.com/cqweekly/WR102406013 (accessed October 12, 2007).

Elkins, Stanley and Eric McKitrick. *The Age of Federalism: The Early American Republic, 1788-1800*. New York: Oxford University Press, 1995.

Elsea, Jennifer K. CRS Report RL32567, *Lawfulness of Interrogation Techniques under the Geneva Conventions*.

__________. CRS Report RL33688, The Military Commissions Act of 2006: Analysis of Procedural Rules and Comparison with Previous DOD Rules and the Uniform Code of Military Justice.

__________. CRS Report RL31367, *Treatment of 'Battlefield Detainees' in the War on Terrorism*.

Elsea, Jennifer K. and Kenneth R. Thomas, Legislative Attorneys, American Law Division, *Enemy Combatant Detainees: Habeas Corpus Challenges in Federal Court*, report prepared for Congress (Congressional Research Service, updated January 28, 2008).

Eskridge, William N., Jr. “Reneging on History? Playing the Court/Congress/President Civil Rights Game.” *California Law Review* 79, no. 3 *Symposium: Civil Rights Legislation in the 1990s* (May 1991): 613-684.

Ferrechio, Susan. "'Born Alive' Bill Would Protect Babies Born at Any Stage." *CQ Weekly Online* (March 16, 2002): 712-713. http://library.cqpress.com/cqweekly/weeklyreport107-000000398649 (accessed October 12, 2007).

Fisher, Louis. *Constitutional Conflicts Between Congress and the President*, 5th ed. Lawrence: University of Kansas Press, 2007.

__________. *Constitutional Dialogues: Interpretation as Political Process*. Princeton: Princeton University Press, 1988.

__________. "Constitutional Interpretation by Members of Congress," *North Carolina Law Review* 63 (1985): 707-747.

__________. "The Cost of Freedom: Civil Liberties, Security and the USA PATRIOT Act," Interview with Louis Fisher, (January 2004).

Fisher, Louis and David Gray Adler. *American Constitutional Law, Vol. 1 Constitutional Structures: Separated Powers and Federalism*, 7th edition Carolina Academic Press: Durham, North Carolina, 2007.

__________. "The War Powers Resolution: Time to Say Goodbye." *Political Science Quarterly* 113, no. 1 (Spring 1998): 1-20.

Foerstel, Karen. "SOCIAL POLICY: As Senate Passes 'Partial-Birth' Ban, One Side Sees Victory Within Reach, The Other Sees a Campaign Issue." *CQ Weekly Online* (October 23, 1999): 2531-2532. http://library.cqpress.com/cqweekly/WR19991023-41ABORTION001 (accessed October 12, 2007).

Freedman, Jacob. "Different Circumstances, Different Rights for Detainees," *CQ Weekly Online* (November 21, 2005): 3117-3117. http://library.cqpress.com/cqweekly/weeklyreport109-000001975392 (accessed October 20, 2008).

Geyh, Charles Gardner. *When Courts & Congress Collide: The Struggle for Control of America's Judicial System*. Ann Arbor, Michigan: The University of Michigan Press, 2006.

Glazer, Sarah. "Roe v. Wade At 25." CQ Researcher Online 7, no. 44 (November 28, 1997): 1033-1056. http://library.cqpress.com/cqresearcher/cqresrre1997112800 (accessed October 12, 2007).

Goldsmith, Jack. *The Terror Presidency: Law and Judgment Inside the Bush Administration*. New York: W.W. Norton, 2007.

Goodgame, Dan. "The White House Nervous and Nasty." TIME (December 2, 1991) Available at http://www.time.com/time/magazine/article/0,9171,974405,00.html.

Govan, Reginald C. "Honorable Compromises and the Moral High Ground: The Conflict Between the Rhetoric and the Content of the Civil Rights Act of 1991." *Rutgers Law Review* 46, no. 1 (1993): 1-242.

Graber, Mark A. *Dred Scott and the Problem of Constitutional Evil.* Cambridge: Cambridge University Press, 2006.

__________. "The Non-Majoritarian Difficulty: Legislative Deference to the Judiciary." *Studies in American Political Development* 7 (1993): 35-72.

Gray, C. Boyden. "Disparate Impact: History and Consequences." *Louisiana Law Review*_54, no. 6 *The Civil Rights Act of 1991: A Symposium* (1993-1994): 1487-1505.

Guéron, Nicole L. "An Idea Whose Time Has Come: A Comparative Procedural History of the Civil Rights Acts of 1960, 1964, and 1991." *The Yale Law Journal* 104, no. 5 (March 1995): 1201-1234.

Hirsh, Michael. "The Hamdan Case: Don't Shoot the Driver." *Newsweek Web Exclusive* August 6, 2008.

Idelson, Holly. "SUPREME COURT: Tension Between Court, Congress Reflected in Civil Rights Cases." *CQ Weekly Online* (October 2, 1993): 2644-2647. Available at http://library.cqpress.com/cqweekly/WR103402521 (accessed October 12, 2007).

Isikoff, Michael and Mark Hosenball. "Mocking Mukasey: The attorney general warns that Gitmo prisoners could go free on U.S. streets. The Dems aren't buying it." *Newsweek Web Exclusive* July 23, 2008.

Johnsen, Dawn. "The hollowing out of Roe v. Wade." *Slate.com* (January 25, 2006).

Jost, Kenneth. (21 March 2003). Abortion debates. *CQ Researcher*, 13, 249-272. Retrieved October 12, 2007, from CQ Researcher Online, http://library.cqpress.com/cqresearcher/cqresrre2003032100.

__________. "Civil Liberties Debates." *CQ Researcher Online* 13, no. 37 (October 24, 2003): 893-916. http://library.cqpress.com/cqresearcher/cqresrre2003102400 (accessed October 12, 2007).

__________. "Rethinking Affirmative Action." *CQ Researcher Online* 5, no. 16 (April 28, 1995): 269-392. Available at http://library.cqpress.com/cqresearcher/cqresrre1995042800 (accessed October 12, 2007).

Jost, Kenneth and Koch, K. (22 September 2006). Abortion showdowns. *CQ Researcher*, *16*, 769-792. Retrieved October 12, 2007, from CQ Researcher Online, http://library.cqpress.com/cqresearcher/cqresrre2006092200.

"Justice Department on Treatment of Post-September 11 Detainees." CQ Electronic Library, CQ Historic Documents Series Online Edition, hsdcp03-229-9912-639137. Originally published in *Historic Documents of 2003* (Washington: CQ Press, 2004). http://library.cqpress.com/historicdocuments/hsdcp03-229-9912-639137 (accessed October 21, 2008).

Kady II, Martin. "Congress Clears Detainee Bill." *CQ Weekly Online* (October 2, 2006): 2624-2625. http://library.cqpress.com/cqweekly/weeklyreport109-000002382860 (accessed October 19, 2007).

Katel, Peter and Kenneth Jost. "Treatment of Detainees." *CQ Researcher Online* 16, no. 29 (August 25, 2006): 673-696. http://library.cqpress.com/cqresearcher/cqresrre2006082500 (accessed October 12, 2007).

Keck, Thomas M. "Party Politics or Judicial Independence? The Regime Politics Literature Hits the Law Schools," review of *From Jim Crow to Civil Rights: The Supreme Court and the Struggle for Racial Equality*, by Michael J. Klarman, *The Most Democratic Branch? How the Courts Serve America*, by Jeffrey Rosen, and *A Court Divided: The Rehnquist Court and the Future of Constitutional Law*, by Mark Tushnet, *Law & Social Inquiry* 32, no. 2 (spring 2007): 511-544.

"Key Moments in the Detainee Rights Battle," *CQ Weekly Online* (December 10, 2007): 3637-3637. http://library.cqpress.com/cqweekly/weeklyreport110-000002638876 (accessed October 20, 2008).

Klarman, Michael J. *From Jim Crow to Civil Rights: The Supreme Court and the Struggle for Racial Equality*. New York: Oxford University Press, 2004.

Kmiec, Douglas W. "Foreward: The 1991 Civil Rights Act: A Constitutional, Statutory, and Philosophical Enigma." *Notre Dame Law Review* 68, no. 5 *Symposium: The Civil Rights Act of 1991: Theory and Practice* (1993): 911-922.

Koszczuk, Jackie. "Lawmakers Struggle to Keep An Eye on Patriot Act," *CQ Weekly Online* (September 7, 2002): 2284-2288. http://library.cqpress.com/cqweekly/weeklyreport107-000000498161 (accessed October 20, 2008).

Leibold, Peter M., Stephen A. Sola, and Reginald E. Jones. "Civil Rights Act of 1991: Race to the Finish – Civil Rights, Quotas, and Disparate Impact in 1991." *Rutgers Law Review* 45, no. 4 (1993): 1043-1087.

Lewis, Karen J. and Jon O. Shimabukuro, Legislative Attorneys, American Law Division, "Abortion Law Development: A Brief Overview," CRS Report for Congress, Prepared for Members and Committees of Congress, Updated January 2, 2001, available at http://www.law.umaryland.edu/marshall/crsreports/crsdocuments/95-724_A.pdf.

Lund, Nelson. "Congressional Self-Exemption from the Employment Discrimination Laws: A Rational Choice Analysis of the Civil Rights Act of 1991." *Louisiana Law Review* 54, no. 6 *The Civil Rights Act of 1991: A Symposium* (1993-1994): 1559-1604.

Maass, Arthur, *Congress and the Common Good*. New York: Basic Books, 1983.

Mann, Robert. *The Walls of Jericho: Lyndon Johnson, Hubert Humphrey, Richard Russell, and the Struggle for Civil Rights*. New York: Harcourt Brace & Company, 1996.

Masci, D., & Marshall, P. (2001, December 14). Civil liberties in wartime. *CQ Researcher*, 11, 1017-1040. Retrieved October 12, 2007, from CQ Researcher Online, http://library.cqpress.com/cqresearcher/cqresrre2001121400.

Mayhew, David R. *America's Congress: Actions in the Public Sphere, James Madison through Newt Gingrich*. New Haven, Conn.: Yale University Press, 2000.

__________. *Congress: The Electoral Connection*. New Haven: Yale University Press, 1974.

McDowell, Douglas S., ed. *The Civil Rights Act of 1991: A Legislative History.* Employment Policy Foundation, 1992.

McGurn, William. "The Two Bobs: Meet Bobs Michel and Dole, establishmentarians extraordinaire. As long as they're the Minority Leaders, they don't seem to mind that their troops are more of a minority with every election." *National Review* (2 December 1991): 34-38.

Mikva, Abner J. and Jeff Bleich. "When Congress Overrules the Court." *California Law Review* 79, no. 3 *Symposium: Civil Rights Legislation in the 1990s* (May 1991): 729-750.

Miller, William Lee. *Arguing About Slavery: The Great Battle in the United States Congress*. New York: Alfred A. Knopf, 1996.

Morgan, Donald. *Congress and the Constitution: A Study of Responsibility*. Cambridge: Belknap Press of Harvard University Press, 1966.

Murphy, Walter F. *Congress and the Court: A Case Study in the American Political Process*. Chicago: The University of Chicago Press, 1962.

__________. "Who Shall Interpret? The Quest for the Ultimate Constitutional Interpreter." *The Review of Politics* 48, no. 3 (Summer 1986): 401-423.

Naff, Katherine C. "From *Bakke* to *Grutter* and *Gratz*: The Supreme Court as a Policy-making Institution," *Review of Policy Research* 21, no. 3 (2004): 405-427.

Nager, Glen D. "Affirmative Action After the Civil Rights Act of 1991: The Effects of a 'Neutral' Statute." *Notre Dame Law Review* 68, no. 5 *Symposium: The Civil Rights Act of 1991: Theory and Practice* (1993): 1057-1094.

__________. "Enforcement Issues: A Practical Overview." *Louisiana Law Review* 54, no. 6 *The Civil Rights Act of 1991: A Symposium* (1993-1994): 1473-1486.

Palmer, Elizabeth A. "Executive Powers in Crises Are Shaped By Precedent, Personality, Public Opinion." *CQ Weekly Online* (September 15, 2001): 2122-2122. http://library.cqpress.com/cqweekly/weeklyreport107-000000309054 (accessed October 20, 2008).

__________. "Supreme Court Hears Case That Could Affect Dozens of 'Partial Birth' Abortion Laws." *CQ Weekly Online* (April 29, 2000): 992-992. http://library.cqpress.com/cqweekly/weeklyreport106-000000073887 (accessed October 12, 2007).

Palmer, Elizabeth A. and Adriel Bettelheim, "War and Civil Liberties: Congress Gropes for a Role," *CQ Weekly Online* (December 1, 2001): 2820-2827. http://library.cqpress.com/cqweekly/weeklyreport107-000000348017 (accessed October 20, 2008).

Palmer, Elizabeth A. and Keith Perine, "Provisions of the Anti-Terrorism Bill," *CQ Weekly Online* (February 2, 2002): 329-335. http://library.cqpress.com/cqweekly/weeklyreport107-000000372964 (accessed October 20, 2008).

"'Partial Birth' Abortion: A Long Legislative History." *CQ Weekly Online* (October 25, 2003): 2635-2635. http://library.cqpress.com/cqweekly/weeklyreport108-000000878454 (accessed October 12, 2007).

Patch, Buel W. "The War Powers of the President." CQ Electronic Library, Researcher Online, cqresrre1940091200. Originally published in *Editorial Research Reports 1940*, vol. II (Washington: CQ Press, 1940). http://library.cqpress.com/cqresearcher/cqresrre1940091200 (accessed October 12, 2007).

Peabody, Bruce. "Congressional Constitutional Interpretation and the Courts: A Preliminary Inquiry into Legislative Attitudes, 1959-2001." *Law and Social Inquiry* 29, no. 1 (2004): 127-175.

Pear, Robert. "With Rights Act Comes Fight To Clarify Congress's Intent." *NY Times* (November 18, 1991) Available at http://www.nytimes.com/1991/11/18/us/with-rights-act-comes-fight-to-clarify-congress-s-intent.html?pagewanted=all.

Perine, Keith. "Appeals Panel Says Detainees Lack Rights to Federal Courts." *CQ Weekly Online* (February 26, 2007): 610-610. http://library.cqpress.com/cq weekly/weeklyreport110-000002457397 (accessed October 12, 2007).

__________. "Bush Yields on Detainee Accord." *CQ Weekly Online* (September 25, 2006): 2554-2555. http://library.cqpress.com/cqweekly/weeklyreport109-000002377083 (accessed October 19, 2007).

__________. "Detainee Rights Pose a Question for '08 Hopefuls," *CQ Weekly Online* (December 10, 2007): 3636-3637. http://library.cqpress.com/cqweekly/weeklyreport110-000002638875 (accessed October 20, 2008).

__________. "Fall Agenda: Habeas Corpus for Detainees." *CQ Weekly Online* (September 3, 2007): 2554-2554. http://library.cqpress.com/cqweekly/weeklyreport110-000002576956 (accessed October 19, 2007).

__________. "High Court Strikes Guantánamo Laws," *CQ Weekly Online* (June 16, 2008): 1638-1638.

__________. "Panel Votes to Undo Restriction of Habeas Rights Enacted in 2006." *CQ Weekly Online* (June 11, 2007): 1772-1772. http://library.cqpres.com/cqweekly/weeklyreport110-000002529082 (accessed October 12, 2007).

__________. "Rules on Detainees May Be Put in Law." *CQ Weekly*

Online (July 10, 2006): 1881-1881. http://library.cqpress.com/cqweekly/weeklyreport109-000002321877 (accessed October 12, 2007).

__________. "Supreme Court Hands Congress the Lead in Rewriting Terror Suspect Detention Rules." *CQ Weekly Online* (July 3, 2004): 1628-1629. http://library.cqpress.com/cqweekly/weeklyreport108-000001233692 (accessed October 12, 2007).

__________. "Supreme Court Takes Second 'Partial Birth' Case." *CQ Weekly Online* (June 26, 2006): 1799-1799. http://library.cqpress.com/cqweekly/weeklyreport109-000002312069 (accessed October 12, 2007).

__________. "Supreme Court Upholds Abortion Ban." *CQ Weekly Online* (April 23, 2007): 1204-1204. http://library.cqpress.com/cqweekly/weeklyreport110-000002494586 (accessed October 12, 2007).

Pickerill, J. Mitchell. *Constitutional Deliberation in Congress: The Impact of Judicial Review in a Separated System*. Durham, North Carolina: Duke University Press, 2004.

Pickerill, J. Mitchell and Cornell W. Clayton. "The Rehnquist Court and the Political Dynamics of Federalism." *Perspectives on Politics* 2, no. 2 (June 2004): 233-248.

Plummer, Anne. "Detainee Rights Remain at Issue," *CQ Weekly Online* (November 21, 2005): 3116-3117. http://library.cqpress.com/cqweekly/weeklyreport109-000001975372 (accessed October 20, 2008).

"PRESIDENTIAL NEWS CONFERENCE: Bush Hails Civil Rights Accord, Sees 'Joyous Day' for Nation." *CQ Weekly Online* (October 26, 1991): 3149-3150. Available at http://library.cqpress.com/cqweekly/WR102405149 (accessed October 23, 2007).

Pritchett, C. Herman. *Congress versus the Supreme Court, 1957-1960*. Minneapolis: University of Minnesota Press, 1961.

Rights of Detainees: A History." *CQ Weekly Online* (June 16, 2008): 1638-1638. http://library.cqpress.com/cqweekly/weeklyreport110-000002897593 (accessed October 20, 2008).

Rotunda, Ronald D. "The Civil Rights Act of 1991: A Brief Introductory Analysis of the Congressional Response to Judicial Interpretation." *Notre Dame Law Review* 68, no. 5 *Symposium: The Civil Rights Act of*

1991: Theory and Practice (1993): 923-953.

Schuler, Kate. "Supreme Court Will Review 'Partial Birth' Abortion Law." *CQ Weekly Online* (February 27, 2006): 554-554. http://library.cqpress.com/cqweekly/weeklyreport109-000002055356 (accessed October 12, 2007).

Shenk, Joshua Wolf, "The Best and Worst of Bob Dole – Dole's Past Experience in Congress." *Washington Monthly* (July-August 1996).

Skowronek, Stephen. *Presidential Leadership in Political Time: Reprise and Reappraisal*, 2nd ed., revised and expanded. Lawrence, KS: University Press of Kansas, 2011.

Stern, Seth. "The Legacy of 'Undue Burden'." *CQ Weekly Online* (November 7, 2005): 2960-2961. http://library.cqpress.com/cqweekly/weeklyreport109-000001950657 (accessed October 12, 2007).

Stewart III, Charles. "Congress and the Constitutional System." In *The Legislative Branch*. eds. Paul J. Quirk and Sarah A. Binder. Oxford: Oxford University Press, 2005.

Sunstein, Cass. *The Partial Constitution*. Cambridge: Harvard University Press, 1993.

Taylor, Jr., Stuart. "A Judicial Overreaction to Bush Abuses?" *National Journal* 39, no. 24 (21-22).

__________. "Bush and the Justices Behaved Badly." *National Journal* (June 21, 2008).

__________. "Ending Bush's War on Due Process." *National Journal* (December 1, 2007).

__________. "In the Balance: Depending on Who Wins the Presidency, the Supreme Court Could Turn Sharply to the Right or See its First Crusading Liberal Justice in Many Years." *National Journal* (July 26, 2008).

__________. "Interrogation: Anti-Bush Overreach." *National Journal* 39, no. 50 (December 15 2007).

__________. "Interrogation: Fixing the Law." *National Journal* (May 3, 2008).

__________. "Nine Justices, 10 Judicial Activists: Two Recent Decisions Lay Bare the Supreme Court's Biases." *National Journal* (Sept. 27, 2008).

__________. "Reforming The State Secrets Privilege." *National Journal* April 14, 2008.

__________. "Terror: We Need New Laws." *National Journal* (August 2, 2008).

__________. "This Time, Let's Get It Right." *National Journal* (December 16, 2006).

Taylor, Paul. "The Historical and Legal Norms Governing the Detention of Suspected Terrorists and the Risks Posed by Recent Efforts to Depart from Them." *Texas Review of Law and Politics* (Spring 2008).

"The Civil Rights Act of 1991: The Business Necessity Standard." *Harvard Law Review* 106, no. 4 (Feb. 1993): 896-913.

Thomas, Evan and Michael Hirsh, "The Debate Over Torture." *Newsweek*, (November 21, 2005).

Thomas, George. "Recovering the Political Constitution: The Madisonian Vision." *Review of Politics* 66, no. 2 (spring 2004): 233-256.

Toobin, Jeffrey, "Killing Habeas Corpus: Arlen Specter's about-face." *The New Yorker* (December 4, 2006).

Tushnet, Mark. "Constitutional Interpretation outside the Courts." Review of *The Constitution [in] Congress: The Federalist Period, 1789-1801*; *The Constitution [in] Congress: The Jeffersonians, 1801-1829*; *The Constitution [in] Congress: Democrats and Whigs, 1829-1861*; *The Constitution [in] Congress: Descent into the Maelstrom, 1829-1861*, by David P. Currie. *Journal of Interdisciplinary History* 37, no. 3 (winter, 2007): 415-422.

__________. "Evaluating Congressional Constitutional Interpretation: Some Criteria and Two Informal Case Studies." *Duke Law Journal* 50, no. 5 (2001): 1395-1425.

__________. *Taking the Constitution Away From the Courts*. Princeton: Princeton University Press, 1999.

25th Anniversary of Roe V. Wade: Has It Stood the Test of Time? Hearing before the Subcommittee on the Constitution, Federalism and Property Rights of the Committee on the Judiciary, United States Senate, 105th Congress, Second Session.

"2000 Legislative Summary: 'Partial-Birth' Abortion Ban." *CQ Weekly Online* (December 16, 2000): 2894-2894. http://library.cqpress.com/cqweekly/weeklyreport106-000000187706 (accessed October 12, 2007).

Wechsler, Herbert. "The Political Safeguards of Federalism: The Role of the States in the Composition and Selection of the National Government." *Columbia Law Review* 54, no. 3 (March 1954): 543-560.

Wert, Justin J. *Habeas Corpus in America: The Politics of Individual Rights*. Lawrence, KS: University Press of Kansas, 2011.

White House Memorandum, "Humane Treatment of al Qaeda and Taliban Detainees" (February 7, 2002), available at http://www.washingtonpost.com/wp-srv/nation/documents/020702bush.pdf.

Whittington, Keith E. "Congress before the Lochner Court." *Boston University Law Review* 85, no. 3 (2005): 821-858.

__________. *Constitutional Construction: Divided Powers and Constitutional Meaning*. Cambridge: Cambridge University Press, 1999.

__________. *Constitutional Interpretation: Textual Meaning, Original Intent, and Judicial Review*. Lawrence: University Press of Kansas, 1999.

__________. *Political Foundations of Judicial Supremacy: The Presidency, the Supreme Court, and Constitutional Leadership in U.S. History*. Princeton: Princeton University Press, 2007.

__________. "Presidential Challenges to Judicial Supremacy and the Politics of Constitutional Meaning." *Polity* 33, no. 3 (Spring 2001): 365-395.

__________. "The Political Foundations of Judicial Supremacy," in Sotirios A. Barber and Robert P. George, eds., *Constitutional Politics: Essays on Constitution Making, Maintenance, and Change* (Princeton: Princeton University Press, 2001): 261-297.

Wittes, Benjamin. *Law and the Long War: The Future of Justice in the Age of Terror*. New York: Penguin Group, 2008.

Wolters, Raymond. *Right Turn: William Bradford Reynolds, the Reagan Administration and Black Civil Rights*. New Brunswick, N.J.: Transaction, 1996.

Zagorin, Adam. "What the Gitmo Ruling Means," *TIME* (June 12, 2008) Available at http://www.time.com/time/nation/article/0,8599,1814253,00.html.

Zeller, Shawn. "A Right-to-Life Rift in Colorado." *CQ Weekly Online* (July 9, 2007): 1990-1990. http://library.cqpress.com/cqweekly/weeklyreport110-000002546547 (accessed October 12, 2007).

Index